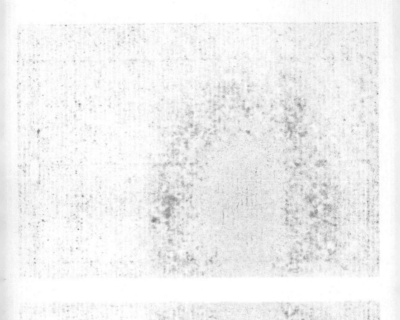

ENGLISH RECUSANT LITERATURE
1558–1640

Selected and Edited by
D. M. ROGERS

Volume 318

OSORIO DA FONSECA
A Learned and Very Eloquent Treatie
1568

OSORIO DA FONSECA

A Learned and Very Eloquent Treatie
1568

The Scolar Press
1976

ISBN o 85967 332 4

Published and printed in Great Britain by
The Scolar Press Limited, 59-61 East Parade,
Ilkley, Yorkshire and
39 Great Russell Street,
London WC1

NOTE

Reproduced (original size) from a copy in the library of Lambeth Palace, by permission of the Librarian. The title-page of this copy is slightly damaged, and in the facsimile the title-page is reproduced from a copy in the British Library, by permission of the Board.

References: Allison and Rogers 587; STC 18889.

A LEARNED AND
VERY ELOQVENT
Treatie`, writen in Latin by
the famouse man *Hieronymus Osorius*
Bishop of Sylua in Portugal, wherein
he confuteth a certayne Aunswere
made by M. Walter Haddon against
the Epistle of the said Bishoppe
vnto the Queenes
Maiestie.

✣

*Translated into English by Iohn Fen stu-
dent of Diuinitie in the Vniuer-
sitie of Louen.*

LOVANII,
Apud Ioannem Foulerum,
Anno 1568.
Cum Gratia & Priuilegio.

TO THE CATHO-
like Reader.

I Was moued (gentle
Reader) to tranſlate
this Booke into our
mother tongue, for
diuers and ſundrie
cauſes. Firſt the fame of the authour
prouoked me thereunto, who is, not
in my priuate opinion, but in the eſti‐
mation of al ſuch as know him, a ver‐
tuous Prieſte and godly Biſhoppe, in
the iudgement of the world, for gra‐
uitie, wiſedome, eloquence and pro‐
found knowledge in al kinde of lear‐
ning in theſe our daies a ſingular,
yea an odde man. Then I thought it
expedient, to impart the benefit ther‐
of vnto my vnlearned countrey men,
* ij   bi‐

bicaufe as it was writen generally for
the commoditie of al the Churche of
Chriſt, ſo it was eſpecially meant and
as it were dedicated to the Churche
and cōmon weal of Englād, vnto the
which, as it may appeere both by the
epiſtle which he wrot before vnto the
Queenes Maieſtie, as alſo by this
Booke, he bare ſingular gōod will.
Moreouer I iudged, that my labour in
tranſlating it ſhuld be the more pro=
fitably emploied, bicauſe there are in
it many goodly exhortations to ſtirre
a mā vp to the loue and feare of God,
many holeſome leſſons, by the whiche
a Chriſtian man may direct and or=
der his life, many points of Catholike
doctrine (whiche are in theſe dayes
called in contrōuerſie by our Aduer=
ſaries) ſo plainly ſet out, that the vn=
lear=

lerned maie take great profit therof,
so lernedly disputed, that such as are
wel exercised in Diuinitie, may find
wherwith to increase their knowlege.
To be short, the thing that most mo=
ued me to take these paines, was, bi=
cause it conteineth a briefe confuta=
tion of manie erroneous opinions, of
much heretical and pestilet doctrine,
comprised in a litle booke, set out
these late yeares in the name of M.
Haddon: wherin was pretended an
answere to the Epistle of Osorius,
(which I spake of before) but in ef=
fecte was nothing els, but a numbre
of stout assertions faintly prooued, be
sprinkled here and there with bitter
tauntes, vnsauerie gyrdes, and other
the like scomme or froth of vndige=
sted affections. These were the things

that cawſed me to ſpare ſome time
from my ſtudy to traſlate this booke
into Engliſhe for the commoditie of
ſuche as vnderſtande not the Latine
tongue: wherof if thou ſhalt receiue
any profit (as thou maiſt very much,
if thou reade it with diligence and
good iudgement) thanke God of it,
and with mindful hart acknowledge
his great mercy and goodnes towards
vs, in that it hath pleaſed him in this
perilous time , not only to ſend vs at
home in our owne countrie moſt vertuous, godlie, and learned men, to be
vnto vs a perfecte rule both of good
life and true beleeſe: but alſo to moue
the heart of this graue Father and
reuerēt Biſhop (whoſe learned writinges haue deſeruedly obteined ſo
great authoritie thoroughout al the
Churche

Church of Christ)to pitie the lamen=
table state of our most miserably de=
caied Church, aud to laie his helping
hand to the repairing of it, employing
thervnto the rare gyftes and graces
of God, with the which (as thou shalt
perceiue by reading this booke) he is
most beawtifully adourned and dec=
ked. And thus I bid the heartily fare=
well, commending my selfe to thy de=
uout praiers , and thee to Almightie
God, whome thou shalt most humbly
besech, that it maie pleafe him, either
of his mercie to turne the heartes of
such as are malicioufly bent against
the true faith of Christe, or els of his
iuftice to turne the wicked deuifes
and diuelifh practifes of Achitophel
and all his confederacie to the glorie

of

To the Catholike Reader.

of his holie name, and aduauncement of the Catholike Churche.

From Louen, the fyrst of Nouember. Anno Domini. 1568.

Jhon Fen.

THE FIRST
BOOKE.

I Thinke it a great grace and benefite of God M. Haddon, that your booke, which ye sette out against me a sewe yeres past, with much a doe at the length, this last daie came vnto my handes. Such care hath God put into the hart of Henrie the Cardinal, who is a most godly Prince and wise gouernour, to vse al possible diligéce, that no such bookes, as may disteine the purenes of godly Religion, be brought in emongest vs. Had it not benne, that Emanuel Almada Bisshoppe of Angra, a man excellently wel furnished with al good qualities and vertues, to me moste intiere, both for the streight friendshippe, as also for the long acqueintaunce be-

A   twene

twene vs begone and continued euen from our Auncestours, had accompaigned the most vertuous Ladie Marie Princesse of Parma, into the low Coūtries of Flaūders, I had not as yet heard any thing either of the booke, or of the Writer. But he, after his arriual into those parties, chauncing vppon the booke, thought he could no lesse doe of friendshippe, but take vpon him my cause, and confute your reprocheful wordes Howbeit in the worke, which he wrote with singular diligence, he tooke vppon him the defence, not so muche of me, as of Religion, of pietie, of godlinesse.

After his returne into his countrie (whiche was much later then we hoped) it was rumored foorthwith, that an English man, whose name was vnknowen, had writen against Hieronymus Osorius, and that the Bishoppe of Angra had earnestly taken vpon him the defence of Osorius, and this much

was

was signified vnto me by my friendes
letters. At the same time, I was painfully occupied in visiting my Diocese,
the which notwithstanding, I was not
so letted, but that I found a time to sa-
lute my frind, and welcome him home
by my letters, in the which I required
of him, that he woulde send me your
booke together with his defence. He
answered me to euery point of my letters, as humanitie, courtesie and frindship required. But as touching your
booke, he said he was moued in con-
science not to send it, vntil he had obteined licence of the Cardinal. whereby ye may perceiue, how heinouse and
wicked offence it is emongest vs, to
reade the bookes of such men, as haue
with many errours infected Religion.

This wise man, albeit he had had very
exact and perfect tryal of my Religion
by long experience, and saw that I was
placed in the roome and dignitie of a
Bishop, and therefore might of mine

owne authoritie fearch and trie out
what foeuer wilines or craft laie hiddē
vnder the couert of your writings: yet
durſt he in no wiſe make me partaker
of your booke, before he vnderſtoode
our Cardinalles pleaſure. You wil here
peraduenture ſcorne and laugh at his
ouermuch ſuperſtition. But I ſhal neuer thinke any diligēce that is employed to put away the contagion of ſuch
a deadlie or mortal peſtilence, to be
ouermuch. After many moneths at the
length when he vnderſtoode the Car-
dinals pleaſure, he ſent me your booke
willing me withal to ſpare ſome time
from mine owne moſt earneſt affaires,
to anſwere you, and ſo did the reſt of
my friendes alſo counſel me to doe.
And although it might ſeme a diſcour-
teſie not to regarde the requeſt of my
friendes, yet I would not haue yelded
vnto them, if in this your woorke my
eſtimation only had ben touched, and
not the puritie of the Catholike Religion

gion violated. I was alſo moued thervnto ſo muche the more, bicauſe I
thought it a point of Chriſtian charitie
to trie, whether you might be brought
through my diligence, to laie downe
ſomewhat of your engraffed lightnes.
For doubtleſſe I may wel gather of
theſe your writinges, that in the writing thereof, ye ſtoode very much in
your owne conceite, yea and that in
ſome places as it were rauiſhed with
good liking of your ſelfe, ye ſtoode ſtil
looking earneſtly about you euen for
the fauourable applauſe of your frinds.
But how much your côceit hath deceiued you, it ſhal foorthwith appeere.

Firſt of al wheras ye ſay that I am a
great framer of wordes and ſentences:
whether ye meane truely, or whether
ye diſſéble, I can not tel, but the praiſe
that you geue me, I doe not acknowledge. If there be in me any cômenda-
ble grace of ſpeache, truly it is bicauſe
I haue beſtowed my time and ſtudie,

A iij   not

not fo much in words, as to atteine the
knowledge of the higheſt pointes of
learning. Beſides that, this qualitie of
ſpeach, how ſimple ſo euer it be in me
(if it be any thing at al) I haue vſed, not
to the damnable forging of falſe Religiõ, but with earneſt and zealous good
heart, to the ſetting foorth of true godlines.

In the very beginning of your booke
ye laie to my charge a great crime of
raſhnes and preſumption : for thus you
ſaie. *You tooke muche vpon you, that be-*
ing a priuate man , ſeparated from vs by
land and ſea, and vnacquainted with our
affaires, durſt ſo boldly ſpeake vnto the
Quenes Maieſtie. Now Sir, I beſeche
you, let me learne this one thing of
you. What meane you by this worde
priuate? Is it a worde of reproche only? Or may it not be applied alſo to
good, vertuous, and noble men? Are
there not emongeſt you many noble
men that beare no office, neither ſerue
in

in any place of the common weale?
Saie you fo Sir? Are al thofe that ferue
not in the Office of Requeftes to be
thruft out by you from the prefence
and fpeach of Kinges? For fo you laie
the name of a priuate man to me, as
though ye eftemed it to be a woord of
villanie and difhonour: as though you
would faie, that my father were fome
vplandifh man, and I brought vp in
bafenes, of fo fmal accompte, that I
was neuer woorthie to looke any
King in the face, and therefore had
committed a fault woorthie of gre-
uoufe punifhment, that durft in my
letters to name Queene Elizabeth,
(whome I alwaies name for honours
fake dewe vnto her Princely Maieftie). But admitte I were not (as I am
in deede) of a verie auncient gentle-
mans howfe: yet it was not the part
of a man brought vp in liberal fciences, to efteme any kind of men, or any
kind of honour more then the orna-

A iiij   mentés

mentes of vertue. For al cognisaunces
or Armes either of nobilitie, or of honour, although they be faire and goodlie in shewe, yet when true vertue is
away, being false, vaine, and void of al
sound fruict, are despised and holden
as worthy of no account with euerie
wise mā. So that, if ye meane to speake
to my rebuke, charge me with some
crime or grieuous offence, laie not vnto me the name of a priuate man. For
before I had the office of a Bishoppe, I
was, both for fauour, authoritie, and
worshippe, preferred before a great
number of your calling. If the name
of a priuate man did signifie dulnes or
lumpishnes of witte, if it did importe
any heinouse crime or dishonestie of
life : then surely, he that shoulde ob-
iect that name to me, should reprochfully speake of me, and contrary to my
desertes. But for so much as we see oftentimes, that, emongest Princes those
mē are in the highest places of honor,
which

which are of al honour moſt vnwor-
thy, and contrariwiſe thoſe voide of al
honour, whiche could moſt faithfully
and honorably ſerue their Princes : it
cōmeth to paſſe, that the name of a pri
uate man ſigniſieth not the vnworthines of the perſons , but the vnluckines
of the Princes. For they are ſo beſette
and holdē with the ſeruice of lewd felowes, that thei can not vſe the vertue
of good men. Now wheras you ſay,
that it is nothing decent, that I being a
ſtraunger ſeperated from you by lande
and ſea , ſhoulde write a letter to your
Queene : I beſeke you Sir, teache me:
were letters deuiſed to aduertiſe mē of
thinges behoueful, in their abſence, or
in their preſence ? Doubtleſſe in their
abſence. Whie then do ye blame me,
that bearing very harty good wil vnto
your Queene, I admoniſhed her being
abſent and ſeperated from me by land
and ſea , of thinges apperteining vnto the eſtabliſhmente of her eſtate ?

If

If I had benne present, I wolde haue humblie besought her, not by letters, but by worde of mowth in presence, that, if she minded to saue her life and mainteine her honour, she should eschew the companie and familiaritie of infamous personnes.

You obiecte also vnto me, that I am not skilled in your affaires. As though I talked not of such matters as are most perfectly knowen of al men.

Last of al you increase the vnworthines of my fact with the name of a Princelie Maiestie : as though your Quene did excel rather in richesse and puissaunce, then in gentlenes and humanitie, and as though I were suche a man as could not by my letters aduertise the greatest Prince in the Christian worlde of things of greatest importaunce. Acknowledge nowe, I pray you, your most vnaduised rashnes in this your talke, for thus muche you seme to saie. Whereas you haue ne-

uer

uer had the practise of the Law, neuer
borne in any common weale office (I
meane such office as apperteine to mē
of Law)neuer offered supplications to
any Prince: Who hath made you so
arrogant and presumptuous, as to take
vpon you to speake vnto the Queenes
Maiestie, a thing graunted to me al only , and to suche as I am , and that for
great good cause ? If you perceiue not
M.Haddon , howe fonde and childish
this your talke is , I must nedes deeme
that you are bestraught of your senses.
But if it greaueth you to see , that the
Quene geueth eare to some other man
that is not of your qualitie , I can not
blame you. For whie , certaine it is,
that you can not long enioy this your
felicitie,if many wise and vertuous mē
shal vnto her good wil and authoritie
ioyne their seruice and industrie. For
the counterfeicted attendaunce of feined vertue , in the presence of true
vertue vanisheth awaie. Wherfore,I
geue

geue you counſel to exclude al honeſt men(ofwhom,as I vnderſtand,there is no ſmal number in England) from the familiaritie of the Prince , expel them, thruſt them out,by proclamatiõs force them to flee out of the Realme.As for me,that am ſo farre of,there is no cauſe whie ye ſhould be greatly careful , for ſo much as it can not be ſuſpected,that I ſhoulde take awaie from you your gaines, after which, as you ſhew your ſelfe , you gape ſo greedilie . But by your pacience Sir , me thinketh ye are of nature very baſe and abiecte , that for ſo meane a promotion take ſo great ſtomake and courage . If ye cannot beare ſo meane a condition , but that you mnſt needes in reſpecte of your office, laie vnto me the name of a priuate man, what would you doe,if you were called to ſome higher degree of worſhippe ?

You ſaie, that I do goe about to appaire the eſtimation of lawes, wheras

in

In deede I doe thinke, that the good e-
ftate of a common weale ftandeth and
is mainteined by lawes, and am hartily
forie, that through thefe peftilēt fectes
al good lawes, cuftomes and ordinaunces are fallen to ruine and decaie.

You faie that I appeache all the
whole Realme of England, I can not
tel, of what, hateful newfanglednes:
the whiche is alfo falfe. For I haue
heard of credible perfonnes, that the
greateft part of that Iland doe continue in the Olde Religion.

Now wheras you require of me to
beare with you, bicaufe you haue talked fomewhat freelie with me, as being an Englifh mā, foftred and brought
vp of the Queenes Maieftie, and of the
affaires of England not ignorant: I com
mend your loue towardes your countrie, I commend your loyaltie towards
your Prince, I cōmend your knowlege
of things gotten by long experience, I
cōmend alfo your freedom in fpeache.

But

But beware you doe not (so muche as in you lieth) ouerthrow your Countrie, beware you bring not the Quene into daunger of her estate and life, and when you are pricked and yearked foorth with the goades of your owne madnes, beware you cloke not your erroneous beleefe and licentious life vnder the honest name of libertie. Ye promise assuredly that you meane to doe it, for no debate or dissension of minde, whereas there can not be deuised any greater dissension then this, you taking vpon you to mainteine, and I contrariwise to inuey against the most wicked and heinouse malefactours of the worlde.

And where you saie, that your purpose is to pul out of mens heartes certaine false opinions that they haue conceiued of the state of England: if you can so doe, you shal doe me a verie friendly pleasure. But this one thing I meruaile much at, that you say, that my

wri-

writings might happẽ to cauſe this falſe
rumor and infamie, that is now bruted
of England. What ſay you Sir? Are
you only ignoraunt, how long time it
is ſence England was firſte charged
with this infamouſe report? How was
it poſsible, when the holie men Iohn
Fiſher Biſhop of Rocheſter, and S. Thomas More were openly put to death
for their conſtancie in their faith and
Religion: when the good Religiouſe
Fathers the Carthuſians were with
moſt cruel tormentes ſlaine and mur-
dred: when the houſes of Religion, in
the whiche was appointed a manſion
or dwelling place of perpetual chaſtitie, were laid wide open, and turned to
prophane vſes: when many other monu
mentes of holines were vtterly ouerthrowen and defaced: how was it poſſible, I ſaie, that England ſhoulde be
without a very exceding great infamie? But without cauſe, ſaie you.
Be it ſo (if it pleaſe you) for I wil not

as

as yet dispute for either part. Yet this muche I saie, that euen at that time there was a great brand of dishonestie burnt into the estimation of English men. But you forsooth, that shoulde haue defended al those thinges with maine pollicie and counsel, were not yet come to beare the swaie, and therfore the matter being destitute of such a spokesman as you are, that opinion that was by the constant reporte and brute of al men diuulged, tooke place in al the Realmes of Christendome. How is it then true, that I should cause this infamie (which is so olde) by my writinges set out but the last daie?

You commend my kinde of writing, the which is more then I require of you. For that I vse in matters wel knowen, words not necessarie (as you thinke) you reproue me. But your reproch I am nothing offended withal: for my desire is to talke of thinges most clere and plaine, and what were to be

put

put into my Oration, and what to be put out, I thinke it dependeth of my iudgement, and not of yours, whiche peraduenture knowe not, what my meaning is.

You saie that, whereas I pretended in the beginning to doe some other thing, I fel at the length to taunting and defacing of Religion. That is trew in deede, if most vile and seditions heresie may be called Religion. You say that it is to no purpose for me to goe about to discharge manie Inglish men of the enuie of the facte, for that, (as you saie) their case and cause is al one. And to proue that, you declare the manner of England to be such, that no law bindeth the people there, vnlesse it be first decreed by the whole communaltie, receiued of the nobilitie, approued by the Clergie, and last of al authorised by the King, and therfore can not stand, that a lawe being made by the ful consent and agreemēt

B   of all

of al, some men should susteine blame,
and some others should be altogether
void thereof. The law I like wel : But
that it is not kept, I thike itmuch to be
misliked. If the geuing of voices were
free , and not wrested and gotten out
frō men by threatning and punishmēt,
I would like your saing wel . But here
to passe ouer with silence the lightnes
and inconstancie of the multitude,
which may verie easilie be brought to
any incōuenience either with the hatred of seueritie, either with the shew
of gentlenes: and withal to leaue that
point vntouched , howe it is a thing
impossible for euerie particular man
to geaue his voice , but of force they
must geue ouer their authoritie of geuing voices vnto a few : I would you
would teach me this one thing, (for
I confesse plainely, that I am a straun-
ger , and nothing expert in matters of
your cōmō weale) what horrible fact
had the bishop of Rochester cōmitted,
that

that neither the grauitie of his perſon, neither the dignitie of a Biſhop could ſaue him from death? Went he about anie treaſon againſt his coūtrey ? Had he conſpired the death of the Prince? Had he entred into talke with foraine ennemies to betraie his owne common weale? Nothing leſſe. But bicauſe he moſt conſtantlie refuſed to yeeld his conſent vnto a wicked ſtatute, the holie and innocent man was ſo puniſhed, as though he had ben the moſt deteſtable traitour in the worlde. What had Thomas More committed, a verie good man, and excellentlie well learned ? Had he forged the Kinges letters patentes? Had he embeſeled the Kinges treaſure ? Had he kylled or greuouſly iniuried any of the Kinges ſubiectes? No ſuche matter. But onelie bicauſe he woulde not claw and flatter the King, but rather woulde ſpeake his minde freelie: they chopped of his

B ij   head

head before al the people, as though he had ben a fellon or traitour. But now what saie you to the Carthusiās, most vertuouse, godly, and religious Fathers, men in pleading at the barre vnacqueinted, in the cōmon affaires and practises of the world vnskilful? Why were thei so cruellie handled? Why were they trussed and hanged vppon gibbets? Whie were they dismēbred and quartered in peaces? Whie were they finally burned and cōsumed with fier? dowbtlesse bicause they would not with their voice allow and make good a thing, that ynto them seemed wicked, heinouse, and vnworthie to be named. What shal I say of the holie bishops, whom you haue lodē with yrōs fetters and chaines, whom you haue shut vp in darke and close prisons, whom you haue robbed both of goods and honour? Haue you any thing elles to laie to their charge, but that they would not geue their assent to your

                                            sta-

ftatutes,which femed to them vniuft?
And therfore it is no wonder, if other
men being with fuch cruel and horrible punifhments put in extreme feare
be not ouer bold to declare their mind
freelie in open place . For where the
geuing of voices is not free,but forced
of men by feare and terrour,there reigneth,not the coūfel of the whole,but
the luft and outrage of a few.You doe
not therefore fufficiently proue , that
thofe lawes were made and allowed
by the cōmon agreement and confent
of al ftates.For it is manifeft, that they
were violently forced , and that who
fo euer did gainefaie them , was extremely punifhed.

As touching my humble fuite vnto
the Queene, wherein I befought her
Maieftie, that, if I were able by good
argumēt to proue,that thefe authours
or brochers of newe fanglednes did
moft daungeroufly and pernicioufly
erre,it might pleafe her to efteme and
B iij   hold

hold their doctrine as vngodly and detestable: you say, that it is a false accusation without strength of argument: that it procedeth of stomake, and not of loue towardes the trewth: that it is grounded vpon a slaunder, and not vpō reason: that it is a reproch, and not a disputation laied vpō the groundworke of religion. You require of me the verie same thing, as I required of your Quene: that is to wit, that if you were able to shew, that I had without good cause found fault with the gouernement of your common weale, I should repent me of myne offence.

First of al, I take Christ Iesus to witnes (who only knoweth the secrettes of my hart) that I wrote those my letters neither for hatred, neither for displeasure, neither for reproche (as you say) but for earnest good zeale and loue I beare to the trewth and to the welfare of the whole realme. For what haue Inglish men hurt me more
then

then other men? What wrong or difpleafure haue thei done me? Trulie neuer a whit. But contrarie wife I haue
ben informed by the letters both of An
tonius Auguftinus Bifhop of Ilerda, a
man for his excellēt vertues and fingular knowledge in the liberal fciences,
wel deferuing the dignitie of a bifhop
together with immortal fame (who
was fometime fent from the bifhop of
Rome legat vnto Quene Marie) as alfo by the letters of Iohn Metellus a
Burgonion, a man, whom for his courteous and fwete conuerfation ioyned
with rare giftes of learning I loue verie intierly: that manie great learned
men in England did geaue me a verie
honourable report. Wherefore there
was good caufe, whie I fhould rather
loue Englifh men, then malice or reuile them. Neither did I euer thinke
to reprooue your common weale,
but the corrupt lewdnes of a fewe,
which difquieteth the whole realme.

           B iiij   And

And whereas you charge me with cu-
riofitie for medling in a ftraunge common weale : I thinke it is no ftraunge
common weale, but myne owne.
For I did not reafon of the lawes of
your Realme and ciuile ordinaunces,
but of Chriftiā religion, for the which
I am not afraid to loofe my life. And
therefore fhal I neuer thinke any thing
to be impertinent to me, whereby I
may mainteine and fet foorth the honour of this common weale. Confider
now, M. Haddon, how iuft your requeft is. This is your demaund. If you
can conuince and manifeftly prooue,
not that I am in any errour (for that
were tolerable) but that I wrote my e-
piftle for hatred, euil wil, and reproch:
you require of me to confeffe my fault
and to faie that I was ouer rafh, when
I tooke vpon me to control your matters, whiche I knew not. Can you
on the other fide prooue, whereas I
meāt louingly, frindly, and religioufly,
                                    that

that it was done flaunderoufly, enui-
oufly and vntruly? But left you fhould
fay, I deale to ftraightly with you, this
much I promife you faithfully. If you
be able to proue, not that I wrote for
any euil intent (for that is impoffible)
but that the rearing vp of this your
newly framed religion is without all
fault and blamelefle, I wil repét me of
my doyng. I am not ignorant, how
daungerous a matter it is, to promife
thus much to a man of law. But bicaufe I haue a good affiaunce, that
you fhal not be able to circumuent me
with any malicious and crafty fetch of
the law, and my defire is to difcharge
honeft men of flaunderous reportes: I
promife you thus much of myne honeftie: if you be able to proue, that
thofe felowes be honeft, godlie, and
religious men, whiche I take to be
lewde and wicked verlettes, I will
neuer fpeake one word againft you.

You take it in fnuffe M. Haddon,
that

that I deale so boisteously with your
new maisters, saing that I doo oftentimes thunder out against them most
horrible and fyerie reproches, yea so
much, that mans hart can not deuise
any thing more detestable. Wherin I
perceiue that you can not well discerne, what an argument, and what a
reproch is. For I contended not with
reprochful woordes, but with argumentes, such as you can not yet answere. Than you saie. *Where are these*
monsters of Religion? What are thei?
How long haue they continued? Where
are those misshapen felowes to be found?
If you thinke to shift the manifold argumētes which I haue vsed, with such
a glittering shew of wordes, you are
much deceiued. For I loke for reasons,
and not for a vaine noise of wordes.
But that, that you bring in vpō this, is a
very toy and mockerie. Your woords
be these. *Declare the thinges, name the*
persones, note the times, adde the circū-
stances,

ſtaces,that we may haue ſome certaintie,
wherin to ſtād with you, as alſo to with-
ſtand you. I thinke, M. Haddon, it was
longe, ere you were ſet to the Rheto-
rike ſchole, and that ye were not verie
apte to learne it. You would be counted a Rhetorician , and yet you know
not that Rhetorique is a prudencie or
diſcretion in ſpeaking: ſo that what ſo
euer is againſt diſcretion, is not conuenient in this arte, whiche you went a-
bout to learne at an incōuenient time.
There is a rule of the law, vſual in iud-
gemētes, which is this. Whē the que-
ſtiō is, not of the law, but of the facte,
the offence being ſecrete, we muſt vſe
al argumētes and coniectures poſſible,
to bring the truth of the facte to light.
For it muſt be cōſidered, of what conuerſation, of what life, of what auda-
citie the partie arreined was : it muſt
be weyed, what feare , what deſire,
what enuie, what hatred might moue
him to committe the facte : it muſt be
declared,

declared, what oportunitie he had, what time, what occaſion, what pollicie to cōceale, what hope to eſcape, what ſuſpiciō went before, what came after, with all other circumſtances, which maie before the iudges increaſe the ſuſpiciō of the fact. Now ſir when your maiſter (which as it ſemeth, was but meanelie ſeene in theſe matters) had taught you this rule : you thought it wolde ſerue in al cauſes, not only in iudgemente, but els where : and therfore you require of me ſuch circumſtances as the cauſe did nothing require. For my meaning was not to accuſe any man, but to aduertiſe the Quene, that ſhe ſhould not ſuffer her ſelfe to be brought to any inconuenience. If you or any ſuch as you are were to be arreined, what? ſhould we, in a matter openlie knowen and not denied, but defended to be lawfully done, vſe ſuch argumentes, coniectures and circumſtances as you require?

quire? Not so. But it were sufficient
to declare, that your doinges were
heinouse and vngodlie. And he that
should otherwise doe, might worthely
be laught to scorne as a trifling and a
foolish babler. Why then Sir? If you
neither vnderstande what is decent,
neither consider what the cause requireth, neither perceiue the difference
of thinges: is it meete, that I shoulde
be punnished for your ignorance? I
thinke not so. But whereas my meaning was, not to arreine any man, but
only to admonishe your Prince, that
she would put awaie from her selfe
and her realme the peril that hangeth
ouer them: could I doo any lesse, but
set the greatnes of the daunger before
her eyes? And bicause the greatest
daunger in the wordle is, to take a
false religion for a true: I shewed certaine markes, by the whiche a man
might discerne false and diuelish heresie, from true and godly religion. Those
                              markes,

markes, if they be falſe, reproue them:
if they be not manifeſt, conuince me
of ignorance: if they offend not you,
hold your peace: if vnwares I touched
you at the quicke, ſhew your greeſe.

Monſters of Religion I know there
are verie manie, it they be not yet
come into England, I am glad for your
countreis ſake: and I confeſſe I was in
an errour, when I thought that your
Iland had ben peſtered with diuers
and ſundrie kindes of ſuch monſters.
But your bare denyal is no ſufficient
Confutation. You muſt vſe manifeſt
proofes: you muſt declare by good
reaſon, that I was in an errour, and
then I will ſaie, that you are an eloquent felow. But if you can not doo
this, but only prate and talke: I am
not bounde to beleeue you. A litle
after ye ſaie thus. *You crie out againſt
religiõ, you fight againſt the ſetters foorth
of religion, in theſe two pointes you vſe
much bitter talke, and yet in neither of
them*

them both do you tel vs either what it is, *or where it is .* Sir either you haue not read my letters, or if you haue , the meaning of them, whiche is verie plaine, you vnderſtande not (ſuche is peraduēture the dulnes of your witte). Could any man ſet foorth more plain-ly with wordes, the infamous doinges of men, the great owtrage, and cruell impietie of their procedinges ? Anon after, ye take a peece as it maie appere out of ſome other mās oration, and ſet it in for your owne, in a place nothing to the purpoſe. theſe be your wordes. *This your accuſation is verie pitiful , the* *which if I anſwere but with one woord,* *ther is no remedie, you muſt needes hold* *your peace.* It is euen ſo , ſir , you haue made a great ſpeake. The thinges that you haue done, the deuiſes and practi-ſes that you haue wrought, al was don in darkenes and huggermugger. Ther are no witneſſes , ther remaineth no footeſteps to tracke you out, no ſignes

and

and tokens by the which a man might come to the knowledge of your doinges. Then you faie thus. *You crie, yea with gaping mowth, and that verie lamentably: that this newly deuifed Religiō is to be fhunned, abandoned, and abhorred, that the begynners of it were mifchieuous perfons, murderers, cutthrotes, poifoners, ouerthrowers of cōmon weales, ennemies of mankind.* Surely this talke that you afcribe vnto me, is yours, and not myne, how be it I am not angry with you for the deuifing of it. For fuch heinoufe offenfes would be fhakē vp with much fharper wordes then thefe be. But fir how anfwere you thefe thinges? Full ftowtly I warrant you, they can not be denied. Yet thus you faie. *I conftantly affirme, that ther is no fuch thing: I beleeue not you, I require to be inftructed. What faie you? What proue you?* Oh what an eloquent felow is this, that cā fo eafily with one claufe or fentence, and that verie fhort, fhut

vp

vp the whole matter? How manfully
you stand to your defence? How warily you kepe out your ennemie? In
good sooth I can not but muse at your
folie,to see, vpon how smal occasion
(when you haue said nothing at all)
you fal to crying out, as though you
had vttered some excellent matter. I
said in that my epistle,that the Virgins
or Nunnes consecrated vnto God,
were defiled with incestuous wedlocke: I said that the images of Saincts,
and of the Crosse, yea and of Christ
him selfe crucified, were pulled out of
their places, and broken in peaces. I
said, that the olde Religion was ouer-
throwne,and a new set vp in the place
of it. Other thinges I let passe, re-
seruing them to their conuenient
places. What saieth M. Haddon to
al this? Al these thinges confuteth he,
like an Oratour, with one word: and
driueth me to the wall, that I can goe
no farder. *I beleue you not,* saieth he, *I*

C   *require*

*require to be instructed. What saie you ?
What proue you ?* Whie then what shall
I doo ? Whether shall I goe ? M Haddon an Inglish man , a man verie expert in the affaires of his countrey ,
saieth plaeinly , that thinges that are
commonly reported to haue ben done
in England , were neuer done. If it be
so , I must bring witnesses. And prin-
cipally I will cite you to geaue witnesse . If you will confesse so muche
as I require of you, you shal ridde me
of great trouble. If you denie it , then
will I call other witnesses to testifie
for me, if nede shall so require. Afterward ye bring in these wordes . *You
crie out as lowd as you can, heaping together all the villanous woordes in the
worlde , whiche , it seemeth, you haue
sorted out, and set a side for the nonce,
to deface this your counterfaict religion,
and to sticke and kill certaine personnes,
which no man knoweth but your selfe.*

I praie

I praie you, M. Haddon, fobre your
felfe a litle, but euen fo longe, as
you maie perufe againe this your
talke. You fhall fee your felfe, that
you were ftarke madde, when you
wrote thefe thinges. For you vtter
fuche matter, as neither I, nor you
your felfe doo vnderftand.

You faie, that I doo deface my
counterfaicte religion with woordes
of villanie. I omitte the name of counterfaicte Religion, as though I had
ben the authour or begynner of any
newe Religion at all. But how fhould
I my felfe deface myne owne Religion, which I doo mainteine and with
dew praife fet out? This would I faine
learne of you.

Then for the perfonnes, which you
faie I fticke, I wold gladly vnderftand
what they are. As for Luther with his
adherétes and folowers I take them for
moft wicked and infamous perfones,

C ij   and

and such in dede I doo a litle pricke in my writinges. These are the persons, which you saie no man knoweth but I. And you forsooth, know them not: and yet you commend them highly, which is a point of meruelouse great ouersight in you to commend such as you know not. But you, will neither saie so, neither can you wel tell, what you wolde saie. Doubtlesse it were better, to be dome, then to vtter such matter, as no man neither sad nor mad can vnderstand.

You accuse me that I haue defamed your most noble Iland, being thervnto brought by pelting rumours of maliciouse persones. Whie then, sir, you graunt, that I haue deuised nothing, but what I haue spoken, I was moued to speake by common report. Moreouer I haue alreadie declared, that I spake not against the whole Iland, as you saie, but only against the brochers of your new fangled Religion.

Now

Now whereas I said, that heresie and sectes are popular, which is verie daungerous and noisome to Princes, that minde to rule like kinges, (wherin you M. Haddon, find great fault with me) if I prooue it not by good reason, I am content, you shal take me, yea and proclaime me as a slaunderer. But of this we wil talke hereafter.

The mischieuouse practise of poison, wherwith it is reported that certaine Princes haue ben killed, you pourge with two examples taken out of your auncient Cronicles. For you saie, that the Emperour Henrie the fourth was made awaie by the treason of a monke, that gaue him the blessed Sacrament infected with poison. You saie also that Iohn king of Englād was by the like man and maner poisoned. I know that both these tales are proued to be slaunderous lyes by good and approued writers. But to my matter, whether it were so or not, it skilleth

C iij   litle.

litle. Neither did I euer faie, that before Martin Luther there was no man
that could ſ kill in poiſon, or that beſides him ther was neuer ill monke or
frier in the wordle. But thus much I
ſaid, that when ſuch offences are committed in common weales, by men
not ſo well trained in godlie life: it
were expedient, that they were refourmed, by the puritie of this your
moſt vnſpotted diſcipline, by the wholſome vertue of your goſpell, by the
goodlie redreſſe that your Doctours
haue brought to the wordle. The
whiche being nothing ſo, but all together to the contrarie, (for it is
manifeſte that within theſe thirtie
yeares laſt paſt manie moe conſpi-
racies haue ben wrought againſt Princes, then in many hundred yeares
before) I maie boldly ſaie, that the
operation of this your medicine is
not ſo effectuall, as you take it to be.
Soone after ye ſaie thus. *But to re-*
herſe

hearſe theſe thinges particularly vnto
you,is not nedeful, whiche being neerer
vnto ſuch miſchiefes then I am,maie the
better learne out of your neighbours
bookes : how often the cuppes of poiſon
haue walked emongeſt the Princes and
rulers of the Churche of Rome : and how
and by whome the ſedes of diſcorde and
warres haue ſuffered thorough all the
common weales of the Chriſtian Domi-
nion. You are a wonderful fellow M.
Haddon . This obſcure and intricate
maner of ſpeaking liketh you meruelouſly well. I praie you what woulde
you ſaie, when you ſaie that I am neerer vnto ſuch miſchiefes ? Meane you
that I am neerer, as acceſſarie to ſuch
faultes? If you ſaie ſo (as your wordes
ſeeme to importe) , you are not well
acqueinted with my manners. If you
ſaie,I am of that countrei, wher poiſon is oftentimes geuen to Princes in
meates and drinkes, that is falſe alſo .
For there is no coūtrey in the worlde,

C iiij   where

where the name of a king is more
reuerenced then here. If you faie that
I am neerer vnto Rome, where such
thinges are fometimes vfed, furely you
haue not wel learned the fituations
and diftances of countreis. For we are
much farder from the citie of Rome
then you are. Whereas you faie, that
the feedes of warres haue fuffered,
what your meaning is, I affure you I
can not tel. Except peraduenture the
printer miftooke, and for this woorde
Difperfa, put in vnwares *perpeffa*.

As towching the heades or prelates
of the Churche, whiche were made
awaie with poifon : I graunt that fuch
wicked actes haue fometimes ben cōmitted. For it chaunceth often, that,
where a man wolde leaft looke for it,
there reigneth moft the heinoufe vices
of coueteoufnes and ambition : out of
the which two fountaines fpringeth al
euils to the deftruction of mankind.
Yet this I warne you, that it is muche
looked

looked for, that the redreſſe of al theſe
euils ſhould procede from your Euan-
gelike diſcipline, which pretendeth in
outward ſhew to make an end of al
enormities.

But ſir, what is it, that you beare
your ſelfe ſo holily, ſo godly, ſo religiouſly, yeelding vnto God thankes
with ſo kind and mindful hart, for the
benefite of this your Goſpel. Thus you
ſaie. *I humbly hold vp my handes vnto*
the immortal God, thanking him hartily,
that it hath pleaſed him, by the riſing of
the ſonne of his Goſpel openly emongeſt
vs, to driue awaie the moſt depe darkenes
of the times paſt: through the lacke of
whoſe knowledge, and through the affi-
aunce of ſuperſtition, we walowed be-
fore without care in the ſinke of vice,
beleeuing that by the lead of Bulles, and
by the mumbling of praiers not vnder-
ſtoode, was purged, what ſo euer ſinne
might be committed in this life. What
more godlie praier could be deuiſed
than

than this? You thanke God, that you
are deliuered frō most perilous darkenes, yea and that through the light and
shining of the gospel, which was writen and set out, not by Matthew, Iohn
or any other holy Euangelist, but by
Luther, Melanchton, Zwinglius, and
suche other worshipful squiers lately
dropte out from heauen. And so being
deliuered through the benefit of this
prosperous and luckie gospel from the
stincking dich of al filthines, in the
which you wallowed before (as you
confesse your selfe) hauing affiaunce in
superstitiō: you are now no more sub-
iecte vnto the brandes of fleshly lust:
you are no more troubled with ambition: you are not occupied in the troublesome cares of coueteousnes: you
are not puffed vp with pride and vaine
glorie: you trust no more to fraude, deceit, and lying For it is like, that hauig
receiued the brightnes of heauenly
light, ye dispised foorthwith al worldly
thinges, and were inflamed with the

desire of heauenlie life, yea and (that
more is) of the diuine nature it selfe.
Who ca deny, if this be so, but that so
wonderful an alteration of life doth
most manifestly declare the verie presence of Christ him selfe? But I would
faine learne this of you, whether you
alone in al England, doe enioye these
so great benefites, or whether thei be
common to al suche, as haue receiued
the brightnes of your new gospel. If
you alone haue the fruitio of this light
with so great fruict of the heauely vertue: the glittering of this newe gospel
hath brought no great commoditie to
your coutrei. for it should haue surde-
red, not any one particular ma, but the
whole comon weale. Oh say you, euerie one. for as the sonne rising driueth
awaie the darkenes from the eyes of
al men : euen so the brightnes of this
gospel putteth awaie the myste that
was cast ouer all mens heartes. Al
thinges are now laid open, al thinges
are

are come to light. Ther are no faultes in the worlde, no wicked offences, no heinouſe crimes, no, none at al . Ther is great good cauſe, if this tale be true, whie we ſhould forſake our owne countrei, and come to dwel in Englãd, that we might be partakers of this your felicitie with you . For what could a man deſire more of God, then alwaies to behold ſuche a countrei, where, for the greater part, neither coueteouſnes, nor ſenſualitie, nor ha-tred, nor pride, nor contention, nor raſhnes, nor any other ſpot of vncleane life may take place. But, Sir, I praie you: What was the let, whie you vſed no iuſtice or godlines, before this new ſonne beames ſhone vpon you ? Hor-rible ſuperſtition, you ſaie . for we be-leeued, that through the vertue of a peece of lead, and the mumbling of a few praiers, whiche we vnderſtoode not, al our offences were forgeauen vs, what ſoeuer we had done in this world.

worlde. What faie you? is it to be thought you were alſo mad, that you wolde thinke a ſinne conceiued in the hart to be forgeauen through the vertue of a peece of lead, or by the pronouncing of praiers, the mind being otherwiſe occupied? What a great dulnes of witte was that? what a ſtraunge folie? who had put that errour into your hartes? Were there no men emongeſt you learned in the holie ſcriptures, to teach you, that al the hope of ſaluation conſiſteth in the grace and mercie of Chriſt? Trulie I hold vp my handes moſt humbly vnto the immortal God (as you pretend to doe) yeelding him moſt hartie thâkes, that it was my chaunce to be borne and brought vp in Spaigne, where no man(if he be a Chriſtian) was euer ſo fooliſh as to thinke, that there is any other waie to pourge ſynne, but only by the grace and goodnes of Chriſt. The which to atteine, the neceſſarie

and

and onely meane is according to the doctrine of Chrift him felfe , to deteft and forfake vice,to confeffe our finnes cómitted with bafhfulnes and forow, to withdraw our felues fró fenfualitie to cótinencie,fró vice to honeftie, fró malice to charitie,to enter into a new trade of life,and to exercife our felues in holy workes.Now fir , of you tru-fted fo much to lead , that ye thought it of force to blot out finne: you were not wel in your wit.If you faie that al England was in the like blindnes, you bring a great flaunder of madnes vpon your countrie , that hath brought you vp and placed you in fo great worfhip. No,fay you,I faie not fo. But I meane by the name of lead , in the whiche we faw the name and image of the bi-fhop of Rome engraued , the authori-tie and iurifdiction of the Pope him felfe, the which manie hundred yeres agoe, was holden and efteemed as a thing verie holie , of our Fathers and

after-

afterward of vs. This authoritie, which
we fometime reuerenced, being now
inftructed by the moft cleere doctrine
of this gofpel, I doe neglecte, defpife,
contemne, and thinke it to be efteemed as a thing of naught of all wife
men. Whie then, M. Haddon, what
needed you the name of lead to fi-
gnifie this authoritie? Did you it,
to make it more odioufe? Or rather
thought you by iefting at the woord
to gette the greater applaufe of your
compagnions? For I knowe, that
pleafaunt fporters, as you be, are
muche delighted with iefting, and
like to contend not fo much with argumentes and fentences, as with
fcoffing, and (as it feemeth to me)
with an vnfauerie kind of pratling. In
fuche like fcoffes and tauntes Martine Luther your youthlie Patriarke
and olde wanton was a great doer.
And I dowbt not but fome of your
clawebackes, when he came to this
place

place, tooke vp a great laughter, and bound it with an oth, that it was meruelous pleasauntly spoken, and excellently wel handled. For al thinges are so farre out of course and dew order, that it is a verie easie matter for a sawcie reprochful scoffer, to get the name of a merie felowe and pleasaunt compagnion.

But as concerning this matter, although the Bishop of Angra hath disputed verie learnedly of the authoritie of the Bishop of Rome: yet wil I reason with you (as with a seculare man and ciuilian) of the said matter in few wordes. First of al let this be a groundeworke or foundation. The Church of Christ is one and not manie. Then let this be agreed vppon. It is not ynough for a Prince, whiche maketh lawes to establish a common weale, to set them out, except he also appoint gouernours and inferiour magistrates. Let this also be the third ground,

The Monarchie of the Church.

ground. (for so much as you like wel
myne opinion as touching the order of
a Monarchie) that it is most expedient
for a common Weale well appointed
with customes and lawes, to be vnder
the rule of one Prince. For many doe
teare and dismembre a cōmon weale,
but one by supreme authoritie vniteth
and as it were with glew, ioineth together the heartes of the people. It was
therfore most agreable to the best maner of gouernement, when the Prince
of al Princes (vnder whose euerlasting
Empire are subiected both heauen and
earth) intended to set vp a heauenlie
cōmon weale in earth : that he should
first make Lawes, and then creat Princes and Magistrates, which might according to the prescribed order of
Lawes and equitie , rule this common
weale. Suche were the Apostles and
the rest of the Disciples of Christe .
Last of al , lest the band of this societie
might be dissolued , and the peace of

D the

the Citie diſtourbed : he appointed a Monarchie, and gaue the ſupreme gouernement thereof vnto Peter. Are not theſe thinges commonly knowen of all men ? Ymagine you to obſcure and darken thinges moſt clearely ſpoken ? Truſt you ſo muche to your malice, that you thinke your ſelfe able to wreſt the wordes of the Goſpell from the true meaning, to ſerue the filthie appetite and luſt of you and your companions ? I pray you what can be ſpoken more plainely and cleerelie then

Mat.16.c. thoſe woordes ? Thou arte Peter, ſaith Chriſt, and vpon this rocke I wil build my Churche. And what ſo euer thou ſhalt bind vpõ the earth, it ſhalbe boñd

Luc.22.d. in heauen. And againe. I haue prayed for thee, that thy faith faile not, and thou being turned, confirme thy brethren. And many other places of like effect, which do manifeſtly proue, that Peter had a Prerogatiue aboue the reſt of the Apoſtles. But you wil ſaie for al

this

this, that these testimonies of the holy
scriptures, which we haue alleged, are
expouded farre otherwise of the new
Apostles. I wil set against the authoritie of your Apostles, the authoritie of
S. Ambrose, Augustine, Hierome, Basile, and all other holie men, that haue
with their writings geuen light to the
Church of Christ. But now your Doctours wil answere, that although it be
true that the supreme authoritie was
graunted to Peter, yet foloweth it not,
that it was geuen to his successours also. Why then I aske you another question. Did Christe set vp a Church to
continue but for one mans life? Or els
minded he to establish it for euer?
If he appointed, that his Church should
stande so little time, he didde not so
great a thing, as was to be looked for
of his infinite bountie and wisedome :
for so muche as he bestowed so much
labour and diligence, yea and shedde
so muche bloud about a common weale,

whose cōtinuance was limited within
the bounds of so short time. If he minded that his church should cōtinue for
euer : then doubtlesse he set it in such
order, as should in al chaunges and alterations of times be mainteined and
kept. If it be then euident(as it is most
euident and plaine) that Peter had a
Superioritie ouer the rest of the Apostles : it must needes folowe, that the
same preeminence or principalitie, of
right apperteineth to al suche as haue
succeded in Peters roome and charge.
Or els, in the Church of Christ, which
is one, it might seeme there was ordeined not the order of the heauēly Monarchie, but the gouernement of manie. And then what knot or band of
concord were there in the Churche ?
By whose authoritie shoulde the tempestes risen in it be asswaged ? By
whome should seditious opinions and
sectes be rooted out ? By whom should
pride and stubbornes be restreined and
kept

kept vnder : if there had ben no man
appointed in the Church from the beginning, by whose authoritie all men
should be kept in order? Nowe for so
much as the church of Christ is simple
and one: and one it can not be, vnlesse
there be in it one only Prince: furthermore being euidente and plaine, that
Christ ordeined one onely ruler in his
Church, whom al men should acknow
ledge and obeie: finally being out of
al doubt, that this preeminence apperteineth to the Successours of Peter,
and that none of al the aūcient Fathers
endewed with the spirit and grace of
God euer doubted, but that the bishops
of Rome were the successours of Peter (as bothe their writinges, and the
common agreement of the vniuersall
Church declareth): with what sprite
were your newe Apostles moued to
bring in this new Gospellish doctrine,
to distourbe the order appointed by
Christe, to breake the bande of vnitie

D iij   and

and concord, to shake the very Rocke
and staie of the Churche.   But lest
some man shuld thinke, that these thinges were wrought of them without
any cause in the world, I wil briefly declare, what their deuise, or rather what
the fetch of Satā was in this enterprise·
It was vnpossible that euer the pestilēt
sects should gather any strēgth, except
the authoritie of the Bishop of Rome
had ben first weakned. For how could
the mischieuous weede haue growen
any long time, whereas it was a very
easy matter with the authoritie of the
Bishop of Rome, forthwith to cut it
doune, so soone as it appeared aboue
the groūd. Take vs (saith the spouse of

Cant,2.d. Christ) the litle foxes, that destroy the
Vineyardes. This request of the spouse
who shalbe able to fulfil, if no man haue
authoritie to suppresse the malice and
lewdnes of heretikes, before it waxe
great? For it is manifest that by the foxes are vnderstode heretikes. And therfore

fore S.Paul in his second epiſtle to the Theſſaloniãs ſaith, that Antichriſt ſhal not come before the great reuoltĩg or departure frõ the catholike Church of Chriſt. It is therefor neceſſari for theſe yong Antichriſts, which(as S. Iohnſaieth)do in figure and ſignificatiõ repreſent the great Antichriſte to come, before they can bring their purpoſed miſchief to paſſe, not only to depart them ſelues frõ the Church, and from the ſupreme ruler of it, but alſo to ſolicite and procure to the like departure all ſuch as they mind to carie away, and make their diſciples: and this is the cauſe that al heretikes, whoſe chiefe endeuour and principal intent is to ouerthrowe the catholike Church, do firſt of al aſſaile this fortreſſe, do here plant their ordinaunce, doo here make their battery, do here vndermine to ouerrhrow the forte. For they ſee, that if this fortreſſe were once ouerthrowen and wonne, they may frely ſow the ſeades

2. *Theſſal.* 2. *b.*

D iiij of

of al naughtines, and to the ruine and
decaie of manie, flee vppe and downe
through the worlde, whether so euer
thei litt, without any cōtrol or checke.
And to passe ouer the olde Heretikes,
this was the cause whie Husse endeuoured to ouerthrow the authority of
the Bishop of Rome. This was also the
meaning of Hierome of Prage, when
he went about to weaken the authority of the said bishop This was the way,
by the which Frier Luther thought vtterly to destroy the Catholike church.
This was the traine, by the whiche in
Englād a gap was vnaduisedly opened
to al suche errours, as sence that time
haue followed. Nowe the railes and
barres being after this manner broken
downe, and the gates laid wide open, it
was a very casie matter for al vile and
desperate felowes to rush in, to mangle
and teare in peeces the vnitie of the
Churche, to bring in so many wicked
errours, suche horrible sectes, suche a
rable

rable of pestilent opinions, one directly
against an other. The Zwinglians fight
against the Lutherãs. The Anabaptists
kepe continual warre with the Zwinglians. What should I here reherse the
heretikes called heauenly Prophetes,
the Interimnists, and such other names
of sectaries? What should I saie of the
hatred, malice, brawling, and discorde
within them selues? What shoulde I
speake of their variety and incõstancy
in opiniõs? Yea and such as are of one
sect, are not al, nor alwaies of one opinion. Many points of their Doctrine
they correct, they alter and chaunge,
thei turne in and out, they blot out the
old, they make newe, nowe they pull
downe, and now they set vp, they can
not wel agree neither with other men,
nor yet with them selues. What saye
you to this Sir? Are not these thinges
true? Can you saie, that al such as are
spróg of Martine Luther, are throughly agreed? that there is emógest them

no

no debate, no difcorde, no diuerfitie of opinions, but contrarily mofte perfect agreement in matters of faith and religion? O M. Haddon how muehe better had it benne to reuerence that peece of lead, whiche you fo muche fcorne at then to open a way to fo many, yea and thofe fo peftilent errours? But let vs returne to your Oration. Thefe are your wordes.

But the authority of the holy Scriptures hath thundred in our eares, and hath made vs fo affraid, that cafting awaie the deuifes of men, we runne onely to the free mercie of God. What is this? Do you fo requite Luther, to whome you are bound for this fingular benefite? For it was he that draue all feare out of your hartes. What terrour is this that you fpeake of? What feare? What carefulneffe of minde? Suche is the faith, that Luther deuifed, as being once well planted in your hearte, no feare in the worlde fhall euer be able

to

to ſhake the quietnes and ſecuritie of
your conſcience. And , me thinketh,
that it is not to be borne, that you ſaie,
you doe deſpiſe the deuiſes of men.
For you are not ſo farre forewarde in
the waie of heauenly life, but that you
make good accompte of ſome men.
For the diuiſes of Luther, Zwinglius,
Bucer, Caluin, and ſuch other as were
the founders of this your new cōmon
weal, you haue learned them, you haue
greedily ſnatched them vppe, yea you
haue with heart and minde embraced
them , ſtriuinge within your ſelues,
who ſhoulde be foremoſte in them,
finallie you haue decreed to frame the
order of your life after their directi-
on . Whereby we gather , you looke
not ſo ſteddilie to heauenwarde , but
that ſometimes you looke downe
vppon menne . And well donne
too ſurelie . For righte and reaſon
requireth , that you ſhoulde alwaies
haue bothe in your eyes and heartes
ſuch

ſuche men as they were, ſo chaſte, ſo
holie, and ſo religious. But yeat this
muche I tel you by the waie, your
minde was not ſo feruently inflamed
with the loue of heauenly thinges, but
that you did highly eſteeme ſome men
withal. Admitte that Frier Luther had
ben a holie man (euen as holie as you
liſt to make him) that Melanchon had
ben void of al earthlie affection : that
Zuinglius for the meruelouſe reporte
of ſincere and chaſte life had ben ad-
mitted to be one of Gods owne priuie
coũſel: that Bucer had excelled al men
in cleane, honeſt, and chaſt conuerſation: that Caluine had paſſed in vertue
and holines Bernarde, Anſelme, Au-
guſtine, Ierome, Baſile, and al other
holy men, that haue lead an angelike
life here vpon the earth: yea adde vnto theſe (if it pleaſe you) euen your
owne Martyr, whoſe rare vertue you
commend ſo highly : Admitte I ſaie,
that theſe men had ben moſt excellently

lently furnished with al the highest
vertues, yea and most chaste withal:
yet were they men, and it is not impossible, but that they might haue ben
in some errours. And yet doo you e-
steeme their lawes, decrees, and ordinances, as a discipline of moste high
wisedome, and as a most holie rule of
mans life. With what face then saie
you, that you despised, and reiected
the deuises of men, whereas you doo
ascribe vnto those menne that I haue
here named, almoste a diuine perfection? But now let vs consider the ende
of your oration. Soone after you bring
in this clause. *Hauing in like manner*
regarde vnto the saying of the Prophete,
where he commaundeth vs, that wee
should confourme the innocencie of our
life vnto holinesse and iustice. In this
place I merueiled excedingly, not at
you, M. Haddon (for it is not credible, that so graue a man as you be,
should lie so impudently) but at the
slaun-

ſlaūderous report of men, which with
feined tales, and forged cōplaintes (ab-
uſing vs being ſtraungers, and ignorāt
(as you ſay) of your affaires haue made
vs beleeue that you conforme you
ſelues, not vnto holines of life by the
law of God, but vnto licentious lewdnes through vnbridled luſte and bolde
preſumption. And the doctrine of that
mad felowe Martine Luther made it
ſeeme the more probable, the whiche
cōdemning wickedly al good workes,
and burning at a ſermō the Canōs and
holie ordinaunces of the Church, and
teaching for a ſownd doctrin this pre-
ſumptuous affiaunce, vnto the which
alone he aſcribeth ſaluation, calling it
raſhly and impudently by the name of
faithe, and putting quitte out of mens
harttes al teare of lawes bothe of God
and man, ſetteth out ſenſualitie in her
ful ſtrength and force, geaueth fleſhlie
luſt free ſcope and libertie, pretendeth
hoope of impunitie, boldeneth men to
al

al synne and wickednes. Wherefore I
thought it impossible, that a man obser
uing his preceptes, should withal geue
his mind to iustice, vertue and religio,
or take great care how to keepe him
selfe chast and honest. For it is the part
of a wise man, when he seeth the cause
to doubte nothing of the euent. And it
is commonly seene, that naughtie be-
gynninges haue the like ending. What
should I then do? Seing iust cause of infamie, hearing it most commonly, yea
and sadly reported, that you are in
farre worse case, then you pretende to
be: weying withal the constant fame,
which is, that such as folowe this new
religion, are not only subiect to fleshly
and vncleane liuing, but also much in-
creased in al wicked and heinouse vices: should I not beleeue it? Should
I stande against moste credible personnes reporting it? Should I without
any groud, without witnesses, vainely
contend, seing the comon agreement
                                    of

of al men confirming this opinion? I could not doe it. Wherfore if that be false, whiche was constantly and not without inward sorow of al good men reported, you must pardon me, and lay the fault vnto the lightnes and impudécie of certaine men bearing you no good wil, whiche were the deuisers of this false report. But if it be true that is reported, then are you a very madde man, if you thinke by lying and facing to wash out the spot of true infamie.

Here you muse againe what I meát to aduertise your Queene, to beware of suche as are infected with these heresies. And here I tel you againe, that, when I come to that place, I wil doo my endeuour so to handle it, that you shal no more muse at it.

You declare vnto me the felicitie of your Quene, that she aboundeth in riches, that she liueth in prosperitie, that she feareth no treason, neither of her owne subiéctes, neither of forenners.

ners. I am right glad of it, and I pray
God graunt her alwaies a good, prosperous and flourishing reigne. Yet is
it the part of a wise Prince, in calme
weather to thinke of a storme, and to
consider long time before, not when
the mariners them selues begynne to
tremble and quake, howe to saue her
selfe: and seing with what tempestes
the maiestie of other Princes hath ben
ruffled in diuers and sundrie realmes,
to mistrust, that her maiestie also maie
experience the like fortune. Of the
tempest in Fraunce, the which you say
is asswaged, I saie nothing elles, but
that you beare witnesse againft your
owne selfe. For, I praie you Sir, who
stirred vp that tempest? Who armed
the Frenche men againft the King of
Fraunce? What discipline or instruction had they, whiche contrary to their
oth taken in the face of the worlde,
conttarie to theyr allegiaunce towards their Prince, finallie contrarie

The re-
bellion in
Fraunce,

E   to

to the maieſtie and reuerence of kingly name, ſet them ſelues in armour a-
gainſt the Kings owne perſon, not only traiterouſly and villanouſly to diſ-
patch the King out of his life, but alſo
to aboliſh the name of a King vtterly
out of the common weale? And you
ſay, the tempeſt is aſſwaged. As though
I had ſaid that, what ſo euer ſuch traitors had moſt wickedly and rebelliuſly
deuiſed, muſt nedes haue a proſperous
ſucceſſe. No, no. Their wicked attempt
was repreſſed by policie and force, and
eſpecially by the great grace and benefite of God: it is nothing long of thē,
that (like rebelles) made warre againſt
their prince. For to haue brought their
purpoſe to a miſchieuous ende, there
lacked not in them any good wil, but
ſtrength and power.

My diſcourſe of the contempte of
wordly thinges and deſire of heauenly
things you miſlike not: but you ar mad
angry with me, bicauſe I cal ſuch men
ene-

enemies of Religion, as you ſaie were
the ſeruaũtes of God, and ſent frõ heauen for the ſaluation of the world, and
it greaueth you, that I ſhould laugh at
their vaine and foliſh attẽpts. Tel me I
pray you Sir, what take thoſe felowes
vpõ them, which were ſent, as you ſay
from heauẽ? Doubtles, to deliuer Chriſtian men from errour, throughly to
purge the Churche, to reſtore the doctrine and rule of the Apoſtles life, to
ſet the truth at libertie, whiche was, as
you ſay, oppreſſed with coueteouſnes
and ambitiõ, to pul dreames and ſuper-
ſtitiõ out of mẽs harts. I ſaid this was a
great vaũt. But Sir, this kingdõ of God
which they tooke vpõ thẽ to maintein:
this glorie of God, for the which they
haue entred into ſo gret a cõflict, doth
it cõſiſt in words õly, or in the workíg
of vertue? Surely if we beleue S. Paul, it
ſtãdeth in the ſtrẽgth and cõſtant working of vertue: wherfor if they mind to
proue themſelues honeſt mẽ, let them

E ij re-

restore the old modestie, humilitie, patience, meekenes, obediéce, chastitie, puritie, innnocentie, the chastising of the bodie, the continual warre bothe against the tyrannie of the flesh, as also against al other vices : let them restore that earnest loue and feruent charitie, that continual meditation of heauenly thinges, that godly exercise of praier vnto God both day and night for the prosperous estate and saluation of al men: Let them take vp the crosse on their shoulders, and crucifie al vncleanes of synnes : let them forsake al pleasures of the world: let them pul vp by the roote the very stringes of carnalitie. finally let them mortifie al the vnbridled passions of their willes: that nothinge liue in them, but the power and wil of Christe, and then wil we beleeue, that they haue fulfilled their promise, and quitte them selues like true men of their worde. But if they haue done no suche thing, but rather

by

by their examples of life and doctrine
haue brought to paſſe, that men liue
more frely in al kind of vice, that they
are the readier to commit ſacrilege,
that they are the bolder to venter vpō
any vile, and heinouſe offence, that
they are the fierſer and creweller (yea
more deſperat then any mans hart can
thinke) to doe villanie and violence to
their Princes, for whoſe ſafetie they
ought to hazard their owne liues: if
they forgetting Religion bend them
ſelues wholly againſt religion: is it not
plaine, that they are not onely to be
ſcorned and laughed at, but alſo to be
abhorred, and deteſted as the moſt
horrible and crewel peſtilence of a
common weale?

Wel wel, ſaie you, *I perceiue at the
length, what this your new ſect is, againſt
the which you haue ſo ſharply whetted
your eloquence.* Oh what a pleaſure
youhaue to ſpeake doubtfully and ob-
ſcurely? What ſaie you M. Haddon?

Say you that you do at legth vnderstãd, what my new secte is? Say you that I do maintein any newfangled sect? that I do allow their wicked actes, which I accurse and detest? That I am fallen frõ the faith and Religion of the holy Catholike Church? And then how stand these thigs together, that I should whet my eloquéce against that secte, which (as you fai) I folow my felf? Moreouer, by what argumét cã you proue it? You haue peraduéture heard faie, that I was a voluptuous mã, geuen to pleasure and vncleanes of life, desirous of nouelties, haftie and headlong to make sedition, debate and discord emõgeft men. And therfore you thinke peraduenture that I am entãgled with the like detestable vices, as your Maisters are. But cõsider, I pray you, how these thinges, that folow, may stãd together with this your moft impudét fuspition. *At the length, say you, I fee the aduersaries, whom you would haue to be cut of from the Quenes maieftie,*

*maieſtie, and driuen out as the corrupters
of the whole realme*. Whie then, if you
ſee, that I am earneſtly bent againſt all
ſuch as are the brochers of new tangled
ſectes: if you ſay plainly, that I would,
they ſhould be driuen farre frō the preſence and familiaritie of the Queene,
that they ſhould be bāniſhed out of the
boundes of England: doubtles, neyther
do theſe innouations like mee, neither
do I allow their wicked doinges. But
how do you defend them your ſelfe?
I am, ſay you, *of a cōtrary opinion. Theſe
profeſſours of the Goſpel are the ſeruantes
of God, ſent vs from heauen, to awake our
ſleapines in theſe daungerous times of the
worlde growing now to olde age, and to
ſtirre vp our ſlownes*. Theſe are wōderful matters that you ſay, if ſlepines may
be awaked, or ſlownes ſtirred vp. So
may feare beare it ſelfe hardily, and the
pleaſure of the bodie reſtreine vice
and vncleanes of life, and mad raſhnes
wel and wiſely gouern a cōmon weal.

Then it foloweth. *They were sent from heauē to cōfute error, to reproue impiety: and therefore they are to be sought out of the Quenes Maiesty, and to be much made of in al the cōmon weale.* When ye spake these wordes, you thought to reproue me of lightnes, for beleuing otherwise, of presumption, for writing vnto the Quene. You say furthermore, that it is not necessarie to discusse particularlie euerie point of my accusation, but only to gather them, as it were into certaine heades, and so briefely to runne them ouer. Then you add these words. *I wil, if I can, put backe the very hornes of your accusation.* I woulde faine see with what manhood and strength you wil beginne the matter. It foloweth. *First of al, you saie we must consider the persones, bicause they promise nobly, and we must weie, whether they be of habilitie to performe it, whether they haue so muche vertue and holinesse as they pretend.* This would I faine see. But for

so

so much as, this holinesse, which you speake of, must be declared in workes, not craked of in woordes (for so doth Christe teache vs to discerne the true *Math.7.c.* prophetes from the false by the fruicte of workes, not by the bragge or vaunt of wordes) I looke you shoulde shewe me the miracles that these holie men haue wrought : the which being declared, you shall be the better able to put backe the hornes of my disputation. For of the woordes I am nothing affraid, the whiche in apparence are merueilous goodly and gaie. And this, I warrant you, is the first lewde point in al Heretiques, to cloke their wilie trappes with most holie wordes. For The wvi-lines of by what other meanes might they al-heretikes lure the mindes of the simple people, but only by a feined shew of holinesse and innocencie ? For vertue naturally inuiteth and draweth al men vnto her. The whiche thing these subtile and craftie fellowes knowing wel inough,

the y

they do on the habit of vertue, the fo-
ner therby to creepe into the bofomes
and hearts of vnlearned folkes . For as
the fowlers deceiue the birdes : either
with fome bait, or els with inftrumēts
refembling the voice and tune of the
birds: euē fo do your doctors by fetting
out the gafe of coūterfeit holines, they
bring vnto their fnares the fimple people, where vnwares and fufpecting no
deceit, thei are takē. For open difhone-
fty could do litle harme, (being of her
felf very foul and deformed to behold)
except fhe did beare the coūtenāce or
face of honefty and innocēcy. But fee I
pray you, what pollicy thefe plaufible
and good felowes haue foūd out to ftir
vp the cōmon people. We were al fo-
ry to fee the maners of mē corrupted,
the ftreightnes of old difciplin relēted,
the Priefts wallowing in vnclean life,
and abufing their dignity immoderatly
to gaine and luker. Nowe, as it happe-
ned fometimes in the Citie of Rome,
                                    the

the furious Tribunes of the peple, whē
the like occasiō was offred thē, to stirr
vp the cōmons against the nobility, did
not let it passe, but the enuy which was
already to much kendled, thei made to
burn, putting vnderneth, the fierbrāds
of their troblesom ād seditious oratiōs:
in like maner these most holy persons,
whom you cōmend so highly, whē thei
saw into how great hatred the church
men were come: thei thought to vse al
meanes possible in the world to bring
them into farder hatred and displesure.
And so, what by finding fault with thē,
and what by putting the peple in hope
of a better world, they shewed themselues as ringleaders in this seditiō and
fallīg frō the church. And the better to
bring their purpose to passe, they vsed
many goodly and holy words, bearing
men in hād, that thei wold expresse the
holy life, not of the Sainctes that came
neere after the Apostles rule (for of thē
they made none accompte) but of the
Apostles

Apostles them selues. And so they had alwaies in their mowthes, Christian pietie, the puritie of the Gospell, the holines of most chast Religion, a heauenlie discipline, the which to disteine with any deuises or superstitions (as they terme it) of man, they tooke it to be a most heinouse offence. After that they brought all men into great hope and expectation, that the very perfection of the Primitiue Churche should by their diligence be restored, and that the wonderful gifts of the holy Ghost, which now were thought to be starke deade, shoulde be reuiued ~~to life~~.

This goodly beginning how plausible it was to the worlde, euery man may iudge. But naughtines can neuer stay long in one degree: but when it hath once begonne to slide, it rusheth forewarde, and falleth downe headlong.

To gette therefore the greater fauour emongest the people, what so euer seemed to them any thing rough or

vnplea-

vnpleafant, they tooke it quite awaie.
To confeffe their finnes, was very tro-
blefome: to punifh their bodie with fa-
fting, was painful : to be tyed with the
bande of Excommunication , was a
vexation of minde : to be fhaken with
the threatninges of Gods iudgement,
was bitter. They did therfore moft earneftly endeuour themfelues, to take al
fuch cares out of mens hartes. Wherfore it is no wonder, if the fimple people , being partlie offended with the
mifhuing of the Church men (whiche
all the worlde talked of) and partlie
brought into great hope of a golden
worlde and moft pleafant libertie, did
willingly applie them felues to the fan-
tafie of thofe men, by whom thei furely trufted to be de'iuered from al euils,
and to haue the fruition of all felicitie
and pleafure. But when the fury of the
cõmon people was nowe armed with
this coũterfeit fhew of Religion (good
Chrift) how garifhly thefe your holie

men

men ranne to the fpoile of the Churches? What greate flaughters of men
they made ? What a great alteratiō of
thinges folowed by and by , with the
decaie of al,Godlines?And yet you M.
Haddon make them equal with Athanafius, Bafile, Ambrofe, Ierome, and
Auguftine. If they are to be tried by
their workes,as Chrift teacheth,who
are rruly fent from God,aud on the o-
ther fide,who are pricked foreward of
the diuel to do mifchiefe:if I can fee no
holie works that your prophetes haue
done: if you your felfe can not declare
any excellēt vertues in them:if you can
bring no holie woorkes for proufe of
their heauenlie vertue : what cometh
into your minde, to compare men for
chaftitie of life moft cleane, for godly
réligion moft holie , for authoritie of
fentences mofte graue , with them ,
whom all the worlde knoweth to be ,
for filthines of life infamous , for their
vngodlie attéptes Churchrobbers, for
their

their vndiscret lawes and ordináces, frã
tik ãd mad mé. But it is worthwhile to
côsider how you proue it:thus you sai.
*Neither shew you any thĩg, why thes may
not be equal with the auncient Fathers.*
Yes surely, I wil shew something, and
shew withal, how shamelesse you are,
which compare vnbridled fleshlinesse,
with cleanesse of life , impietie with
godlynes, raiging madnes with godly
wisedome. Then you saie.

But I wil bring you away from these
*odious comparisons, for this is no place to
reason these matters.* Yes M.Haddon, I
wil be so bold as to reason with you. If
this be true, that in geuíg of counsel the
manners and behauiour of the geuer,
is to be weied, and that nothing indu-
ceth vs more to credit the counsel geué,
then the tried honesty of the person: I
say plaíly, that it is a questió worthy to
be asked, of what maners and côuersa-
tió thei are, that giue vs counsel to folow
their opinion. You say afterward. *I wil
vphold*

vphold that our Doctours doe agree with the reuerende Fathers, that they take the verie same way that they did, that they teach in effecte the selfe same religion. I would you were able to defende, that the auncient fathers and your doctours were wel agreed. Then it foloweth. *The whiche if it be true, it booteth not to make comparison betwen such as are alone. If it be not so, tel vs wherein they disagree.* You say wel, if it be so. But before I begynne to declare, how muche the auncient Fathers dissented from your new maisters, I wil tarie a litle to see howe you can proue this goodlie agreement. *S. Augustine,* saie you, *complaineth in his time, that flouddes of ceremonies ouerflowed the Churche, in so muche that the Christians were almost in worse case, then euer were the Iewes.* You neuer read that in S. Augustine, that the Ceremonies, whiche we now vse, are like to the Iewish ceremonies, and therfore to be reiected:
but

but your maisters haue brought you
like an ignorant felowe to beleeue it.
S.Hierome, saie you, *wissheth that the
holie scriptures, which your Churche hi-
deth frō al men, might be learned without the booke, euen of children and women.* S. Ierome writing to Paulinus,
disputeth to the contrarie, where he
complaineth of the rashnes and bold-
hardines of men, which tooke vppon
them without any good witte or vertue to handle the Scriptures with to
much libertie: and of the vndiscrete
chatting of foolish women, which taking vppon them to expounde Scriptures, defined manie thinges verie vnaduisedly. It foloweth. *Basile imploied
his vacant time in the most godlie exercise of reading and teaching diuinitie.* It
was wel don truly. for Basil was none
ofthem that take vpon them arrogantly to teache doctrine that they neuer
learned. Then you adde these wordes.

If Monkes had leued according to

F   the

the rules of Bafile , no man woulde euer haue touched them with so much as his finger. As though your quarel had ben againft men , and not againft chaftitie it felfe . But admit that their manners were loofe , their behauiour diffolute, their life wanton . What then ? was there none emógeft them al, that kept their chaftitie ? There were without doubt And that the loue of cleane, and chaft life was not vtterly decaied e-mongeft monkes, the end of the holie fathers the Carthufians declared full wel, who, if thei would haue yeelded their cófent to the wicked decrees, ne-ded neuer to haue fuffered other pu-nifhmét but only to be married. It was not therefore the mifliking of filthie pleafure , that ftirred you to fuch bar-barous crueltie, but the hatred of cha-ftitie and virginitie. And I know wel, that not only thei were chaft and per-feét men, but alfo many other that are now banniſhed emong vs : the which

wher-

wherſoeuer they ſet their foote, they
leaue behind them moſt manifeſt foot-
ſteppes of baſhfulnes and honeſty. But
admit that the greater part of them had
ben drowned in vice: was it therefore
good reaſon by and by, to ouerthrow
the whol order? How much had it ben
more for your honeſty, to haue don as
the moſt puiſſaunt King Fernandus did
ſometime in Spaigne and Elizabeth his
wife, a Princeſſe cōſecrated to euerlaſ-
ſting fame? as the moſt honorable king
and renoumed Prince Emanuel : as
Iohn the third his ſonne, a King for his
religion and godlines worthy of moſt
high cōmendation: as Charles the fifth
an emperour born to immortal glorie:
as Euricus the Cardinal ſonne of king
Emanuel, in whom ſhineth a wōderful
light of al vertue and holines: finally as
all other moſte religious Princes did :
who ſeing the manners of monkes to
tende towardes a niceneſſe, ſent for
certaine perfecte religious menne, by

whofe diligence their vnbridled affection and licentioufnes was tied vp,
their loofe manners by ftreighter difcipline reftreined, and their fleapie
mindes ftyrred vp to the moft feruent
loue of godlines. And fo there are now
emongeft vs moft holie and religious
Monkes, whiche folow Bafile, Benet,
and Bernarde, and Dominique, and
Frauncis, in the puritie of moft chafte
religion, in moft earneft and zealous
loue of God, in moft notable examples
of al vertue. Whie then would you rather cut of that, that might haue ben
healed? Bicaufe, as I faid a litle before,
it was not anie difpleafure toward filthie luft or life, but the hatred of perpetual chaftitie, that ftyrred you to
deface and vtterlie to ouerthrow the
name of Mounkes. For (as S. Hierome faith) all Heretiques haue a naturall hatred and grudge againft chaftitie. Wherefore there is no doubt,
but that, if your Mounkes had liued

Heretike
enemies
to cha-
ftitie.

ac-

accerding to the rules of S. Basile: the
greater their perfection had ben, the
more displeasure and hatred you wold
haue born them. Afterward you bring
in these wordes.

We reuerence the Crede of Atha-
nasius as it ought to be, neither is there
any controuersie betwene them and vs.
What great discorde there is betwene
your menne and Athanasius, I haue
partely declared in that my letter,
whiche you so muche reuile. Neither skilleth it muche, whether you
be agreed in some pointes yea or no.
For I neuer saide, that your Champi-
onsdissented from the opinion of the
holie Fathers in al matters. But to
what end tendeth al this talke? what
would you prooue? For sooth, that
Luther, Bucer, Zwinglius, Oecolampadius, Caluine and other the Ministers of this your gospel, are in vertue, holines, chastitie, and religion, nothing inferiour to S. Augustine, Hie-

rome, Basile, and Athanasius and other holie Fathers, whose writinges seeme to send forth the verie swete sauour of the holie ghost. But how do you proue it? *S. Augustine* you say, *cōplaineth, that whole flouddes of ceremonies ouerflowed the Church: S. Ierome thought it expedient, that women and children should learne the scriptures without the booke: If Monkes liued according to the rule of S. Basile, no man woulde once laie his finger on them: and we reuerēce the Crede of Athanasius .* What then? Can you proue by these propositions, that Luther and Bucer, and the rest of your Worthies are to be compared with S. Augustine, Ierome, Basile, Athanasius in vertue, cōstancie, chastitie, cleanes of life, religion and wisedom? A goodlie pregnāt wit of a yong Logician: he shaketh out his argumentes so fearsly, that he maketh them fitte to cōclude, what so euer him listeth to prooue. Let this sourme of reasoning be once

recei-

receiued, and what thing is ther in the
worlde fo muche contrarie to al reafon, that maie not eafily be prooued ?
As if we fhould faie for example: Mahumete faieth, that God created the
worlde. S. Bafile holdeth the fame.
Bafile therefore and Mahumete are
mofte like in godlie life. Arius confeffed, that Chrift fhed his bloud for
the redemption of mankinde. Athanafius affirmeth the fame. *E*,
Arius fhined in vertuoufe conuerfation no leffe then Athanafius. Luther difputeth that all good thinges
are to be referred to the grace of
Chrifte: the verie fame doth S Auguftine declare moft wifely. It followeth therefore, that Luther hath
deferued no leffe commendation of
holines, then S. Auguftine. See you
not, vnderftande you not, confider
you not, howe childifhly you haue
concluded, howe weakelie you haue
defended your newe Maifters?

F iiij   Are

Are you wont in ſkirmiſh ſo to put backe the hornes of your ennemies? This was the principall and chiefeſt point of al, in the whiche you ſhould haue ſhewed al the force and ſtrength of your witte, to haue brought al the world in admiration of you.

You ſaie afterward that I doe taunt and reuile the ſoule of Luther. As though the minde of Luther did not yet liue in al ſuche as folowe his doctrine. You cal the ſame Luther the man of God. I knowe not what you are M. Haddon. But if it were lawful to eſteeme by coniecture, what maner of man you are, I ſee no cauſe why I ſhould greatly commend either your witte, or your life. for he that geaueth the teſtimonie of diuine vertue or heauenlie conuerſation to a moſt filthie and infamous perſonne, we may worthely ſuſpecte, that he is him ſelfe ſubiecte vnto the like vices. Your woordes are theſe. *This man of God, whome you*
re-

reprochefully call a mad man, in open af-semble before Charles the fifte, gaue a fo-bre and fownd account of his faith. That is falſe. You might better ſaie, that in the preſence of the Emperour him ſelſe, he moſt impudently betraied his owne madnes. And, that he was not puniſhed for ſo doing, it was, bicauſe he had receiued before hand the Em-perours ſafeconduicte for his indem-nitie, in caſe he ſpake anie thing not agreable to holie religion. You ſaie. *Thus madde man ſtoode faſt and in ſafetie thirtie yeares, in ſpite of all the politike and wiſe patrones of your Church, were they neuer ſo madly bent to make him out of the waie.* In theſe wordes you doe not defende Luther, but you reioiſe and triūph at the ruine of the Church. I knowe that the outrage of Luther hath ben fortified and mainteined by the aide of Princes, and by the furie of the common people : and I confeſſe that it hath ſo come to paſſe for our ſynnes.

fynnes. For as God in the old time to punifh the fynnes of his people, ftyrred vp ennemies againft them, minding by punifhment and plagues to bring them backe to honeft ciuilitie and godlie religiõ: euen fo in our time hath he fuffred Luther, and permitted his madnes to be bolftered and borne out by the helpe of manie men, meaning by plagues of his wifedome appointed, to cal vs home againe to the feruẽt loue and folowing of true godlines. But wheras you faie, that Luther ftoode faft and in fafetie: furely you know not wherin fafetie ftandeth, if you be of that mind, that it is rather a miferie to be pounifhed for fynne, then to liue in fynne. Furthermore the patrones of the Church (as it liketh you to call them) perced him thorough with their writinges, and fet out his name to all the pofteritie, difhonefted with the fowle fpottes of his moft heinoufe and filthie life. As

for

for the thirtie yeares, in the which you
boaſt he ſtoode ſo faſte, you needs
bragge no more. For the name of Mahumete, which hath cōtinnued aboue
nine hundred yeares, remaineth yet in
verie greate honour and eſtimation
emongeſt ſuche men, as doe followe
that wicked and deteſtable ſecte. *But
Eraſmus,* ſaie you, *geaueth vnto this
madde man a ſingular good teſtimonie of
innocencie by theſe wordes. The doctrine
of Luther manie men miſlike, but his life
they doe with one voice allow.* I doe not
ſo much eſteme Eraſmus, that I thinke
my ſelfe bounde to ſet my hand to his
teſtimoniall in all matters. And yet I
know, that Eraſmus wrote againſt Luther, (how beit not ſo earneſtly as the
cauſe required). For he feared the
furious and reprochfull talke of the
felow.

You accuſe me for ſaing, that Luther was Popular, and withall you
demaunde of me, what I meane by
the

the worde Popular. I wil do soo much for you, that you maie vnderstãd, how fitly the worde maie be applied to Luther . They were sometimes called Popular, which sought the common profitte of the people, and endeuoured them selues by strength and diligence to rescue the impotent and poore men, when wrong was offered them by such as were of greater force and power. This name therfore was in those daies much estemed and highly commended Now whereas it is the propertie of flatterie to counterfaicte vertue, and vnder the pretensed coulour of honestie and gentlenes priuily to creepe into the hartes of the simple people : the craftie and malitiouse felowes, whose only bent was to attein to honour , perceiuing that suche as were Popular, were in greatest estimation emongest the people , and by common agreement promoted to the highest romes of honour: endeuoured them

Popular vvhat it is.

them ſelues to ſeeme Popular. And
theſe men conſidered verie curiouſly,
not what was in dede good and profitable for the people, but what they liked and longed moſt after as profitable
vnto them. And as it fareth now a
daies with manie ſeruitours in court
that hunte after the fauour of Kinges,
they ſpie out diligently, not what ſtā-
deth moſt with the kinges profite and
honour, but what they moſt couet,
what they loue, and what they would
faineſt bring to paſſe, ſeruing only
their vnlawfull pleaſure and vnruled
affection : euen ſo emongeſt free peoples did thoſe men, whome we cal popular, the Grecians called them δη-
μαſωγοὺς, that is to witte, leaders of the
people : they applied them ſelues, not
to the profitte, but to the pleaſure of
the people. For the profitte of the
people conſiſteth in a good and diſcrete moderation of thinges : but
through inordinate greedines of the
thing

Clavvꝰ
backes of
the court.

thing that they luft after, and through
the name of libertie, it is brought to
naught The common people enuied
fuch as were men of power. Thefe Populares made lawes, by the whiche
they were either depriued of their
goods, or bannifhed out of their coū-
trie, or put to death. The people could
not awaie with feueritie of lawes. The
lawes therfore, that feemed any thing
ftreight, in reftreining the vnbridled
affections of the people, the Populares
tooke quite awaie. The people hated
vertue, bicaufe they fawe, it ftoode directely againft their vntamed outrages : the Populares with their decrees
and ordinaunces difpatched all vertue
out of their common weales, and fo
by the meanes of thefe Populares, the
people might without cōtrol or check
doe what them lifted But to cōclude,
fuch as came to honor by this meanes,
ferued the filthie luft, the vicious defire, the vncleane affectiō, and the fu-
rioufe

riouse rage of the base people: and did
so beare them selues in euerie office,
that it might ful wel appere, that they
were no free men, but the verie bond-
slaues of the vndiscret and mad peple.
And the better to bring this matter to
passe they marked verie diligétly , not
only what the people longed for , but
also whome they enuied at for wealth
and richesse: and so brought al men of
power and richesse to be enuied, stvr-
red vp the most earnest hatred of the
commons against their Princes, set fire
vnto the hote rage of the multitude,
therwith to cósume and wast al such as
were in high authoritie and honour in
their cómon weales. But how did they
profit the peple? Ful wel I warrát you.
For euen those thinges, that the peple
most thirstily gaped after, were vtterli
ouerthowé. For wheras the nature of
the peple is such, that thei cã not beare
to much welth and prosperity : hauing
once atteined the libertie : whiche
they

they so much wished for , they fal together by the eares within themselues,
they rage and ruffle , they tosse and
turmoile , and in the end they wrecke
their angre and malice euen vpō them,
that were the procurers of this libertie. And so, (whereas nothing can
longe continew , where discord and
madnes reigneth) it cometh to passe,
that they leese not onely the libertie
and impunitie by the diligence and
flatterie of these Populars procured,
but also their honest and lawfull libertie, whiche they might otherwise
haue kepte long time. These are they,
that are wont to be called Populars.

Now it remaineth, that we declare,
whether frier Luther were Popular
after this manner. Is there anie doubt
in the wordle of the matter ? What
other thing, I praie you, intended Luther, but only to flatter the people? Al
such thinges as the people hated and
lothed , did he not take them quite
awaie ?

awaie? The authoritie of the Bishop
of Rome, did he not vtterly deface it?
The holie Canons, did he not abrogate
and disannull them? Did he not stirre
vp hatred and enuie against the Princes of the Church? did he not quench
in mens hartes al feare of lawes both
of God and man? did he not make a
faith, which assured men of saluation,
were they neuer so wicked, yea and
obstinately bent to cötinew in naughtines? did he not shew to al the wordle
a great hope of licentiousnes? did he
not with his doctrine make those men
disobedient and rebellious, which he
him selfe had begoten, fostred and
brought vp? Is it not wel knowë, that
such as had geuen them selues wholly
to his doctrine, prooued so desperate
and headlong, that he him selfe could
not rule them? But how worthely you
defend him M. Haddon? *If he be popu-*
lar, say you, *that regardeth the health of*
the people, there is no man more popular

G   *then*

then he: but if you meane, by popular, such a one as stirreth the people to ciuile dis-cord, read his booke, in the which he in-ueieth against the tumultes of the cōmon people in Germanie, and slaunder him no more. Oh what a wise mã is this? How wittily he quiteth the Prince of his re-ligiõ? I cal him Popular, whose scholers by hearing his doctrine become sediti-ous. You answere me, that Luther cõ-plained of the tumultes in Germanie, whiche his scholers and folowers stir-red vp. And you are so blockishe, that you perceue not that you speke for me against your selfe. Luther, say you, spe-keth earnestly against the tumultes in Germanie. Why then he cõfesseth, that the selfe same religiõ, which he had ta-ken vpõ him to gouerne, which he had instructed with diuine ordinaunces, which he had brought backe to the old puritie of the gospel, is stirring and sedi tious. Then did Luther brĩg meruelous goodly frutes to his coũtrei men. for he
made

made them not modeft, but reproch-
ful:not gentle,but impatiét: not quiet,
but feditious:yea fo much,that he him
felfe was forced to fet out bookes,and
to reprehéd their defperat madnes. O
what a holefome gofpelifhe doctrine
was this? what a wonderful light caft
this diuine má into the wordle? what a
foueraigne falue laied he to the woun-
ded cófciences ? Is this, to pourge the
Church throughly of vices? to reftore
againe the olde puritie of the gofpel?
to proppe vp the doctrine of the Apoftles,begynning to fal ? to caufe by his
doctrine fuch men, as were of nature
quiet,to become fo prowd and infolét,
fuch brawlers and quarellers,that their
captaine, yea their owne deere father
could not hold them backe ? For how
manie thowfand men were flaine by
ciuile warres in Switzerland ftyrred
vppe by Zwinglius and Oecolampadius ? What a companie of hufband
men in Sueuia folowing their captaine

Herefie
caufe of
ciuile
vvarres
ãd bloud;
fhead.

G ij   Muncer

Muncer were cut of by the nobilitie?
What place was there in al Germanie
free from this contagious and peſtilēt
diſcorde? The begynners and ringleaders thereof what were they, out of
what fountaine ſprang they? Doubtleſſe out of the rage, madnes, and preſumption, of Luther, out of the ſhop
wher the moſt infamous Lutheraniſme
was wrought and cõtriued. But ſome
of the forenamed perſonnes ſel out
afterward with Luther. Yea and no
meruaile. For it was impoſſible, that
ſuch naughtie felowes being al agreed
in miſchiefe, ſhould long agree within
them ſelues: where euerie one of them
ſought to be the Captaine. What did
Luther him ſelfe? did he not make ſeditious ſermons? did he not ſtirre vp
the commõs againſt their Princes? did
he not vſe verie reprochful and villanous talke againſt moſt honorable perſonages? did he not moſt ſpitefully reuile th'Emperour him ſelfe, Hérie king
of

of England, George Duke of Saxonie,
and manie other noble Princes ? Is it
not wel knowē, that al his fermons tē-
ded to the ftirring vp of difcord and fedition ? What is then more plaine and
euident then that the fecte of Luther
is altogether Populare , feditious and
troublefome? And how daungerous it
is to Princes, it nedeth no declaration.
For what fo euer is, after this fort, populare, is, (as I declared in my letters)
verie much contrarie, not only to the
good eftate of the common weale, but
alfo to the maieftie of Princes. If you
be not of fuch conuenient witte , that
you are able to forefee by the caufes
going before, what euent is like to folow : you wil neuer fully vnderftād it,
though I fhould declare it with infinit
examples. Is it vnknowen, thinke you
that through the naughtines and outrage of Luther , Ludouicus King of
hūgarie was flaine in the fielde with a
great multitude of Chriftian men? For

Herefse
ouer-
throvve
of Kings
and king
domes.

G iij   when

whē Solimanus Emperour of the Turks brought againſt the King a great huge armie, ād great daūger was bēt againſt al Germany: yet the cities of Germani, being partly entāgled with ciuile wars within themſelues (the which Luthers ſect had cauſed) ād partly imbrued with the doctrine of Luther (who mainteined in diſputatiō, that it was not lauful to withſtād the force of the Turkes) either could not, or would not aide Ludouicus. If therfore this victorie of the Turkes hath brought ſuch great diſhonour to the name of Chriſtians: if by it ther is laied open a gap into Chriſtendom, to the vtter decaie and ruine of Auſtria, and to the great daunger of all Germanie: if the noble kingdome of Hungarie (for the greater part of it) be brought vnder the rule and gouernement of a moſt barbarous and crewell ennemie: for al this we maie thāke the naughtines and owtrage of Martine Luther. But peraduenture you neuer heard of this geare, and therfore you

wil bide by it, that your new gospel is
no hinderáce to Princes. What? cá you
be ignorant of that also, how Edward
your owne king was in his childhood
most traiterously made away with poi
son? know not you, by whom Charles
the Emperour a most worthie Prince
was both betraid and assaulted? heard
you neuer saie, with how crewel treason quene Marie a womā most excel-
létly furnished with princelie vertues,
was first assaulted with poison and afterward besieged of her own subiects?
Is it possible that you should know no
thíg of the cóspiracy, in the which was
contriued by a cópanie of most filthie
traitors the murder both of the quene
and of Cardinall Poole a most noble,
godlie, and wisemā? what nede I to reherse vnto you the rebellió of the fréch
mé, the dissoialty, the cruelty, the wast
ād spoile of churches and holy thinges
in Fráce? what should I say of the king
of Scotlád, who was by most cruel vil
lanie murdered and slaine? Now they

that haue ſtirred vp ſuch great broiles
and tumultes, they that haue committed ſuch barbarous and horrible actes,
frō whens haue they their originall or
begynning? Is it not euident to the
wordle, that the verie fountaine and
ſpring of al theſe miſchiefes was in Luther? And yet it liketh you to cal him
the man of God, one ſent from heauen
for the ſaluation of mankind. Tel me, I
praie you, what vertues appeared in
him ſo great, that you ſhould conceiue
ſuch opinion of him as you doe? what
continencie of life? what grauitie of
māners? What ſeueritie? what gentlenes? what contempte of wordlie thinges? what contemplation of heauenly
thinges? what time ſpent in cōtinnual
praiers? what daies and nightes paſſed
ouer in weeping and teares for the
health of the people? What faſting?
what gronīg and ſighing? Finally what
deedes of moſt feruēt charitie hath cō-
mended this man vnto you ſo much,
                                        that

that you dare saie of him, that he maie
wel be compared for his excellencie
in vertue and godlines, with Basile, and
Athanasius, and al other holie men?

First of all, he was, as his owne
paiges do confesse, of nature crewel, in
his talke rough, wrathful, haughtie and
prowde, yea so muche, that he esteemed not Melanchton to be a man.
Then his vowe solempnely made vnto Christ he brake it, and like a most
filthie ribaude coupled him selfe with
a woman, whiche had in like manner
vowed perpetual chastitie vnto Christ
in a monasterie of Vrgines: and by
this example shewed him selfe to be
a captaine and ringleader to al suche,
as would doe the like. To be short,
he was infamous for many other most
heinouse vices and detestable crimes.
But least his commendable qualities
might seeme to be vtterly defaced
with the blemish of manie vices: I cō-
fesse, he could with a goodlie shew of
                                        hu-

humanity somtimes hide his rough and
boisteous mad nature, and so set forth
hiself to the simple people. For he was
a pleasant cōpagniō, and at a bāket a io-
lie prater in al kind of myrth verie fine,
if reprochful taūting may be called ciuil finenes. He pleasured much in scof-
fing and taūting, in reuiling the Princes
and gouerners of the Church, in moc-
kig and scornig of honest plain folkes,
such as were true Christiā mē. But our
lord, saith Salomō, abhorreth scorners,
and cōmunicateth the secretes of his
coūsel with the simple. Wherby it may
be gathered that Luther was not reple
nished with the light of heauē. And yet
you thík hí worthy to be cōpared with
the most holy fathers. Of felowship tel
me, which of al the ancíét fathers disteined himselfe with ribaudrie and in-
cest? Which of them brought the cōmō people in hope of licétious liuing?
Which of them stirred vp with his sermons sedition and hurlyburly in diuers

Prou.3.d.

uers and sundrie places?which of them
taught mē to put the hope of their sal-
uatiō in faith,that is to say,in a only rash
and folish presumptiō? Which of them
tied vp the wil of mā,which god wold
haue to be free,with I cā not tel what
bādes of destenie?which of them durst
euer affirme,that God was the author
or chief cause of al sinne?which of thē
euer held that al good works wrought
and done of holy mē by the grace and
instinct of the holyghost were vnclean
and spotted with sinne?which of them
euer toke away the true iustice,which
by the grace and goodnes of Christ is
ascribed vnto faithful mē,and cōsisteth
in clean life,innocēt cōuersation , and
exercise of holy workes:and in steede
of it substituted a newly deuised iustice
such as was neuer heard of before? For
whē Luther denied,that syn was quite
blotted out in holy mē by the grace of
Christ,he affirmed,that ther was none
other iustice , but onely the singular
                              iustice

iuſtice of Chriſte , applied to euerie
particular man by faith, were he neuer
ſo ſynnefull and wicked : the whiche
being but one in all men , it was impoſſible , that there ſhoulde be anie
difference in the worlde betwene the
iuſtice of anie common man , and the
iuſtice of Paule or Peter, yea or of the
moſt holie Virgine mother of God.
And you demaund of me what thoſe
monſters of religion are. Al theſe thinges, whiche I haue here moſt briefely
compriſed, I ſaie, are the moſt horrible
monſters of religion: and the father of
them is not villanous , but villanie it
ſelfe : not frantike and madde, but verie frantikenes and madnes it ſelfe.
What ſhew of baſhfulnes, honeſtie or
modeſtie could you ſee in this man being the ouerthrower of all honeſtie,
continencie , and modeſtie ? What
glimſe of vertue could he ſo daſel your
eyes withal , that you woulde ſuffer
your ſelfe to be ſo daungerouſly de-
cei-

ceiued in him? And yet wil you continewe in your errour as you haue begonne. And yet wil you acquite suche
a pestilét secte as blamelesse and without faulte? And yet will you liken
the good holie Fathers to Luther a
moste vile and infamous caitiue.

But you triumph excedingly, that
he stoode so stiffe thirtie yeares together, and was neuer punished for his
naughtines and owtrage. Can you
imagin anie greater punishment in the
worlde, then the remembrance of a
synneful and filthie life? The remorse
of his heinouse offences made him terribly afraied. The feendes of hell tor-
menters of damned sowles vexed his
mind. The ennemie the diuel shooke
him vp, and would not suffer him once
to breath or rest him selfe. Truth it is,
he woulde banket and make good
cheere with his freendes, and there-
with somewhat relent his intensise
cares. But neither chambering, nor bá-
ket-

ketting is of that force, that it is able to raife vp a mans hart weied downe with the peife of synne. But what kind of death died this noble holie Father? Being at supper with his frinds ouer night he quaffed fomewhat free-ly, and the nexte morning was founde dead.

Luthers death.

You faie afterward, that there were brought into England by the goodnes of God a golden couple of olde men, Martin Bucere, and Peter Martyr, whofe vertues you comend aboue the fkies. Of them I haue nothing elles to fay, but that I thinke them to be verie lewde and naughtie felowes, if for no-thing els, yet for this caufe onely, that you fo highly commend them. for he that commendeth Luther, it is not pof-fible, that he fhould comend any thing that is godly, honeft, or holy.

Whereas you put me in mind that I fhould fomewhat temper my ftyle, and not cal fuch men arrogát and prowde,

as

as you esteeme for gentle and modest, signifying withal after a sort the
daunger that by them might ensewe
towardes me: I woulde ye would aduisedly consider, howe illsauouredly
your woordes hang together. For if
they be verie gentle (as you saie they
are) then although I shall reuile them,
they will neuer be moued withall, but
wil merueloufly well keepe their pacience and constancie. But if they
wil fearcely sette vppon me with villanous and reprochfull language: then
are they not so gentle, as you make
them to be. I knowe verie wel, that
vnder the couert of a sheepes skynne
(as Christe saieth) lieth hidden the
rough and crewell nature of wolues.
It is also by experience well tried,
that there is nothing in the worlde
more shamelesse, then these fellowes
are. For when anie reason is brought
against them, thei endeuour thē selues
to answere it, not by reason, but by

Mat.7.6

multi-

multiplying of woordes . And therefore, when they are preſſed with argumentes, then beginne they to chafe
and ſweat, to feare and fainte , to
raile and raue , and in the ende fall to
plaine ſcolding, vntil thei haue founde
for their impudent aſſertion ſome
ſhameles ſhifte. But beleéue me I feare
no mans ſlaunderous tongue . For I
haue committed myne honeſtie and
eſtimation to the keeping of Ieſus
Chriſt, and therefore no man ſhal euer
be able to thruſt me out of my place
by the violence of his tongue. And as
for your reprochful woordes , they
moue me no more then the rauing of
one that were frantike or out of his
witte . Were it not that the loue of
godlines had moued me , had I euer
written ſo much as one letter againſt
you ? No, not one . I tooke vpon me
this charge of writing , not minding
thereby to mainteine myne owne
good fame or eſtimation, but to confute

fute your wicked and vngodlie talke.
Wherefore be bolde and fpare not, to
taunt me at your pleafure, to perce my
good name with fowl words, to tour-
moile it with villanie, to rente and
teare it with al difhoneftie: and I geue
good leaue and licence not onely to
you, but alfo to all your Bucers and
Martyrs, moft gentle and fofte creatures (as you cal them) to bende them
felues as fiercely againft me as thei can
deuife. Wherefore there is no caufe
why you fhuld goe about to make me
affraied of them: for fo muche as, vnto
their tauntes, for the which I care not,
I wil neuer anfwere: and their reafons
are very peuifh, and alreadi cõfuted by
the bookes of many learned men: and I
my felf am at this point, that I fear nothing in the worlde but only Chrifte.
  As touching their perfons, if there be
any fenfe of humanitie in you, you fee
how il you haue defended thẽ. You fay
afterwarde, that it is nothing true, that
you

you shuld stand to the holy Scriptures
only : for so muche as you do receiue
many sentences of the holy Fathers
withal. What a doubling and incóstan-
cie is this? Now you reiect many thinges, for this reason only , bicause they
are(as you say)the deuises of men: and
by and by , you receiue what you lift,
and say , that you haue not reiected al
the traditions of menne . You are so
doubteful , so diuers , and so slipperie,
that you can not wel tel your selues,
what you thinke , and what you mind
to stand to . And yet when you spake
those wordes, you commended them
that acknowledge nothing elles but
the holy Scriptures, and refuse al holy
traditions and ordinaunces. These are
your wordes. *Truely if it were so, then*
folowed they the example of our Lorde
Iesus Christe , then folowed they the cu-
stome of the Apostles, and of the auncient
Fathers in the primitiue Church . How
many things you laie out at a venture?
　　　　　　　　　　　　　　　　It

It is like forsooth that Chrift, the mind
and wifedome of God the Father, by
whofe power and difpéfation the law
it felfe was made, by whom the Prophetes declared thinges to come, of
whom al holie men of old time receiued their light, was content to abyde
that lawe him felfe, that he would not
be fo hardie, as to fpeake one woorde,
which he founde not regiftred in the
holy Scriptures. I befech you Sir, wher
read he in the Scriptures, that a man Vnvvritē
for being angry only, although he vtte- truthes.
red not one reprochful word, fhuld in-
cur the dāger of Gods iudgemēt? wher
found he it written, that a man for cafting his eye alitle afide wātonly, fhuld *Mat.5.d*
be accounted as an adulterer? By what
wordes in the Law was a man forbidden to geue a bil of diuorfe to his wife?
In what place was it euer writen, that
a man minding the perfect obferuatió
of the Lawe, fhould fell all his goodes,
and beftowe the money made thereof

to the vſe of the poore, reſeruing to him
ſelfe nothing? Haue you euer read, either in the law, or in the Pſalmes, or in
the Prophets, that the way to ſaluatiõ
is a narrowe waie, or that you ought,
when a man hath ſtriken one cheeke,
to holde him vppe the other, or that
you ought to pray vnto God for their
life, that ſpeake il of you, and woorke
your deſtruction? But nowe to come
to other pointes, of the birth and proceding of God : of the regeneration of
men in heauenlie life, the whiche Ni-
Io.3.a codemus a man exactlie ſeene in the
doctrine of the lawe vnderſtood not :
of the time, in the whiche God would
Io.4.c. be woorſhipped neither at Hieruſalem, nor in the mountaine of Sama-
ria : of the bread of heauen, whiche is
the foode and ſuſtenaunce of our life :
of al theſe thinges what woorde haue
you expreſſely written in any place
of the olde Teſtamente ? But when
Chriſt ſpake theſe wordes, there was
                                    no

no Gofpell yet written, neyther did any writen monumente confirme the fayinges of Chrift, but looke what he ordeined by woordes, was afterward put in writing, to the ende that men fhould not forgette it. I doe here let paffe many thinges (minding not to profecute al that might be faied, for fo muche as I haue alreadie fpoken fufficientlie) to the intent you might vnderftand howe vnaduifedly you haue faied, that our Lorde Iefus Chrift did alfo obferue fuch a rule in his doinges. What fhall I faie of the Apoftles? Where had S. Paule read, that fuch as *Galat.5.a* kepte the circumcifion of the Lawe, were to be feparated from the communion of Chrifte? In whiche of all the holie Writers found he, that it is vnfeemely for a woman to worfhippe God bare headed, or for a man to co- *1.Cor.11.c* uer his head, when he praieth to God? What fhoulde I rehearfe vnto you, howe he commendeth fuche men as

H iij were

were mindful of his Doctrine, deliuered vnto them either by writing, or by
worde? What should I speake of that,
that the Apostles say in their Councel?
It hath seemed good to the holy Ghost
and vs? They saie not: It is writen in
the holie Scripture : but, It hath seemed good to the holie Ghost and vs.
Nowe as touching the holie Fathers,
which peraduenture you neuer read,
how durst you affirme of them, that
they neuer brought in any thing for
the gouernement of the Churche, but
what thei had found writen in the holie Scriptures? How many things reherseth S. Basile, and disputeth that thei
were deliuered from the Apostles vnto the Churche, onely by woorde of
mouth? How many such things are re-
cited of Cyprian, Chrysostom, Augustine, and the rest of the holie Fathers?
How much do they reuerence al such
holy ordinaunces, as were decreed in
general Coūcels? I do here omitte an
                                    infinite

Act. 15. e.

infinite nūber of testimonies, which do
plainly cōuince this madnes of you, or
rather of your Maisters, for so much as
not onely the greatest learned men of
our age, but also the most holy Fathers
of other ages, haue in these points very
learnedly disputed against your opinion. For in times past, al heretikes in a
manner held this opinion, that nothing
ought to be receiued, vnlesse it were
written in the holie Scriptures, minding withal to wrest and corrupt the
holie Scriptures with their owne in-
terpretation. But the holie Fathers
most earnestly defended the contrary,
alleaging Argumentes and Examples
brought euen from the Apostles time,
and by the decrees of Coūcels directed
they al their doinges. Wherfore suche
thinges as you report of Christ, of his
Disciples, and of the holie Fathers, are
al most euidently false.   You say, it
is not true, that your Doctours should
take any thing vppon them, aboue the
                    H iiij   com-

cõmon sort of men. Can you ymagine
any greater arrogancie in the worlde,
thē to presume to reforme the church,
being somewhat impaired, with newe
lawes and statutes, whiche neither
Athanasius, nor Basile, nor Cyprian,
nor any other of the holi Fathers euer
thought vpon: and to set such wordes,
and countenance vpon the doctrine of
their new Gospell as though they had
done al thinges by ordre and appoint-
ment of Christ him selfe?

You say that I am not able to shew
any fault or dishonestie in the worlde
in their life. That is true, if we must
needes stand to your opinion: For so
much as emongest you neither filthie
pleasure of the bodie, nor rebellion,
nor any other disordre or outrage are
accompted as faults.

You find faulte with me, for that I
cease not to trifle daungerously, and
to hinder the estimation of most graue
personages, by whose diligence your
Church

Churche hath ben set in a maruelous
goodly ordre. You could say no lesse,
for such as you doe commend (being
your selfe both for vertue and authoritie a very graue sire) must needes be
verie graue men. Then you saie.

You laie to aur charge that the compa-
nies of virgins and monkes, which were
sometimes inclosed in Monasteries to
keepe the Diuine seruice of God, and to
mainteine the chastitie of their bodies,
were by our men let out to the vncleane
pleasure of the flesh, and al other licenti-
ous liuing: that their howses were laied
wide open for gaine, that lawes were
made, that no religion shoulde hinder the
pleasure of the bodie. What you meane
by their gaine, I vnderstand not. For I
neuer suspected, that they did for their
gaine comit any vile or filthy acte. But
you doe in this as you doe commoly.
You can not wel tel, neither what
you do say, nor what you would say.
Then how impudently is that spoken
that

that foloweth? *Out vpon this ouer male-part and licentiouse desire , whiche you haue to peruert all thinges . We confesse, yea and with all our heartes confesse, that , through the moste holie aduer-tisement of our menne , those downge-ous of all wickednes are fallen downe, into the whiche the tender young mai-dens , and the seelie boyes were violent-ly thrust in , to their so great hinde-raunce in good manners, as I can not for bashfulnesse well declare .* Oh what a shamefaste and maydenlie fel-low is this ? What is that, I praie you, that you woulde not for shamefastnes expresse ? Nothing in the wordle. for immediatly after ·you bring in these woordes . *Those same shoppes of lewd-nes had litle other thing in them, but on-ly a certaine pharisaical continuance of praiers in an vnknowen tongue. Their o-ther more secrete exercises might wel be likened to the old reuelles of Bacchus in Rome.* Tel me I praie you (most pre-

sump-

sumptuous and impudent railer)could
you hane vttered any more spiteful
reproche against the poore monasteries of holi virgins, if your goodly mai-
denlines and modestie had not staied
you? Compare you the greene arbour
of Christ, the house of chastitie, the re-
presentation of heauély life, with the
most horrible and filthy reuels of Ba-
chus, whiche were sometime moste
sharply pounished by the lawes of the
Romaines? And yet you say forsooth,
that your maydenlie modestie wil not
suffer you to expresse their secrete vices. Pleasure you so much in your stin-
king eloquence ? Like you so wel to
taunt and reuile chastitie, to ioyne the
defence of your most barbarus and vile
acte, with the reproche of Christ ? As
though the worlde knewe not, that
you ouerthrow those holy Monasteries, not for any displeasure you beare
to naughtines and vice, but for the
hatred you beare towardes chastitie.

And

And of like the greadie defire you had of the goods and poffeffions, with the which the Nonnes and Monkes were mainteined, holpe the matter well foreward. If you had had no face at al, no fhame, no bafhfulnes in the world, how could you with more vile and filthie language haue difhonefted fo holie a trade of life? The exercife of Religious and chaft life you cal the downgeon of wickednes: that is to fay, a fincke of al vice, a cannel of filthines, a ftanding poole of vnclean pleafures. Could any thing be more impudently fpoken? And yet you content not your felfe with al this ftincking fturre of wordes, but you fay moreouer, that the tender young maidens, and the feelie boies were violently thruft into the faid Monafteries, to their greate hinderance in good manners. What meane you by this? What would you fay? What geaue you the worlde to vnderftande? Is there any vice fo hei-

noufe

nouſe, that it may not be wel compriſed in this your ſhameleſſe talke? After
this there ſoloweth the moſte beaſtlie
word of all the reſt, where you cal the
holie diſcipline of cleane life and continencie, a ſhoppe of naughtines. As for
the Phariſaical continuance of praier,
which is but a tricke proceding of Luthers railing ſprit, I wil let it paſſe. But
wherto tēdeth the compariſon, which
you make with the moſt vncleane and
deteſtable rebels of Bacchus? Is mans
heart able to deuiſe any thing ſo abho-
minable, that you may not wel cōpre-
hende it within the compaſſe of this
your moſte baſe and vile language?
Why then what is that, which you can
not expreſſe for baſhfulnes? Doutleſſe
nothing: wherof it foloweth, that vou
are vtterly void of al ſhame, baſhfulnes
and honeſtie. For I can not tel how it
cometh to paſſe, that the more a man
vſeth the companie and familiaritie of
ſuch men as you commende, the more
                                        ſhameleſſe

shamelesse is his behauiour. But to the intent you may the better see, howe heinouse and wicked an offence you haue cõmitted againſt your owne self: I think it good to declare the original of the name and inſtitutiõ of Monkes.

The original and inſtitutiõ of mõkes.

There are two kind of men within the folde of Chriſtes church. The one is of them, which liuing a cõmon life, cõtent them ſelues with the commendable exerciſe of meane vertue and godlines. The other is of ſuch, as endeuour them ſelfe to excell in the folowing of heauenly life and diſcipline. Now for ſo much as the ende, whiche euery Chriſtian man ought to ſet before his eyes, is the likenes of the perfection and iuſtice of God, the which they atteine muche ſooner, which are prõpter and redier to behold the beautie of the wil of God: the which beautie no man can wel cõceiue in his hart, ſo long as he is as it were tied downe with the bandes of ſtreight frindſhip and familiaritie of the bodie: it came to

paſſe, that ſuche as had an earnſt and
feruent deſire to ioyne them ſelues vnto God, called away their mindes (as
much as was poſsible) from the familiar acqueintance of the body, to the intent they mighte the better faſten the
eyes of their hearts in the cléerenes of
God. Theſe are they, which (as our
Lord ſaith.) haue ghelded them ſelues
for the loue and earneſt deſire of the
kingdome of heauen. For the pleaſure of the bodie weyeth downe the
heart euen to the earth, and with her
importunitie carieth away the minde
from the contéplation of the brightnes
of God. The which thing is ſo true, *Hèb.13.a.*
that, although Mariage be honorable,
and the bed vndefiled, and he that de-
fraudeth his wiſe of the right of Mariage, committeth no ſmall ſinne, yet it
is ſometimes neceſſarie for ſuche as
dō minde to receiue this cleereneſſe
of God within them ſelues to abſteine
from their owne wiues.

For

Exod.19.6 For this caufe Moyfes, before he receiued the law, gaue commaundemēt
to al men, to abfteine from the companie of their wiues, vntil God had geuē
out the law. For this confideration S.
Paule alfo, when he forbiddeth the
husbandes to forfake the companie of
1.Cor.7.4 their wiues, addeth this claufe. except
it be for a time to geaue your felues
whollie to praier. In the which place
the holie Apoftle teacheth plainely
that the verie lawful and holy companie of man and wife, doth hinder the
mind, that it can not fo freely and fpe-
dily pearce the heauēs, and there talke
familiarly with God. And therefore
faieth he in the fame Epiftle, he that
ioineth his virginitie in marriage, doth
wel: and he that ioyneth not, doth better. The reafon, whiche the Apoftle
geueth, why it were better for a maide
to continewe vnmarried, is this. Bicaufe that, fuch as are entangled with
the cares of marriage, are oftentimes
ca-

caried awaie from the remembrāce of heauenly thinges. But such as are free from mariage, are troubled with none other care, but how to pleaſe God. And, the ſingle woman, ſaith S. Paule, thinketh vpon the thinges that apperteine vnto God: how ſhe may be holly in bodie and in ſoule. And a few lines after, he ſetteth before our eyes, the goodli fruit of this moſt holy freedom, which is, a libertie to praie vnto God at all times without any impediment or lette. That this ſo great a gifte, and benefitte ought to be aſcribed, not to the merite of man, but to the mercie of God, our Lorde him ſelfe declareth, ſaying. Euerie man receiueth not this word, but they only to whom it is geauen. Whereby it is manifeſt, that, ſuche as doe ſo conquere the tyranny of fleſhly pleaſure, that they are able to continue their lyfe in chaſtitie, they dooe it by a ſingular benefitte of God, and for that cauſe are moſt wor

Mat. 19. b

I   thie

thie of honoure and reuerence.

But you wil saie peraduenture, that I spend muche talke in thinges too wel knowen, and not necessarie. They are, I graunte you, thinges verie well knowen, and thoroughly debated in the writinges of holie menne. But that they are nothing necessarie, then maie you geue iudgement, when you shall perfectly vnderstande, that they are impertinēt to those matters, which I haue taken vpon me to treate of.

Whereas therefore in the Primitiue Churche, the greatest parte of men that became Christians, liued vprightly and godly, but yet so, that they differred little from the common lyfe of men: there was no smal number which were inflamed with most ernest desire of the greater dignitie and higher perfection. Nowe these (being therevnto moued by the spirit and grace of God) fearing lest the luste of the bodie, and care thereof, might be some hinderāce

vnto

vnto them, and hoping withal that thei
ſhuld more manfully vanquiſh the ſen-
ſualıty of the fleſh, abſteined thē ſelues
frō mariage: to thentent that although
their bodies walked vp and downe in
the earth, yet their minds ād thoughts
might be cōuerſant with God in heauē.
The which thing that they might the
more cōmodiouſly bring to paſſe, they
ſeparated themſelues frō the company
and cōuerſation of men, and with one
accord pitched in one place: that ther
might be made of al their mindes, one
ſure and perfecte agreemente of heart
and will . And the order that was taken in the beginninge at Hieruſalem ,
that no man ſhoulde haue any poſſeſ-
ſion ſeuerall to him , (whiche coulde
not be long kept of all , for the greate
multitude of men) was of theſe men
reſtored and putte in vre againe .
Their lyſe was nothing elles , but onlie a perpetual warre againſt the bodily
pleaſures and ſinne ; with an earneſt

and continual meditation of heauenlie thinges. Their bodie therefore they subdued with fasting, watching and labour: but their mindes they stirred vp to behold the bewtie and brightnes of God by prayers and spiritual songes, hymnes and meditation of godly matters. Hereof proceded that most feruent flame of loue: hereof came that earnest desire to folow godlines and vertue: hereof arose the ioyning of mans wil with the wil of God: hereof sprang a certaine cleere and bright sonneshine in the sowle of man: finally hereof issued that knot or coniunction with God, then the whiche mannes hart is able to ymagin no thing streighter or faster.

These men were at the first called in greeke Monkes, that is to say, solitarie liuers: not so much bicause they haunted desert places, as bicause they forsoke and despised al wordly things, and were knitte with a most streight

band

band of loue vnto God al only, according to tbe saying of Dauid. It is good Psal.72.d
for me to cleaue vnto God. And S.
Paul saith in like manner. He that clea- 1.Cor.6. d
ueth vnto God, is one spirit with God.
These monkes therfor, which I speake
of, that they might the better atteine
vnto a state, in the whiche no man
might disquiet or pul them away from
this coniunction of the spirite of God:
tooke such ordre of life, as I haue here
declared. S. Dionysius of Areopagus
whom I esteeme, after the Apostles, as
prince of al Diuines, doth not only expound the name of a Monke after this
sort, but declareth also, what ceremonie the Bishops vsed at the professing
of monkes. This name of a monke hath
ben sometimes in great reuerence and
estimation : and howses were builded
for them to dwell in, the whiche, as
Philo writeth, were at the first called
Monasteries. There were also many
virgins inflamed with the loue of God,

          I iij the

the which subdewing the sensual pleasure of the bodie, taming the affections of the mind, despising the richesse
of the world: gaue themselues wholly
to the seruice of Christ: and the better to bring their purpose to good effecte, thei came together in one place,
where they liued alwayes in the contemplation of God. S. Basile a very
holie and great learned man, after many yeares drewe out a rule in writing
for Monkes, to the ende they should
no more alter and chaunge their discipline, but be well setled and bound
alwaies to one vniforme fasshion of religion. His Epistles are yet extante,
in the whiche he doth moste grauelie
confute the slaunderouse talke of certaine lewde felowes, the which misliked his doinges herein. For the
worlde was neuer, nor is nowe, nor
neuer shall be without some seedmen
and seruitors of Satans retinew, which
endeuoure them selues to vndoe the

Decrees

Decrees and ordinaunces of holy men.
This life of Monkes how highly doth
Chryfoftome commend it? With how
greate woordes doth Auguftine bring
men in admiration of it? How often,
how grauely, how eloquently doth S.
Hierome fet out the excellencie of it?
Who did not only c̄omend it in words,
but alfo folowed him felf that trade of
life, and liued and died in the company
of Monks. And fo did Gregorie of Na-
zianzen, the moft worthy piller of Diuinitie, the goodly paterne of vertue
and eloquence. What fhould I here reherfe al other men, that haue excelled
in learning and holines? Was ther euer
any vertuoufe and perfect man in the
world, which gaue not exceding great
commendation to the rule and life of
Monks? Truth it is, that the erneft loue
of this perfect religion hath ben flaked
and quenched (as it happeneth) diuers
times: but there neuer lacked holie
men to ftir it vp and kendle it againe.

I iiij　　From

from thence came that wõderful good
Father Benet, from thence came Bernard and Brunus, and after them Fran-
cis and Dominike, the whiche did not
only set an order in the life of Monks,
but also with most earnest and feruent
desire, laboured to reforme the church
of Priestes which was very slacke and
negligent. How many Martyrs came
from thence ? How many Writers ?
How many excellent men in al kinde
of vertues ? For if there was any thing
in the Church in their time, that tended
either to example of excellent vertue,
or to a rule of high wisedome, al that
may we thanke the Monkes of : or (to
speake better) thanke Christ him selfe,
which stirred the hartes and mindes of
Monkes to follow such a goodly discipline of vertue and wisedome.

But, to abridge this our discourse, being now made plaine, that there were
euen in the Primitiue Churche, two
kind of Christians: the one which con-
ten-

téting them selues with meane doings, liued a cōmon life without crime : the other, which tending to heauenwarde with greater feruécie, withdrew their minds from the familiariti of the body, and them selues from al resort of men, and cōsecrated their whole life, to the seruice and loue of Christ : being also euidently proued, that this life of perfection farre passeth the other cōmon life : surely it is veri manifest, how great honour and reuerence men ought to haue borne to those houses of Virgins and Monkes. For they were in this kinde of life, which is more noble and excellent, yea and commeth farre neerer to the nature and likenesse of Angelles, as it were common Scholes or working howses of heauenlie vertue, and cleane life. This is that, that induced manie Christian Princes most vertuous and godly men, to build Monasteries, and to endew them with possessions, by the whiche the Virgins

and

and monkes might liue and ferue God continuallie. When this was donne, thofe princes were for victories moft renowmed, for chiualrie and feates of armes moft honorable, and their countreis excellently wel gouerned. But nowe we fee in many places where men do bafely fwarue from the godlines of their auncetours, that it cometh farre otherwife to paffe. For with increafing of rentes and reuenewes cõtendeth nedines: with the multitude of men, diſhonefty: with pride, the weaknes of the whole cõmon weale: finally with the ſhew of holines impudently faced and borne out, facrilege.

But you wil faye, that this kinde of monks are al decaied and worne away. Not emong vs, I aſſure you. For fence the Kinges of Spaigne haue bent them felues earneſtly towards the reformation of religion: there is found fo great religion and godlines in diuers Monaſteries, that manie younge men of the

the nobility brought vp in great welth,
standing in good hope of muche worſhip and honour in the cōmon weale,
being inflamed with the loue of ſuche
wōderful vertue as they ſee with their
eyes, doe forſake richeſſe, deſpiſe honour, reiecte pleaſures, litle regard the
teares of their parents, and flie for ſuc-
cour into ſome holy cōpanie of monks,
as it were from the ſtormy tempeſt of
filthie vice, into the quiet hauen of
cleane life. In like maner many virgins
of excellent bewtie and comely behauiour, being ſewed vnto for marriage
of diuerſe yong men of the Nobilitie,
haue forſaken al the allurements of this
life, that they might in the company of
holie virgins much more pleaſantly ſo-
lace them ſelues in the ſpirituall and
ſweet familiarity of Chriſt.

But you will ſaye peraduenture,
that theſe exaumples of greate vertue, are verie fewe in compariſon of
them, that are thruſt into Monaſteries
against

againſt their wil and repining at it. And
no meruaile. For why, in euerie kind,
looke what is exellente, is alſo rare.
Then whereas you talke of violence
vſed in putting the Virgins into Monaſteries, it was neuer permitted by any
Lawe, nor yet allowed of wiſe men,
and the holie Councell of Trent hath
from hence foorth vtterlie forbidde it,
and therfore it is now no more vſed.

But what fruiƈte and commoditie
haue theſe Virgins by this kind of life?
Doubtleſſe ſuch as can not in wordes
be expreſſed. For manie of them are
ſo inflamed in ſpirit, that they are ſomtimes taken quite awaie from their bodies, and liſted vp into heauen, where
in the contemplation of the goodnes
of God they reioyſe excedingly, and
beholding the bewtie and brightnes of
God (ſo much as they may) are aſto-
niſhed, yea ſo much that ſomtimes thei
are beſides them ſelues. I haue good
aoquaintáce my ſelfe with a Monke, a
ſimple

simple and plaine man, the whiche, so
often as mentiõ is made of the loue of
God, his senses failing him, he falleth v-
pon the grownd, and yet in the meane
time, his memorie is fresh, and is in cõ-
templation of heauenlie and godlie
thinges. It were an infinite matter, if I
wold reherse, how manie holie men I
haue seene in those companies which
you laugh to scorne, and howe manie
virgins I haue talked withal, which are
wonderful for religion and holines.

If these thinges be true (as they are
most true) why haue you taken away
this so excellét an example of religiõ?
Whie haue you defaced so wonderful
a rule of chastitie and cleane life, in the
which is conteined that, that is in the
religiõ of Christ the highest perfectiõ,
and (as I said before) most of all to be
esteemed? whie haue you violétly and
furiously rushed into those holy howses to abolish vtterly out of the worlde
the very remébrance of perpetual cha
stitie?

ſtity ? Oh,ſay you,they liued not after
the rule of S.Baſil.I graūt you,for emō-
geſt vs alſo ſomtime,the Nūnes forgetting their duety,waxed ſomwhat wan
ton , and ſome Monkes alſo liued very
diſordredly:howbeit the moſt holy order and diſciplin was not for that cauſe
vtterly taken away and ouerthrowen.
Neither are the members of the body,
which may be healed , ſo ſone as they
fal into any diſeaſe,forthwith to be cut
of. What?Thinke you it wel done,for
a ſmal blemiſh or eyeſore to grubbe vp
the whole order by the root ? Were it
not better,wene you to bring the mē-
bers,that are diſeaſed, to their naturall
ſtrēgth again?If you had vſed the ſame
medicine, as our Prīces did:why might
not the cōmendable vertues of chaſtity
and holines haue floriſhed emōgſt you,
as thei do with vs?But it was neuer no
part of your thought. Neither did reaſon moue you to doe well , but hatred
and couetouſnes pricked you forward
to miſchiefe.

Nowe as touching the Pharisaicall continuance of praiers (for so it liketh you to terme the continual exercise in the Diuine seruice of God)this much I answere. If the defence of Religion do consist in vnreasonable and reprochful woordes, then are you to to muche to good for vs. For you haue had in that honest faculty, an excellent scholemaster called Luther, from whom proceded al these termes, Pharisee, hypocrit, Papist, and such other (which I do let passe as wordes not meet to be spoken of any honest and bashfull man) with the which he reuiled holy men. And yet you to mainteine one mischiefe by an other, to defende Sacrilege with a heape of slaunders and false witnesse, you saie, that the disorder of Monkes in their Celles, and of Nunnes in their Cloisters was so great, that they might well be compared with the reuelles of Bacchus. Howe then haue you left such heinous offences vnpunished?

Where-

Wherefore did you not suppresse such fowle and horrible vices with moste extreme and sharpe punishmentes? Wherefore did you not procede with al seueritie and rigor against such detestable conueticles (for so you ful vnreuerently cal them) wherfore did you not make them exáples to the worlde, lest the libertie of vnbridled and filthy pleasure might ouerflow your coūtrei to the vtter vndoing of your common weale? Are you so rechlesse and negligent in the gouernemēt of your realm, that you thought it meete to appoint no punishmēt at al for that most detestable shop (as you cal it) of filthie vice? Wil you in that Iland, in the which a Queene (whome the king loued verie well for her beawtie, witte, and courtelie behauiour) for the onelie suspicion of a great deale lighter offence then this is, was by the sentence of the iudges, at the commaundement of the King him selfe her housband,

ſande , openlie in the face of the
world, by the hand of a hangman executed and beheaded : wil you, I ſaie,
in that Iland ſuffer ſuch heinouſe offences, as are not to be named , to eſcape vnpuniſhed, yea ād that in a kind
of men, which are not only contemp-
tible and abiecte , but alſo odious and
hateful? It is not like.

Moreouer , this feate of pulling
downe monaſteries beganne not emõgeſt you , but you had it from other
menne . For Carolſtadius and Luther
and other the head Sectaries attempted this goodlie enterpriſe firſte of al:
ſo that you maie not robbe them of
the honour thereof , and take it to
your ſelfe . It was not therefore the
hatred of vncleane pleaſure , but the
example of theſe noble perſonages ſet
out as a rule in this your new diſcipline and Religion , that ſtirred your
mindes to the ouerthrowe of perpetual chaſtitie. Beſides this , the grea-

K   uous

uous difpleafure you had conceiued againft the Bifhoppe of Rome for entermedling and geauing fentence against you : the cafting of your eyes vpon the goods and poffefsions, with the whiche the Mounkes liued : the flatterie of certaine naughtie and defperate fellowes : the fonde pleafure and appetite to make alterations and chaunges, helped the matter wel forwarde . In olde tyme emongeft the Romaines (whiche were men vtterly void of the light and knowledge of God) the Virgins of Vefta were had in fuch eftimation, that euerie man did geaue them the waie, the place, and feate, with verie great reuerence . And you haue difteined the Virgins of Chrifte with a notorious and perpetuall infamie . Thofe Virgins, bicaufe they mainteined the fier of Vefta, the citezins did not onely honour and attende vpon religioufly, but alfo reuerenced their iudgementes: and

you

you haue not suffered the holie virgins of Christe to keepe their virginitie solemly vowed, to maintaine the euerlasting fier of heauenlie loue in their heartes enkendled. It was lawful for those Virgins to marrie after thirtie yeares, and yet of their owne accord they did absteine from marriage: you haue maried the virgins of Christ, to whome it was in al ages vnlawful, to filthie ribaudes. Those virgins, if they were at anie tyme by intisement deflowred, they were buried aliue and so ended their life with a horrible kinde of death: and you haue taken them, whiche were dishonested (as you saie) with moste vile brothelrie, and haue for punishment of so great a vice pleasauntly rewarded them with sporting and daliaunce. And yet you say.

Wherefore God hath stirred the harts of our men, that these so great bãds or cõpanies, which laie lurking in blind stĩking

corners , were through their godlie exhortations called foorth, from idlenes to
labour, from vice to vertue , from wicked brothelrie to most honest marriage.
You say , God hath stirred the heartes
of our men . I would faine learne of
you, what God that was. for there are
manie, as S. Paule saith, that are called
Goddes . For to some men the bellie
is a God : to some other monie is a
God : yea and to some riot and ruf-
fling and hawtines is a God . I would
therefore faine knowe , what God
that was , that put it into the heartes
of your menne , to abolishe and rake
vp in the earth the loue of most holie and perpetuall chastitie . Was it
Bacchus , or Cupide , or Mercurie?
For of Christ the sonne of God, who
is verie muche delyted in perpetuall
chastitie and cleane life, I am right wel
assured, that he neuer moued you to
any such heinouse acte.

The idlenes , which you speake of,
was

was not a fruteles sitting stil, void of al
holie workes, but it was a continuall
exercise in the contemplation of godlie thinges.

As touching the most filthie brothelrie (as you cal it) you are in one
sentence conuinced both of a lie, and
of impudencie withall. For, if there
had benne anie suche offence committed of them, you woulde not
haue suffered it vnpounithed. And
then howe impudent and shamelesse
you be, the forging of so filthie a
crime doth plainelie declare. It is not
therefore true that you saie, that
your doinges stande well with the
profitte of the common weale. But
contrariewise you haue by violence
and authoritie drawen out those bandes or companies (as you cal them)
from holie quietnes to a busines defiled with wicked sacrilege : from the
exercise of godlines, to the libertie of vice : from the discipline of per-

petuall continencie to the bondage of
moſte vncleane voluptuouſneſſe .
Howe be it by this , I due not excuſe
your Religiouſe menne . For it had
ben muche better for them to ſuffer
intolerable paines , yea and to let their
lyues in tormentes , then to forſake
their Faith , whiche they haue openly
profeſſed to Chriſte . For if they had
withſtood your warninges and counſell , your threates and authoritie with
good courage and conſtante heartes,
dowbteleſſe they had died an honourable death for the glorie of Chriſte .
For you are wont to punniſh extreme-
lie the chaſte and cleane lyfe : but filthie and vile brothelrie , as you confeſſe your ſelfe , you are wonte mer-
cifullie to pardonne . The Carthuſians‘, moſte chaſte and holie Fathers,
you put to death : but thoſe moſt wicked bandes and companies , as you
terme them , you called foorth to be
married,

married, and to liue in pleasure.
Wherefore there is no dowbt, but
that, if your Mounkes had liued after S. Basiles ruse, they had benne
dispatched emongest you euerie one.
And yet you glorie that by this your
so goodlie an acte you are restored
againe to libertie. As thoughe you
vnderstoode, what thinge true libertie were. But of that we shall
see hereafter. Nowe before I enter
into that discourse, I wilbe so bolde
as to demaunde of you one question.

This libertie of the gospell, whiche
you haue alwaies in your mowth,
doth it take place in all thinges, so,
that it maie be lawfull for euerie man
at al tymes to do what him listeth? Or
els is it limited by some certaine rule
of lawe and reason? As for example
in Matrimonie. Shall it be laweful for
the husband to put awaye his wife
for euerie cause that hym lysteth

K iiij   to

to alleage? No without doubte. For the euerlasting law of the Gospell will not beare it. If then the band of Matrimonie beinge once knitte by the mutuall consent of man and wife, can not be dissolued: by what meanes, I praie you, may that bande, with the which Virgins are willingly consecrated vnto Christe with solemne ceremonies, and faithful promise, be broken by the presumption of menne, without great and heinouse offence? S. Paule commaunded Timothee to auoide yonge widowes. For when they haue liued rioteouslie, saieth he, to the reproche of Christe, they will marrie. What then? Is it not lawefull for widowes to marrie? Doubtlesse it is lawfull. For the same S. Paule saieth. If her husbande be asleape, shee is free from the lawe of her husbande. Shee may marrie to whome shee will, onely in our Lorde.

1. Tim. 3. b

1. Cor. 7. g

If then it be lawful for Widowes to marrie

marrie without ſinne, what is the mat-
that S. Paule findeth faulte with theſe
widowes, bicauſe they would marrie?
for he addeth, that they haue their dā-
natiō. Whie ſo I praie you? what haue
they donne? what offence haue they
cōmitted? Bicauſe they haue, ſaith he,
broken their firſt faith. what ſaith I beſeke you? Expound the meaning of S.
Paule, if you can. What manner of promiſe was this, whiche the Widowes
haue broken with none other offence,
but bicauſe they would haue married.
Is it the promiſe, which they made to
their houſbandes, that they would neuer ſpot the bed of wedlocke with ad-
ulterie? No. For of that promiſe they
were quite diſcharged by the death of
their houſbandes. Whie then it foloweth, that this promiſe was not made
to anie man, but to the ſonne of God,
that they ſhoulde keepe the chaſtitie
both of bodie and mind perpetually to
his glorie. The whiche promiſe when
                    they

1. *Tim.* 5. *b.*

they had decreed to breake, they did a
greuous reproche, not to men, but to
Chriſt him ſelfe. And therfore it ſee-
med to the Apoſtle, that they had de-
ſerued, (as being condemned for the
offence of a moſt wicked adultery)not
to be receiued into the cōpany of chaſt
widowes, but rather to be ſorebidden
to enter into the church. And that you
maie the more meruaile at it, note,
that S. Paule ſaied not, that thoſe widowes after the firſt mariage had married to other mē cōtrarie to their pro-
miſe made, but onely that they would
haue married : wherby it is geauen vs
to vnderſtand, that this religious promiſe is moſt wickedly and heinouſly
broken by the onlie will and deſire to
be married againe. It was therfore lawful for widowes to marrie, before they
had promiſed and cōſecrated their cha
ſtitie vnto Chriſte , but after the time
that the promiſe was paſt , it was no
more lawful. Now then ſir: Think you
that the offence of the Virgins is anie

thing leſſe, which haue not only a deſire to marrie, but doe marrie in deede
to the great reproch of Chriſt? Doubtleſſe it is farre greater: by ſo much as, it
is a more wicked offence for an vndefiled virgin to plaie the harlot to the
diſhonour of Chriſte, then not to kepe
the chaſtitie of a bodie, whiche is not
vntowched. How long then laſteth
this libertie? So long as it is in our free
choiſe, to take what way we wil. But
when we haue once either yoked our
ſelues in matrimonie, or els offered vp
our bodies by vow to ſerue God in religiõ: as it is not laeful to break the promiſe of matrimony, ſo is it not lauful to
violate the ſacramẽt of perpetual chaſtitie. And who ſo euer preſumeth to
due it, cõmitteth a moſt wicked crime,
that deſerueth the iudgemẽt and ven-
geance of God. He that hath cõſtantly 1. Cor. 7. g
determined in his heart, ſaith S. Paule,
hauing no cõſtreint, but hauing power
ouer his owne wil, and hath aduiſedly
deter-

determined in his hart to kepe his virgin, doth wel. He laieth no necessitie at al vpon vs : but by his authoritie
approueth the wil of that man, which
weying and considering the matter
wel, and taking withall the will of the
virgin (for otherwise it maie not be) de-
dicateth the said virgin vnto Christe,
which he kepeth vnder his rule and
power. But after the virgin hath once
bound her selfe with the vowe of perpetual chastitie, S. Paule saieth not, that
she is at her choise to marrie if she wil.
For if he should so saie, he should speke
verie muche against him selfe . But al
these thinges are verie easily confuted
in the opinion of such as are addicted
to Luther. For it is not lawful, say thei,
for any man to bind him selfe by vowe
to that religion , which he is not able
to kepe . And to resist the tyrannie of
fleshlie lust, they saie, is graunted to no
man. This is the talke of a mã not only
incõtinent and dissolute, but also wickedly

kedly bent againſt God. For he diſtru-
ſteth the goodnes and power of God,
and meaſureth the ſtrength of vertue
and continencie, not by the almighti-
nes and power of God, but by his own
weakenes and filthie appetit. And this
is the propertie of al naughty felowes,
by their owne beaſtly life to iudge the
conuerſation of other men. Nero was
fully perſwaded, that al men were as
euil as him ſelfe, but that their vnbridled luſt was reſtrained by the lacke of
thinges, that it could not breake out at
al times into deedes. And this opinion
cauſeth, that when vicious men heare
tel of anie man or woman that is verie
continent, they doe not only not beleeue it, but they wil deuiſe oftētimes
ſome infamous crime to burden him
withal. I graunt you thus muche, that
neither Luther, nor Bucer, nor Zwinglius, nor Oecolampadius, nor Caluin,
nor your Martyr him ſelfe was able to
ſuſteine the aſſault of the fleſh. For the
heauenly

heauenly gifte of perpetual chastitie, is
iustly denied to al suche, as haue most
wickedly diuided them selues from
the church. But vnto such as are within the boundes of holy Churche, and
are desirous to be ioyned with most
feruent loue to Christ the chiefe and
principal worker of honestie and holines, for so much as they are sensed on
euerie side with the strong bulwarke
of God, it is very easie to put fleshlie
pleasure to flight, to pul vp the verie
strings and rootes of al vncleane vice.
Otherwise S. Paule had neuer geauen
counsel to virgins to continew in the
state of virginitie : he had neuer said,
that they were farre happiest of al o-
ther, that folowed the cleanes of his
life: he had neuer condéned widowes,
only for that they had a wil, to be married contrary to their promise: he had
neuer preferred the state of Virgins
before widowhod : no our Lord him
selfe had neuer approued that kind of
gel-

1. Cor. 7. b

1. Tim. 5. b
1. Cor. 7. g

geldinges, whiche haue gelded them Math.19.
selues for the kingdom of heauen. And *b.*
yet wil you here lament (like a Popular felowe , a restorer of libertie) the
wretched bódage of those virgins that
desire to serue Christ more painfully
and more chastly,then you doe . You
are altogether ignorãt,what libertie is,
which doe condemne the most excellent kind of liberty,calling it bondage.
For if it be true libertie to doe , what
fleshlie lust cõmaundeth,what naughtines forceth , what wrathsulnes moueth, what hatred perswadeth , what
the mad rage of a wilful and headlong
mind driueth a man to deuise and doe:
then I graunt you,that they are bond-
men,which haue crucified their affections , and haue fastened them selues
with such streight bandes vnto Christ,
that they can not be tossed to and fro
with the swaie of pestilēt and filthy lustes. But if libertie be a power of that True li-
part of the minde,which hath the rule bertie.
                                    and

and gouernment, and tendeth to come
to that end, to the which both the ex-
cellécie of natural inclination, and also the likenes of God in the mind calleth it: I would learne of you, whome
you thinke to be more free : that woman, that being, as it were, pulled in
sunder with a thowsand diuers busines, serueth alwaies with great care
her husband, her children, and her fa-
milie : or her, that being discharged
of al these troubles, casteth her selfe
downe at the feete of Christ, and hath
no more but one onely care, how she
may at al times singularly wel please
Christ her heauenly spouse. That woman, whome the force of pleasure being by law permitted, yea and of dewtie required, constreineth oftentimes
to forget heauenly thinges: or her,
whome no force of pleasure is able (so
long as she is bound vnto Christe) to
hinder from the cötemplation of God.
Finally, that woman, who is thorough
the

the loue of her husband drawen two
waies, or her, which hath set her whol
loue vpon the beawtie of Christ. Who
can denie, but that liberty is then geuē
to the mind in dede, when reason beareth rule in all the state of the minde ?
Whervpō it foloweth, that where reason keepeth downe the fleshlie lustes
most, ther is the mind freest. Wherfore
it must needes be, that the frutefull libertie whiche you haue vnseasonably
brought foorth for holie Virgins and
Monkes, against all right and reason,
against the holie order of Christian religion, is no libertie at al, but a detestable and pitiful bondage. We haue ben
somewhat long in the confirmatiō of
this part, bicause I sawe, that vpon this
lewd point was laied the verie foundatiō and growndworke of al Luthers
most pestilent doctrine. For this holie
chaplain of Venus (I meane not Venus
of Cyprus norPaphos, nor Ericine, but
Venus the Regét of hel) when he had

L   most

moſt filthylie ſpotted him ſelſe with leacherie and ribawdrie, he thought that not ynough, but vſed violent per-ſwaſions with ſo manie as were of his retinew, to doe the like. And as we reade in Euripedes, that Venus tooke great diſpleſure, bicauſe ſhe was deſpi-ſed of Hippolitus, and therfore deuiſed craftily, to ſende certaine monſtruous ſeacalues out of the ſea, to gallowe his chariot horſes, by the whiche traine Hippolitus was for the onlie loue of chaſtitie, torne al in peeces and cruelly ſlaine: euen ſo hath this helliſh Venus pricked foreward Luther and Carol-ſtadius, and the reſte of theſe horrible monſters, not againſt anie one chaſte man, but againſt chaſtitie it ſelte, mea-ning by them vtterly to aboliſh out of the wordle that heauenly example of chaſtitie, of honeſtie, and of virginitie.

Moreouer ther was a bitter hatred côceiued againſt the Biſhop of Rome, whoſe ſtate Luther ymagined might by by this goodlie pollicie be verie much weakened.

Laſt ofal Luther, according to the diuels phyſick(who vſeth to cure one euel diſeaſe with an other woorſe)deuiſed to heale the infamie of incontinencie with impietie and miſbeleefe: to thintent that, when he had perſwaded al ſuch as folowed him,that it was not only lawful and honeſt , but alſo that very dewtie and godlines,yea and neceſsitie it ſelfe required,that al Nunnes and Mõkes ſhould be maried,there ſhould no man be able to blame him for his incontinent and vicious liuing. The verie ſame trade and waie haue you takẽ,folowing the ſteppes of your maiſter,to aboliſh al good affection towardes perpetual chaſtitie : and now, that , that was verie vngodly and heinouſly done , you defende it to be done , for godlie and iuſt cauſes. To ſlide and fall procedeth of the weakenes of man, and to continewe in anie

vice il begonne, is an argument of an
vnbridled mind and vnrulie affection:
But to reioife and glorie in wickednes,
and to geue the name of honeftie and
godlines to moft filthie vices, is fo prefumptuous and horrible offence, that
it cã not by wordes be expreffed. And
yet bicaufe I did in my letters but only
lament this fo great a ruine and decaie
of religió, you laie out againft me with
open mowth. And yet you make out-
cries, and in fo doing you woulde be
taken for an erneft and vehemẽt man.
And yet you wold beare men in hãd,
that the thinges that you haue done
for hatred, malice and rafhnes, were
done charitably, prouidently, and adui-
fedly. You faie.

Out vpon this ouer malepart and licẽ-
tioufe defire, which you haue to peruert
all thinges. I faie on the other fide. Out
vpó your barbarous and crewel boldnes.
Out vpon your intolerable impudécie. Out vpó your moft wicked and
deuilifh

deuilifh practifes, deuifed and wronght
by the labour, ftudie, and diligence of
Satan. What rage hath fo driuen you,
what madnes hath fo ftirred you, that
you durft fet vpon fo wicked an en-
terprife? For you haue made open
warres againft honeftie and chaftitie:
you haue furioufly broké into the holy
Monafteries: you haue ouerthrowen
bafhfulnes, honeftie, and continencie:
you haue chafed awaie that moft excellent loue of perpetual virginitie:
you haue geuen the goods of religions
perfonnes to whome you lifted: and
now, when you triumph at the fall of
chaftitie and Religion, you fo vaunt
your felues in it, as though you had by
this noble victorie, gotten euerlafting
fame and honour.

Now foloweth the difputation of **Images.**
the pulling downe of Images, whiche
you like verie well, and are offended
with me, bicaufe I fhould faie, that
when the images are také awaie, there

is nothing left, wherby the mind might be ftirred vppe to thinke vpon godlie thinges. The which I neuer fpake: For there are manie other thinges, whiche you haue ouerthrowen together with the ymages, that moue our mindes more vehemently then they doe. But this much I faied: For fo much as Images are verie good and effectuall to bring al men, efpecially the vnlearned, to the remembraunce of the wonderful vertue, which fhone fometimes in the holy Saintes: and it were expediét that the benefit of Chrift fhould be reprefented vnto vs by al fignes, in al places: it was wickedly done of them, that pulled downe Croffes and Images. For we doe neither praie, nor offer, nor facrifice vnto them: but we are by them put in remembraunce of thofe thinges that are of dew to be worfhipped. *It us,* faie you, *againft the expreffe commaundement of God.* I would your doctours wonld inftructe you better in Diuinitie,

nitie, that you might no more babble
out fuch childifh toyes. Tell me, I
praie you, haue you neuer read, that
there were in the tabernacle of God,
Images of Cherubines fet before the
Arke of promife? The vele, whiche
diuided the inner part from the refte
of the tabernacle, was is not wrought
betwene, with manie Images of Cherubines? Was there not made the
Image of a Serpent in braffe by the
commaundement of God in the wil-
dernes, vpon the whiche, fuche as
were bitten of ferpentes, looked, and
were healed? What Images then hath
God forbidden to be made? Thofe
Images without dowbte, by the
whiche men blinded with fynne went
abowte to expreffe a thinge, that
can neither be deuifed, nor painted,
nor engrauen, nor expreffed wyth
woordes, nor conceiued with the
heart, that is, the infinite Maieftie of
God. Befides this, there was greate

*Exod.25.
b.*

*Numer.
21.b.*

L iiij   daunger

daunger, left the people being now acqueinted with the manners of the Aegiptians, being alfo abowt to goe into a land, which was infected with the felfe fame errours, might through familiaritie and neighbourhood of thefe vngodlie nations, fall into the like errour, and offer vp facrifice vnto goddes made of ftockes and ftones: or at the leaft make the ymages of fome naughty and vile men, and fet them vp in the place of God. The feare of this daunger caufed manie thinges to be taken quite awaie, which had ben otherwife lawfull and tolerated. The ymage of the brafen ferpent was diligently kept, as a goodlie monument of the benefite of God, and fingular facrament of the faluation to come. But after manie yeares, when the people were come to fuch madnes, that they thought there had benne fome diuinitie in the ymage, and therfore offered facrifice vnto it: it was by the holie

holie King Ezechias broken and made
into powder. Shew you now, that we
doe goe about to expresse the nature
of God by signes, or that we thinke
that ther is anie godhead in dome images, and then may you wel conuince
vs of blindnesse and folie. So long as
you doe not this, there is no cause,
whie you should feare the dotage of
idolatrie (as you terme it) or laie blindnesse to our charge with suche mon-
struous wordes. For we doe that, that
is by right and reason ordeined, by
the holie Churche approoued, by sentence of holy Fathers determined. *The*
gospell, say you, *commaundeth vs to ab-*
steine from Images. That is true. But
what must we vnderstand to be ordeined by this commaundement? For
sooth this, that no man should offer
vp sacrifice to Images, or for anie pre-
tense of religion, make as though he
did follow the errour, that was in o-
ther men. For the faithful men were
not

4. Reg.
18. 4.

not then commaunded to ouerthrow
and breake their Images, but to forsake the detestable Sacrifices. Moreouer, what Images were those? Of
Iuppiter, Apollo, Minerua, Mars,
and Mercurie, and other the like
Goddes, which were thought of old
time to be verie true goddes in deede.
But we doe neither offer vp sacrifice
vnto idols, neither doe we thinke the
Images of vncleane and vicious men
to be worthie of any reuerence in the
world. You say afterward.

*But this feare being taken awaie, yet
must the doctrine of Christ haue ful authoritie emongest Christian men : in the
which it is plainlie said, that God is a spirite, and that the true order of praying
to God is, to worship him in spirite and
trewth.* Of like we know not that, M.
Haddon, and therefore doe we make
God like a man both in bodie and māners. Would God, you had learned,
what it is to worship God in spirite,
and

and then had you neuer fallē into such
vngodly opinions. You say, that the
true ordre of praying nedeth not these
helpes of outward thinges. Although
you and such as you are, hauing nowe
waded so farre in the exercise of spiritual life, neede not these outwarde
helpes, but may without them presse
euen to the throne of God: yet should
you remembre, that there are manie,
that are not yet come to so high a degree of heauenlie perfection as you
be, and therfore haue neede to be holpen by all meanes possible. *Not so,*
saie you, *but raither while our owt-*
warde man is to muche occupied in
these shadowes of holie thinges, the
feruencie of the minde waxeth colde
within. Not so, M. Haddon, but
rather while the minde waxeth colde
within, it is, by these outwarde re-
presentations of holie thinges, to be
stirred vp, to remembre those thinges
that were forgotten. for, as Dionysius
tea-

teacheth vs, so long as we are inclosed
within the frame of this bodie, and
can not altogether withdrawe our
minde from the acqueintance of the
bodie, we are to be stirred vp nowe
and then by bodilie Images to the re-
memhrance of the inuisible God. This
not withstanding you goe forewarde,
and saie.

*Let vs put examples. The old Church
of the Apostles and Martyrs had none
of all these monumentes, and yet was
their spirite moste earnestly inflamed
with the loue of God. In the wane of
pure Religion pictures crope in by litle
and litle, and so appalled in the heartes of
men that former boyling heat of Religion.* Not so sir, but then were Images
and pictures necessarie, to stirre vp a-
gaine by al meanes the feruencie of religion, which was, as you say, appalled.
For so long as the Image of the Crosse
was printed and engraué in the hearts
of all men, this multitude of Images
was

was not so necessarie. But you doe
much like, as if a man should say, that
the remedies of diseases were the causes of diseases. for the picture did not
cause men to forgette holie thinges:
but rather it was wisely deuised, that
men might not forgette them. If the
vse of images quenched, as you saie,
that seruécie of spirit, with the which
men were inflamed in the olde tyme:
then must it needes folow, that, when
Images were first ouerthrowē of you,
you were by and by verie hote in spirite. Tel me therefore, if it please you:
When you first brake downe the Images, tables and other monumentes of
Saintes: when you defaced them, má-
gled them, and dasshed them in a thou-
sand peeces: when you burned the relikes of the most holie Martyr S. Thomas: was there foorthwith enkendled
in you so great a heat as you speake of?
were you by and by wholly inflamed
with fier from heauen? I beleeue there
fel

fell from aboue, not onely fierie tongues, but alſo fierie heartes and bowelles, the heate and flames whereof
wrought with you ſo extremely, that
you are not able by any meanes to a-
bide this ſtraũge force of loue, which
burneth within you. Neither do you
now liue vpon the earth, but in hearte
and mind you are in heauen. For euen
as vpon the ouerthrow of the authoritie of the biſhop of Rome, ther aroſe
out of hand a new ſonne emõgeſt you:
ſo muſt it nedes folow, that vpon the
pulling downe of Images, vppon the
breaking of the monumentes of Chriſt
crucified, vpon the digging vp of the
graue of the holy Martyr, and burning
of his bones: you cõceiued foorthwith
ſuch a fier of heauenly loue in your
bowelles, that there is nothing in the
world to be ſeene in your heartes, but
only that ſame hoat and fierie loue of
God. If it be ſo, I commend the vehe-
mencie of your ſpirite, I allowe your
doing,

doing, I thinke, this worthie acte of
yours deserueth immortall fame and
honour. for what so euer quencheth
the feruencie of the spirite, what so e-
uer doth any thing breake or weaken
the force of loue, it would be put back
with the whole bent of the hart. Neither ought we to beare anie thing in
the world, that might cause a dulnes
or slakenes in the minde. But if it be
nothing so, if, after the breaking
downe and defacing of the goodlie
monumentes of vertue, you were
not inflamed by and by with fier from
heauen: then it is most euident, that
the Images and reliques of holie men
buried vnder the grownde, did nothing hinder you from that feruent
loue of God. Whie then, what (the
diuell) madnes came into your heads,
that you should be so earnestly bent to
make a waste and spoile of thinges,
whereof you could take no commoditie in the worlde?

At

At the length, you speake verie earneſtly (as you doe often) againſt the diuinitie of the ſchoole doctours, wherin I can not much blame you: for you
haue good cauſe to be offended with
them, whoſe whole drifte both of
mindes and diſputation is altogether
againſt you. For they haue receiued a
pure and true Doctrine from holie
men: you haue taken a pudlie and ſtin-
king doctrine of moſt wicked perſons.
They are bound to the verie auncient
Religion, that was deliuered from the
Apoſtles: you falling from the auncient religion, are wickedly flitted to
this newfangled ſecte. They, for the
moſt part of them, doe worſhip Chriſt
with honeſt conuerſation and vpright
coſcience: but you haue done and ſpoken manie thinges verie impudentlie
and raſhly, to the reproche and diſhonour of Chriſt. Nowe whereas you
impute the cauſe of Images to them,
you ſhew your ſelfe to be not only verie

ry shamelesse, but also very witlesse. for
you doe not accompt emongest the
schoole Doctours Cyrillus or Athanasius, or Ierome, or Ambrose, or Augustine. Whome then? Dowbtlesse such
as folowed Petrus Lombardus, and beganne manie yeares after his tyme to
expound openly in schooles his Sentences (as they cal them) gathered out
of the bookes of the holie Fathers, and
brought into one volume. Petrus Lō-
bardus flourished about the yeare of
our Lord. 1141. And the second Councel of Nice was kept in the yeare. 781.
Neither was it firste decreed in that
coūcel, that Images shuld be set vp, but
that they should not be pulled down.
And the heresie of such as would haue
them to be ouerthrowen, was there
condemned by the ful agreement of al
the fathers. Of the which errour, as it
appeared by the testimonials brought
into the Councel, the firste brochers
were certaine Manichees and Mar-

M   cio-

cioniftes. It was there declared at that time, by the authoritie of Bafile, Gregorie of Niffa, Cyril, Ierom, Auguftin, and by the cuftome receiued in the Church euen from the Apoftles time: that the Images of Chrift, of his moft bleffed Mother, and of other holie men had ben fet vp, vpon a great good confideration, to call the mindes of men continually to remébre the goodnes of God. In the felfe fame Councel alfo, was read an oratió of Athanafius, of a miracle, whiche was wrought at Berith a citie of Syria, when certaine Iewes pearced the Image of Chrifte with a fpeare. For out of the wound flowed out bloud, whervpó the Iewes were turned vnto Chrifte. And although in the Apoftles time, fuche fignes were nothing neceffarie, and as then it was not lawful through the tyrannie of Princes to builde Churches, and to bewtifie them with comely ornaments: yet doe the auncient monu-

mentes

mentes declare, that euen at that time
there was some vse of Images. As for
the Images of the Crosse, there is no
doubt, for so much as the most auncier
monumentes both of Aethiopia and
India make mention of them.

In that part of India, which is within the riuers Indus and Ganges towardes the east, there is a towne called
Mailapur, and belongeth to the great
kingdō of Narsingua, where the bodie
of S. Thomas was buried. Ther, not ma
ny yeares ago, was digged out by the
prouidéce of God a great Crosse made
of stone: whose top and both sides, an
arke hewen out of the same stone co-
uered: wherein were engrauen letters
of verie great antiquitie, whiche no
man could reade but such as were lerned in the auncièt letters of the Brac-
mans. The meaning of the letters, as
it was afterwardes sounde, was a sto-
rie of the death of S. Thomas: whiche
declared, howe a holie man named

M ij Tho-

Thomas, in the time of King Sangam ruler of thofe landes, was fent of the fonne of God to vifite thofe countreis, and to bring the people vnto the knowledge of God: and how the ennemies of religion crucified him vpon the fame Croffe. And the Croffe euen at this daie is fmeared with fpottes of bloud.

Eufebius alfo writeth, that, in a citie called Philips Cefarea, there was a brafen Image of Chrift fet vpõ a foote, of a good heith, and before it an other Image of a woman, the whiche being fometime ficke of a bloudie fluxe, was cured by the benefit of our Lord. This Image was made in manner of a woman fuppliaunt and holding vppe her handes vnto the Image of Chrift. He declareth furthermore, that neere vnto the foote of the faid Image there was wont to growe a certaine kind of herbe, the which when it was growẽ fo high, that it touched the hemme of

the

the garment of Chrift, it conceiued a great vertue, and was verie foueraigne againft diuers and fundrie difeafes. The felfe fame Eufebius reporteth, that he him felfe had feene the Images of the Apoftles excellently wel painted, the which manner he cōmendeth highly.

It is alfo writen that Conftantine the Emperour fawe in a vifion Peter and Paule, whofe Images when he beheld afterwarde, being fhewed vnto him by Syluefter the Pope, refembling in al pointes that, that he had feene, he was excedingly aftoined.

What faie you M. Haddon? Are you not afhamed of your ignorance? It is euident, that there were Images fet vp in places of common refort, euē in the times of holie men (which you graunt to be happie tymes) efpecially after it was lawful to buyld great and fumptuous Churches: it is euidēt, that they were mifliked and refifted of verie olde heretikes, and worrhely main-

M iij   tei-

teined by moſt excellent men both for
holines and learning:finally it is euidēt
that the ſecond Councel of Nice ac-
curſed and excōmunicated al ſuche as
dyd condemne the Images of holie
men,and the monumētes of Chriſt:and
wil you vnaduiſedly aſcribe the cauſe,
and original of them vnto the ſchoole-
doctours,which beganne to diſpute of
diuinitie in ſchooles manie yeares,yea
many hundred yeares after that tyme?
what dulnes is this? what negligence?
what ignorance of antiquitie ? But
to let paſſe your ignorance in ſtories,
what maie be ſaid of your vndiſcreete
boldnes in theſe your doinges? For
whereas Images are ſo effectuall in
bringing vs to the remembrance of
thinges,that euē thei that reade bokes
continually,that ſerue God with great
feruencie, that may be brought to remembre heauenly thinges by many o-
ther monumentes,yet are they cheer-
fully preuoked to the loue of godlines,
by

by looking vpon the outward fignes
of heauély thinges, and Images of holie men: what came into your heades,
to pulaway frō the vnlearued people,
which haue not fo many ftaies to lean
vnto, thefe healpes and fuccour of memorie, thefe monumentes of perfecte
religion? For(to paffe ouer with filéce
al other monumentes)where fhal you
find one emongeft an hundred, that is
not moued by looking vpō the Image
of Chrift nailed on the Croffe? that is
nōt inwardly ftirred to deuotiō by the
remembrance of fo great goodnes and
mercie of God? that is not fometime
wholly· molten and refolued into
teares? Wherefore then will you
take awaie from the vnlearned and
weake, this goodlie healpe, with the
whiche, the learned them felues, yea
and fuche as are well hardened in the
exercife of godlineffe, are oftentimes
moued? Efpecially, for fo much as you
are neuer the feruenter in faith and
M iiij charitie,

charitie, after this your so honorable
an enterprise, for the which you take
so much vpon you.

But how wittily you conclude all
this question with a twoforked argument, saying, that our pictures, if the
spirite be present, neede not: if it be
absent, they boote not. Not so sir, but
if the spirite be present, they doe no
hurt, if it be absent, thei maie do much
good. For what so euer reneweth in
vs the remembrance of the goodnes
and mercie of God, profitteth vs not a
litle, and prepareth the waie verie
wel to atteine to the grace
of the spirite it
selfe.

§

THE

THE SECOND
BOOKE.

IN good faith I am a-
shamed to vse so many
wordes in the confu-
tation of that your
booke, for the which
you stoode so muche
in your owne conceite. But for so
much as you haue hudled vp together
so manie thinges in it, whiche I must
nedes laie abrode ech thing by it selfe,
I could not comprise so manie and so
diuers pointes of vngodlines and heresie in fewe wordes.

But to come vnto other matters,
you meruaile, that I should lament in
those my letters, that all holie thinges,
ceremonies, godlie custumes, solemne
feastes, and Sacramentes of Religion
were vtterly decaied. You saie therefore. *What doe I heare? Is it like that*
there

*there should liue anie kind of professours
of Diuinitie in the Christian worlde, the
which would vtterly abolish holy things,
ceremonies, and all Sacramentes of the
Churche?* By these your wordes, M.
Haddon, a man maie coniecture, that
it were such a horrible acte to doe it,
that the verie remembrance of it maketh you to tremble and quake. For
you thinke it a thing impossible, that
anie man (which is called by the name
of a Christian) shoulde be so wicked
and barbarous, so farre from true faith
and religion, so spitefully bent against
al godlines, that he would goe abowt
to dishonest, to depraue, to corrupte
and deface the solemne custumes of
the Churche, the religious vsage of
holie thinges, the inuiolable reuerence
of ceremonies. Looke what you graũt
vs we take it, and we thinke you to
be worthie of no meane commendation, bicause you thinke that their offence is not meane, which do despise
auncient

auncient ceremonies. Otherwife you
would not haue afked with a certaine
admiration, whether there were anie
kind of profeffours of Diuinitie in the
Chriftian worlde, that would commit
an offence fo wicked and barbarous.
And although you vfed craft, wheras
you faied, that the ceremonies were
not al ouerthrowen)as though it were
no fault to take awaie fome, and to re-
taiñe fome):yet I doubt not, but when
it fhal appeere euidêtly, that the verie
principal facramentes haue ben quite
ouerthrowê by fuch as beare the name
of Chriftian men, it fhal feeme euen to
you a very horrible offence. You mer-
uel(and not without caufe)at the gret-
nes of their heinoufe act. But I meruail
excedingly, not at the wicked acte of a
fort of defperat felowes, but at the foly
of a graue and wife mã. What fay you?
Are you only ignorãt in al Chriftendõ,
what hath ben done? Are you only a
ftranger and vnacqueinted in matters

ſo notoriouſly well knowen? Heard you neuer ſaie, how Luther a paſſing holie man (as you thinke) hath geauen a prowd ſaie to plucke awaie al the ſacramentes of the church? Neither can it be ſaied, that he keepeth the ſacramétes, the which wickedly and lewdly appaireth the vertue and ſtrength of them. If you neuer vnderſtoode this, what ſaie you to that? heard you neuer tel, that Carolſtadius, Zwinglius, Oecolampadius, and laſt of all your owne Martyr (to paſſe ouer a great nombre of others) did rent and teare the bleſſed Sacrament of the aulter with moſt vile and reprochful wordes? It is like you neuer heard of it. For how had it ben poſſible, that M. Haddon a chaſt and vpright man, a má moſt zealouſly bent towardes religion, (if he had vnderſtoode, that Peter Martyr had ben diſteined with ſo fowle a crime) could haue fownd in his hearr, I ſaie not to commend him, but only

to

to bid him good morrow after a familiar and frindlie fort? Tufh, faie you,
this is al falfe. For they keepe their facramentes ftill, and we vfe the felfe
fame facramentes with al our heartes.
For footh I am right glad of it, and I
praie God, much good maie it do you.
How beit I would faine know, what
is to be vnderftãded, by the facramẽts,
whiche you keepe ftil. Are they only
bare Images of thinges? Or is there
fome diuine power or vertue mingled
withal? If they be only bare Images,
is it not a fhame for men, whiche are
now paft al earthlie confectiõs, which
with pure mindes talke with the fprite
without anie meffengers betwene, to
vfe Images? For what fkilleth it, what
manner of Images they be? Truth it is,
that there are Images, which doe con-
fift both of wordes and bodilie things,
and fuch are much leffe ftable and per-
manent, then thofe whiche you haue
ouerthrowen. If you faie, that they
haue

haue anie ſtrength or power towardes
ſaluation: it is not poſsible, that anie
thing ſhoulde healpe towardes ſaluation, whiche is void of the grace and
mercie of Chriſt. But Luther denieth,
that the grace of Chriſt is procured by
them. Wherupō it foloweth, that ther
is conteined in them no ſownd fruicte
of iuſtification, but onlie bare Images
and tokens. And therfore it is to no
purpoſe for you to keepe them, if you
beleeue Luther. But bicauſe it were
tedious to make a diſcourſe vpon all
the reſt of the Sacramétes I wil ſpeake
only of two, which are of gret weight
and importaunce tewardes ſaluation.
The one is the confeſsion of ſynnes,
wherin is conteined the ſacrament of
penaunce: (it maie pleaſe your fine
and piked eloquence to beare with
theſe termes of plaine ſchoolemen)the
other is the Sacrament of the Aulter.

And to ſpeake ſomewhat firſt of
Confeſsion, I ſaie and affirme, that
there is no remedie appointed in the

Confeſsi-
on.

Church so effectuall to put awaie the
diseases of the sowle, and to recouer
the health thereof by the grace of
Christ, as confession is. The whiche
we prooue by reason, and trie also by
daile experience. I saie nothing here,
how in the time of the old lawe, in the
sacrifices which were oftentimes offered vp for the purgation of synnes,
there was a certaine confession of vn- *Nnm.5.a*
clene life made vnto the Priestes. Neither do I think it needefull to rehearse
in this place, how ernestly such as came
to the baptisme of Iohn, did first con- *Math.3.b*
fesse their sinnes. Neither wil I declare
as now what is writen in the Actes of
the Apostles as towching cōfession of *Act.19.d.*
synnes, which was made vnto the disciples of Christe by suche as became
Christians. That commaundemēt also
of S. Iames concerning confession I *Iacob.5.a*
wil passe ouer with silence. Neither
wil I here alleage those place in the
which Christ hath most vndowbtedly
com-

committed the rule and iurifdictió of
fowles vnto the Prieftes, the whiche,
as you know verie well by the ftudie
of the law, can not be executed, without the examination of the caufe.

The pro-
fit of cõ-
fefsion.

This one thing wil I faie, that the profitte of this wholefome cõfefsion is fo
great , that anie wife man maie eafily
coniecture, without anie teftimonials,
that it was ordeined by the prouident
wil and bowntiful mercie of the holie
Ghofte. For firft of al, how muche the
knowledge of euerfe mans owne felfe
auaileth to faluation, it can not wel be
expreffed with wordes . For euen as
felfe ignorãce blindeth the mind with
errours, and maketh it prowd and infolent : fo doth the remembrance of
the wekenes and miferie of man bring
men to the learning of wifedome. Furthermore, for fo much as no man can
atteine the grace of God , except he
doe firfte lowly abbafe and plucke
downe his minde ; there is nothing to

be

be regarded with greater care, ſtudie,
and diligence of ſuch as deſire to get
the grace of Chriſt, then a moſt feruent loue and earneſt deſire to come
vnto this vertue of humilitie, in the
which reſteth the verie foundatiō of Humilitie
Chriſtian pietie. And this humilitie is
cauſed in vs by ſetting before our eyes
the deformitie of our ſynnes, by ſhame
which riſeth in vs by beholding the
ilſauourednes of then, by dew conſi-
deratiō of the daunger, into the which
we ranne headlong. But al theſe things
are conteined in the confeſſion of our
wickednes and ſynnes. For confeſſion
conteineth in it ſelfe a diſcrete exami-
natiō and acknowleging of our ſelues,
a learning of humilitie and modeſtie, a
baſhful rehearſal of the ſynne committed, a feare of the daunger hanging
ouer our heades. By this confeſſion,
ſuch as lie downe, are ſtirred vp: ſuche
as be faint, are cheered foreward: ſuch
as be prowd, are pulled downe: ſuch as

N   be

be vnlearned , are instructed wyth
wholesome lessons. And this is well
knowen, that when the time draweth
nere in the which confession is to be
made, men are more modest and côti-
nent then at other times. And the har-
der it is to bring manie men vnto it,
the better it is seene, that it was ordeined by the prouidence of God. For
whereas there is naturally in al men a
certaine loue of honestie , and a careful desire to conceale dishonestie , no
man could be brought to open the deformitie of his sinnes vnto Priestes, vnlesse he were driuen therevnto by order, disposition, power and wil of the
holie Ghost. Moreouer what stronger
bridle can be deuised to asswage and
represse the haughtinesse of men of
power , to restreigne and moderate
their rash and wilfull presumpteousnes? For we see the highest Princes,
when they haue caste them selues
downe at the feete of the Priestes, to
be

be fore afraied of their rebukés, to be
reſtreigned by their lawes, to be inſtru
cted by their aduertiſementes, to be
reclaimed by their commaundemétes
frō vnlawfull luſt and libertie to good
order and ciuilitie. This Sacramét cau- The ef-
ſeth baſhfulnes, it draweth out teares, fectes of
yt endeth aduouteries, yt reſtoreth cōſeſsion.
money embeſeled, it quencheth ha-
tred, yt maketh peace, yt quieteth
rage, it ſetteth in comelie order the
whole conuerſation of the inwarde
man. But now, if a man not contenting him ſelfe to be confeſſed once in
the yeare, wil oftentimes confeſſe all
the vncleanes of his minde, wil examine his conſcience diligently, to the
end that he maie cōfeſſe with the gre-
ter fruict, wil keepe an earneſt battaile
againſt ſynne : he ſhal ſee a dailie amé-
demét in him ſelf, with a more cleane,
chaſt and vpright conuerſation. I take
Ieſus Chriſt my Lord and my God to
witneſſe, that by the often coming

to this most wholesome confession I
haue risen and escaped from a meruelous nombre of sinnes. In so much that,
if I haue at anie time repressed the ple-
sure of the flesh, if I haue despised vncleane lustes, if I haue ben earnestly
bent towardes the loue of chast life, if
I haue ben enkedled with anie sparcle
of the loue of God: I maie thanke this
Sacrament of it, by the whiche the
holie Ghost hath imparted vnto me a
great deale of his mercie and goodnes.
Neither haue I only receiued this so
great commoditie of confession, but
whome so euer I do see geauen to this
most holie exercise, (of the whiche
there is a meruelouse numbre emongest vs) I perceiue that they are deliuered from al worldlie pleasures, that
they flourish in all vertues, and that
they become better and better dailie,
to the great wonder of manie men.
And this is that, that moueth me to vse
moste earnest perswasions with my
sub-

ſubiectes, to induce them to reſort oftentimes to confeſſion : wherof I receiue no ſmal profitte . For manie of
them haue nowe withdrawen them
ſelues from the companie of vnchaſt
women , manie haue remoued them
ſelues from exactinge of vſurie, manie
haue recōciled them ſelues vnto ſuch,
as they did beare mortal hatred vnto.
And I know , that emongeſt vs, many
worthie Biſhops both for learning and
vertue doth the like . Neither are we
ſuch as can contēt our ſelues with the
confeſſion of ſynnes only , but we require alſo the fruictes of penance, the
whiche we are wont to call ſatisſacti-   Satisſacti
ons, how ſo euer it pleſe your maiſters   on.
to ſcorne and ſcoffe at that word . But
beleeue me, we are nothing troubled
with the laughter of vngodlie mē. We
herken to S. Iohn, which commaūded
ſuch as had alreadie confeſſed their
ſynnes to doe the worthy fruictes of   *Math.3.b*
penáce. We willingly receiue the ſelfo
                    N iij   ſame

same wordes pronownced and repeted by that most high maister of iustice, the redeemer of mankind. For
while we obei the commaundemetes
of Christe, we so litle esteeme the
tauntes and scoffes of lewd felowes,
that we are not only not moued with
their reprochful talke, but also we re-
ioise excedingly in it.

Now then, seing that this sacramet
is of so great importaunce to saluatio,
seing that we see so great fruicte to be
gathered out of it, if we doe feruently
desire the saluation of al men: can you
blame me, if I sorow and lament, that
this great gate of saluatio is closed vp
to manie Christians through the lewdnes and misbelefe of a few men? I talk
not with you now, for so much as you
kepe, as you saie your selfe, the sacramentes of the Churche. But if some
man of an other disposition shal be so
crewell and vngodlie, that he wil attempte

tempte to damme vp this waie to ſaluation, caſting before it piles or heapes
of earth , wil you ſuffer it ? Will you,
ſeeing ſuch a deteſtable offence, ſo refraine your ſelfe, that you wil not crie
out vpon it ? Blame not me then , if I
doe, as you your ſelfe wil doe, if it be
true, that you ſaie, that you doe keepe
and obſerue diligently the ſacrametes
of the church. But if you ſpeake otherwiſe then truth, I will not much meruaile at it, for your doctours are excellent framers, not only of impietie , but
alſo of vanitie.

But you will ſaye peraduenture,
that muche euyll and myſchiefe ariſeth by the occaſion of this confeſſion. If it be ſo , it is not muche to be
merueiled at. For there is nothing in
the worlde ſoo holye , the whiche
men agreed in wickedneſſe maie not
abuſe to naughtines and miſchiefe.
But it foloweth not by and by , that
for the defaulte of a fewe lewde
N iiij   per-

perſonnes, thinges ordeined of God
for the ſaluation of men ſhould be vtterly caſt awaie. For ſo, ther had ben
no good thing left this daie in the
worlde. For al thinges, that are by nature wholeſome, are vnto corrupt and
vicious men hurtful and peſtilent. And
to let paſſe all other thinges, howe
manie men are wont to abuſe the
verie mercie of God, when he differreth to puniſh them for ſynne, to the
increaſe of their damnation ? And yet
is not God for all that remoued from
his good will and purpoſe to deale
mercifully with vs.

But ſome will ſaie: we confeſſe vnto
God only. Yea, but God, for ſo much
as he can not be perfectely ſeene of
vs, hath appointed his Deputies vpon
the earth, to exerciſe his authoritie
and iuriſdiction, to threaten and feare,
to geaue gentle admonitions, to in-
courage, to raiſe vppe, to geaue
ſentence: in ſo muche that, who ſo
euer

so euer doth despise them, are to be taken (and that for great good cause) as
though they did despise God him self,
and refuse his order and commaunde-
mét. Furthermore it were dágerous to
leaue euerie man to his owne wil in
this case. For howe manie shall you
find, that shalbe able to search out and
consider their owne synnes ? that wil
confesse them with such shamefastnes
and contrition of heart, as Dauid saith
is a moste acceptable Sacrifice vnto
God? that wil geaue sentence lawfully vpon them selues , for that they are
in their owne causes verie parciall
iudges ? It remaineth therefore , that
he , that lyueth not vnder the obedience of the Church, and wil not abide
the iudgement of a Prieste : neither
would he at anie tyme be confessed of
his synnes vnto God, as he ought to
be. Dowbtlesse Basile the great sawe
ful wel , what profitte ariseth by this
confession, when in his Ethikes he ascribed

cribed vnto it the very beginning and foundation of iustice. So thought Origen, when he willed vs that we shuld not delaie it from daie to daie: but so soone as we were fallen, we should foorthwith haue recourse vnto the Priest. Such was the iudgement of all holie men, the which exhort vs so often to this godly exercise. Neither did the bishop of Rome first ordeine this Sacrament: but being before ordeined and commonly receiued, he decreed verie prouidently, that it should be put in vre at the least once in the yeare, lest it might be neglected to the great decaie of godlines.

But to coclude this matter, I would faine learne of you, howe you thinke *Esai*.11.b. that place of Esaie to be vnderstanded, where he saieth, that it shall come to passe after the birth of Christe, that a wained child shal thrust his hand into the Cockatrise hole, and pul him out. If you wil solow the Iewes, you shall

vnder-

vnderſtand it thus: that euen as the
Poetes reporte, that Hercules being
yet in his cradle caught twoo great
ſnakes that were ſent vnto him by
Iuno, and daſht them together: ſo ſhal
euery ſucking babe take venemous ſerpentes in his handes out of their holes
and kil them. But if you wil expound
the place like a Chriſtian man, by
the children you muſte vnderſtande
thoſe menne, to whome Chriſte hath
geauen power to treade vppon ſerpentes and ſcorpions, that is to ſaie,
vppon the beaſtlines of ſynnes, vpon
the crafte and creweltie of Diuelles,
that lie lurking in the ſecrete couerte
of ſowles. And although they be
ſimple as children, yet are they endewed with ſuche great power and
ſtrength, that they can eaſilie pull
owt thoſe vipers out of the moſte
priuie corners and innermoſt creekes
of mennes heartes and kill them, that
they may not infecte and poiſon ſuch,

as

as haue ioyned them selues to Chrift
by earneft and true faith . Nowe this
thing as it maie be done of the Prieftes
of Chrift manie waies , fo there can
no waie be deuifed by anie wife man
more commodious then that , whiche
is by the wholefome confeſsion of
fynnes . for in confeſsion the Prieftes
doe thruſt their handes into the innermoſt partes of mens heartes, that they
may draw out the ſerpentes of ſynne,
and daſſh them againſt a ſtone, and kil
them.

The Sa-
crament
of the
Aulter.

But now let vs come to that wonderful Sacrament of the Aulter . But
before I enter into this matter, it liketh me to ſet here a goodlie ſaying of
Simias written of Plato in his booke
intituled Phœdo. Plato bringeth in Simias reaſoning thus with Socrates. Me
thinketh, Socrates, as I iudge you think
alfo, that it is impoſsible , or ſurely exceding hard, for a man, ſo long as he is
in this life , to vnderſtand the truthe
clerely

clerely and perfectely . The which although it be true , yet me thinketh it
were the parte of a weake and faint
hearted man , not to discusse and examine by reasoning on both sides, what
so euer is wont to be disputed in these
darke matters, vntil at the length , the
matter being diligently weyed and
considered, we may be able either to
lerne the truth of other, or els to find it
our selues. If we can not atteine vnto
this, yet at the left wise, we must haue
great regard , emongest the reasons of
diuers men to take some one that seemeth better and surer: with the which
as it were with a boate we maie gouerne our life in these waues with
some daunger , vntil we may either
find an other ship of more assuraunce
and lesse daunger, or els be instructed
by the wordes and aduise of God him
selfe, how to directe our course without anie errour . Thus much said he.
But to what purpose , say you , haue
you

you alleaged this place out of Plato?
That you may vnderstand, that men of
excellent wits did euen in those daies
perceiue, how litle we ought to trust
to mãs reason, and how earnestly we
ought to praie, that our life might be
gouerned, not by the staie of our owne
wit, but by the rule of the woorde of
God. So we doe, say you. Would God
ye did. But it is not so. But rather when
it is left cõuenient, you wil weakē reason and take it awaie quite, and runne
like mad mē into darkenes: againe whē
reason is to be bridled by the faith of
Christ, you yeald so much to reason,
that what so euer reason is not able
to atteyne, you will foorthwith geaue
it ouer. Now for somuch as reason is
driuen into a narrowe and streight
roome, and the boundes of Christian
faith are passing great and endles : it is
a token not onely of a naughtie and
wicked man, but also of a blunt and
dul wit, to directe his life, not by faith,
but by

but by reason . For what man a liue is
able to trie out perfectly the caufes of
the left thinges in the worlde ? to def-
cribe exactely the firft fpring , the increafe,the varietie, the beawtie , the
fruict,the profitte and vfe of trees and
plātes?to expreffe in wordes the ordre
and waie,by the which eche thing in
his kinde is holdē together and made to
cōtinue?what man in the world is able
to atteine by wit, to fearch out the fecret force and caufe,how a liuing thīg
is made , nourifhed and knit together
with bones and finewes ? by what cūning or fubtilty the vaines are fpread
through the whole body, how the ar-
teries are fo wonderfully wouen one
within an other,.and how they do cō-
uey the fpirite of life to al the partes of
the body,being fo merueloufly accor-
ded the one to ferueth'other,ād fo finely cōpacted together within thēfelues.
Then to come to the nourifhment,in-
creafe,mouīg,goīg,diuerfity,ād multitude

tude of liuing thinges, and the naturall
knowledge and pollicie that ech thing
hath to keepe and defend it selfe: what
man was euer able to find out by vn-
doubted reasons the very ground and
perfecte knowledge of these thinges?
Great learned men haue disputed verie much as touching the mind of mã:
of the nature, disposition, wit, reason,
inuention, memorie, and other powers
of it : but of al this disputation we receiue none other commoditie but this,
that we may wel perceiue by their
long studie and diligent search, howe
great darkenes and ignoraunce there
is in mans reason . For we see in them
a goodlie endeuour of mind to consider the nature of mans mind : but of
the perfecte knowledge of the thing,
which thev seeke for, we are neuer
the neere. Wherevpon it is gathered,
that no man is able to know him selfe
perfectly.

　　And yet there are some men so hard
　　　　　　　　　　　　headed,

headed, that, if a thing be tolde them,
which is wont to grow or to be done
in farre Countries, they wil not beleue
it : as though the thinges whiche they
fee with their eyes, and yet are ignorant of the caufes, were leffe to be wo-
dred at, then thofe thinges, which are
reported to be done in other places.
But now to omit to fpeake of the firm-
nes of the earth, the paffing great wid-
nes of the fea, the nature of the ayer
that enuironeth vs, the burning of the
fkie, the due proportion and agreemet
of thefe bodies, the chaunge and alteration of one nature into an other as it
were by courfe and order of Lawe:
What fhall we faie of the brightneffe,
bewtie, hugenes, and compaffe of the
heauen? You, if ye leane vnto reafon
onely, what woulde you haue done in
this cafe? Ymagine you had ben borne
and bred in the darke countries of Ci-
meria (as the Poetes feine) and fome
man had tolde you, that there were a

O   huge

huge greate frame conteining within his compasse al the whole world, merueloullie decked and garnished with many fiers, of such hugenes that al the landes and seas in comparison of it, are but as a pinnes point, of such swiftnes in mouinge, that within the space of fower and twentie howers it turneth the whole bodie round about, of such force and violence, that seuen other huge bodies of the same nature, which are conteined within his compasse, hauinge a contrarye course, it beareth them al backe with his onely mouing, if a manne should tell you this tale, would you beleeue him? No truly, if you trust onely to reason and senses. For so would you perswade your selues, that the thinges, the causes wherof you are not able to conceiue, were impossible, (before you see them with your eyes).

What if he shoulde tell you of the sonneshine, a thing both healthful and
comfortable

comfortable to al liuing creatures, and
of the goodly order, which the sonne
keepeth in goinge by litle and litle towards the North, and again how he re-
turneth by the same way to the south,
casting his bright beames vpō al things
in the world? What if he should report
how the moone with her increase and
decrease diuideth the times of the yere
and how she geueth ripenes to al thĩgs
which the land and sea bringeth forth?
What if he should declare, how diuers-
lie the heauenly bodies aboue are moued and tourned, and how notwithstanding they are all reduced to a most
perfecte harmonie and agreemente?
Would you beleeue it? No truely,
if you can be perswaded in nothing,
except it may either be proued by reason, or perceiued by sense.

It is surely a token of a base mind to
esteme the knowlege of things, by the
narrow and streight measure of mans
vnderstanding, and not according to

the almighty power of him that made them. And out of this dulnes or weaknes of nature procedeth al such opinions, as are contrary to holy Religion.

For all heretikes, either they esteeme the almightie power of God by their owne weakenes, or els they measure the infinite mercie of God by their own naughtines. As though thei were able to make any resemblance in the world of the power of God, or vnderstand how great the goodnes is of that moste bountifull Father, whiche doth with special regard, as it were, walke vp and downe throughout al his creatures, and prouidētly mainteineth eche thing in his kinde and nature. And to passe ouer all other thinges, me thinketh, that in that last geuing of shape and fourme to euery liuing thing, I see a miracle, which sheweth plainly the power and cūning of that most excellent workeman, in whose handes the liuing creature was made and fashioned.

ned. Neither dothe the multitude of liuing thinges minish the estimation of Gods worke, but rather augment and increase it. For the benefites of almigh-tie God, the more they are in number, and the better they are knowen, the better is the greatnes of his power and mercy sene, although the reason of his workes be not vnderstood. What shal I here speake of those thinges, that are for the excellency of their nature farre aboue the sense and vnderstanding of man? Who wil beleue that there is an infinite multitude of heauenly spirites, whiche being of vnderstanding moste cleere, of holines most pure, of vertue and power very exellent, of comelines and bewty most like vnto God, are al-waies occupied in the Seruice of God? euermore singing and praising his Ma-iestie, continually burning with the flame of the loue of God? What? Can you conceiue by reason, how the only sonne of God, the veri expresse Image

O iij   of

of the Father, the brightnes of euerlasting light, being equal with the Father
in nature, power, kingdome, and maiestie : toke vpon him the shape of man,
suffered in his mortal bodie labour, mi-
sery, punishment for vs, redemed with
his bloud our soules which were fouly
spotted in sinne? If these thinges are to
be weyed by mans reason onely, they
are nothing like to be true : but if we
will consider them according to the
faith, which we haue of the bowntiful
goodnes of God, there is nothing more
credible. For passing great benefits are
to be required and loked for of passing
great bountie. He that spared not (saith

Rom.8 .f.

S. Paul) his owne sonne, but gaue him
vp for vs al: How gaue he not vnto vs
al things with him ? Wherfore to such
as beleue vprightly, I thinke ther is nothing els nedeful to be considered, but
how the thing, that they are willed to
beleue , standeth with the bountie of
God : the which doing, it is not possible

ſible that any man ſhould doubt of any
myſterie of our ſaluation.

These thinges being thus determined, I will now talke, not with you,
M. Haddon, of whome, as you ſaie,
the Sacramentes of the Churche are
kepte : butte I will take ſoome one
of them to talke withall, that rayleth
with blaſphemouſe mouth againſt the
bleſſed Sacramente of the Aulter.
And bicauſe I wil ſeeke no further, let
it be your golden Martyr, whom you
commend ſo highlie. Ymagine therefore, that I talke with him after this
ſorte.

O moſte vile and naughtie felowe,
what came into thy minde to go about
to deface, to violate, and to depraue
that moſte holy Myſterie, the monumente of the loue of God towardes
vs, the comforte of our banniſhment,
the ſtaie of the frailtie of manne, the
bankette of heauen, ordeyned for vs
in that laſt Supper by the handes of
O iiij   our

Our Lord him selfe ? Was there none in so many hundred yeres but thou and thy Maisters, that durst attempt so heinouse, vile, and barbarouse an acte ? Was there none that vnderstoode the sense of the holie Scripture, the meaning of the Gospell, the order of the blessed Sacramentes, but you ? Were so many holy Martyrs, so many Religious persons, so many great wise men (in whome shone the beames of the brightnes of God) ignorant in matters of so great importance ? It is like forsooth, that the light of the holie Ghost shewed it selfe first vnto suche saucie, desperate, rash and presumptuous varlettes, as you are, and suffered so many thousandes of holie and vertuous men to lye in darkenes and ignorance. Tel me, I pray thee, what great thing had Christ done for vs, if at what time he determined to leaue to his Disciples a speciall pleadge of his loue towardes thẽ, he had left them nothing els, but a

bare

bare remembrance of his death in the consecration of that bread? It had ben a signe only, meet to be nūbred emōgest those that you defaced and ouerthrew, and nothing worthie to be celebrated with so great reueréce of that moste holie and euerlasting Prieste. Moreouer I wold faine learne of thee, whether it be a wicked offence to call to remembrance the death of Christe, so long as a man is in sinne? No truly, but cōtrariwise we can deuise no better medicine, then that is, to driue awai sinne, and to recouer our health by the grace of Christ. What moued S. Paul then, if there be nothing elles in this sacrament, but only a bare remembrāce of that death that Christ suffred vpon the Crosse, to threaten so grieuous and horrible paines to suche as woulde receiue this heauēly bread vnworthily? Who so euer shall eate, saieth he, the bread, and drinke the cup of our Lord vnworthylie, shal be giltie. What? Is

1. *Cor.* 11. 4.

it

it such a greiuous offence, when I am sicke, to thinke vpon the medicine, with the which only I may be healed? What other thing did I, when I receiued that bread, (if there be nothing els in it, but a remēbrance of those wordes, by the which only my wounds may be healed) but cal to remēbraunce the only remedy of life? Wilt thou blame me, when I am sicke, bicause I seeke the remedie of my disease, and humblie call for succour? Thou canst not do it. And yet, if I receiue that bread vnworthily, that is to say, as thou expoundest it, if I remember being in synne, that Christ suffered death and crewel tormentes for me: S. Paule maketh me terribly afraid, by charging me with a crime. But with what a crime I pray thee? Some light or cōmon crime peraduēture, the which offendeth not verie much. No, such a crime as is of al other most heinouse and wicked He shalbe giltle, saieth he, of the bodie and bloude of our Lord,

1. Co. 11. f.

Lorde, that is to say, he shalbe gyltie of no lesse crime, then if he had crucified Christ. For what cause? Bicause as the wicked souldiers, pricked forewarde with vnbeleefe, put to death the Lord and maker of al thinges : so do they, that presume to touch with vncleane mindes that moste excellent cleanes, seeme to bring vpon them selues the selfe same plague for the likenes of their heinouse offence. For bothe of them do alike despise Christe, and vn-reuerently abuse his holines and maiesty. For otherwise what harme were it to synful men to receiue that bread? None at al. The Apostle therfore, bi-cause he sawe, how grieuouse a faulte it was, to touch the bodie of our Lord with an vncleane soule, denouced the punishment, to fray al men from doing such a presumptuous acte. And there-fore he saith anon after : Let a manne first trie him selfe, and so eate of that breade, and drinke of that cuppe. 1. *Co.* 11. *g.*

And,

Mat.26.e
Mar.14.c
Luc.22.b.
1.Co.11.c.
And, what can be more plaine then the wordes of our Lord? This is, saith he, my bodie: and doe this in remembrance of me. How then? Wilt thou presume to take the wordes of Christ, being nothing doubtful, but plaine and euident, and expoũd them maliciusly? Wilt thou set the meaning of S. Paul at naught, which expoũdeth the mysterie exceeding plainly and wel? Wilt thou preferre this thy vnsetled fantasie and mad gare, before the most sincere meaning of the Apostle of God? If he be giltie of the bodie and bloud of our Lord, which receiueth this bread vnworthelie: He that slaundereth and depraueth it, he that reuileth and (so muche as in him lyeth) rendeth it in peeces, he that treadeth vnder his foote the bodie and bloude of Christe, he that goeth about to take away and vtterlie to abolishe the vertue of that so wonderfull a Sacramente: howe shall he be punnished according to his wicked

wicked and horrible facte?

What is it so? If thou vnderstande not, by what meanes the moste holie bodie of Christ is in this Sacramēt, not placed or limited according to the mea sure and proportion of the greatnesse thereof, but presente in the eyes of a faithfull heart through the almightie power of the woorde of God: if thou see not that merueilouse chaunge of earthly breade into the natnre of hea-uenlie bread: if thou perceiue not, by what meanes the most excellent Ma-iestie of Christ, which filleth al things, multiplieth the giftes of his whole bo-die, that he may therewirh feede and refresh the faithfull soules, and glewe them all together with charitie within them selues, and tye them fast to him selfe with the band of euerlasting loue: is it therfore reason,that thou shouldst slaunder and depraue this so wonder-ful a benefite of God? What thing doest thou vnderstande? What thing
doest

doeſt thou conceiue by diſcourſe and reaſon? What thing is there in all the worlde, whiche thy minde is able to perceue exactly, and to know perfectlie? Why then doeſt thou not order thy life, by cleere faithe, and not by troubled reaſon? Tel mee, I pray thee, doeſt thou miſtruſt Gods power or mercie, or elles doth the greatneſſe of the benefite trouble thee? Neyther can the power of God be hindred by any let or ſtaie, neyther can his mercy be limited with any bowndes: and the greatnes of the benefite is a very good proofe of the truth thereof. For why, there is nothing more agreeable to the greate bountifulneſſe of God, then the greatnes of the thing, which he geaueth.

Then I aſke thee an other queſtion: What is the cauſe, thinkeſt thou, why I doe beleue, that the bodie and bloud of Chriſte is after a wonderfull manner conteined in this Sacrament, and thou

thou beleeueſt it not ? It is not ſurely , bicauſe I will ſuffer my ſelfe to be
abuſed for lacke of witte . For thou
doeſt not paſſe mee either in witte, or
learning . But this is the cauſe . Thou
truſteſt thy ſenſes , and I directe al my
doinges according to the faith of holie
Churche . Thou doeſt caſte of the
yoke , and ſpurne againſt it : but I doe
of myne owne accorde put my heade
into the moſte ſweete yoke of Chriſt.
Thou doeſt refuſe his benefites , but I
doe praie vnto him to encreaſe my
faieth .

Moreouer, we ſee this by daily experience . The more a man yeldeth to
vice and vncleanes of life : the feinter
is his beleefe as touching this dreadfull
Myſterie . Wherevppon it is concluded , that he , that geaueth him ſelfe
wholie ouer to the pleaſure of the bodie , and therefore falleth from the
vnitie of the Churche , wil beleue nothing at all of it . But on the other
ſide

fide we fee , that the chafter and cleaner life any mã leadeth, the more fure
and conftant is his belefe in this point:
in fo much that he perfuadeth him felf,
that he beholdeth in this Sacrament,
euen Chrift him felfe nailed vpon the
Croffe.

Surely this agreement of the mind
and wil of man, is a thing to be woon-
dered at. The mind feeketh the thing
that is true : the wil defireth the thing
that is good: and the wel gouerned wil
foloweth the iudgement of the truly
directed mind. It foloweth therefore
that they only fee the truth perfectly,
which are wel ordered in their life and
conuerfation: for vicious and naughty
men are cõmonly tourned away from
the truth, bicaufe they haue their mind
difordered with vnruly defires .

Now therefore confider to whom
it is better to geaue eare. To thofe holy men, the which being of mind moft
pure, of life moft chaft , in holie Scriptures

ptures moſt excellently wel learned,
haue from the time of the primitiue
Church folowed this faith : or elles to
theſe madbraines and frantik felowes,
to theſe filthie licentiouſe ribawdes,
to the newe vpſtart doctours, which
haue moſt wickedly and heinouſly violated this faith? This Sacramente the
holie Fathers, whiche were taught of
the Apoſtles, called *Synaxim*, that is
to ſay, a bringing together, bicauſe it *Synaxis.*
linked the mindes of men together wi
in themſelues, and brought them to be
ioyned al in Chriſt. In like māner they
called it *Euchariſtiam*, that is, a than- *Euchariſtia.*
keſgeuing: bicauſe there is no benefite
of God in this life, for the whiche we
are bound to yeald vnto his Maieſtie
greater praiſe and hartier thankes. For
it ſupporteth the ſtate of the ſowle, it The effectes of the
eſtabliſheth the powers of the minde, Sacramēt
it clereth the vnderſtāding, it ſtrēgth- of the
neth faith, it ſtirreth vppe hope, it en- Aulter.
kendleth charitie, it inflameth hartes,

P   it fil-it filleth the godlie and deuout mindes with meruelouſe great ſweetenes and comfort . With this heauenlie ſoode, S. Cyprian (ſo often as any tempeſt or perſecution was towarde) thought it good to fortifie them , that were appointed to ſuffer tormentes for the name of Chriſte. And therefore dyd he the ſooner admit into the Churche againe , ſuch as were yet penitentes, that is to witte, menne ſeparated from the Church for a tyme, to do penance for ſome offence committed : to the intent that, being ſtrengthned by this cōmunion of the body of Chriſt, they might ſtand valiātly to the end againſt al the power of Satan. For the holy mā was of this mind, that the ſoode of this heauēly bread gaue ſuch ſtrēgth ād courage, as could not be brokē or weakened by any force of our enemie the deuil. What ſhould I here rehearſe other holy Martyrs without nūbre, al holie writers, the faith and agreemēt of the

vni-

vniuerſal Church continued euen frõ
the Apoſtles time to our daies? And
yet wilt thou keepe open war, againſt
the ordinaunce of Chriſte, againſt the
doctrine of S. Paule, againſt the ineſti-
mable greatneſſe of the fruictes in this
myſterie cõteined, againſt the experi-
éce of ſuch wõderful profit and ſweet-
nes, againſt the pure and ſincere faith
of the Catholik Church? And yet wilt
thou reprochfully reuile the body and
bloud of Chriſt, and depraue like a mad
mã the moſt excellent and higheſt be-
nifit, that euer the goodnes of God beſtowed vpon man? And yet wilt thou
reioyſe in thy wickednes, and poiſon
many other men with the contagion
of this thy moſt peſtilent hereſie?

These thinges, M. Haddon, thinke
them not ſpoken to you, but to your
Martyr. And now let him ſtand a ſide,
and I wil thus reaſon with you. Could
you, M. Haddon, knowing, as you
doe verie wel, not only the vertue of

P ij   this

this wonderful Sacrament, whiche is of al other the greateſt, but alſo the ſtrength and operation of al other Sacramentes: being withall of that opinion, that to deſpiſe the Sacramentes, is a moſte heinouſe treſpaſſe: when you vnderſtoode, that there was a man in the worlde ſo lewde and wicked, that he woulde goe aboute to take awaie and aboliſh this moſt worthie pleadge of the loue of God, this moſt ſure ſtaie of all Chriſtian Religion, conteining in it all the graces and benefiites of God: could you, I ſaie, ſpeake familiarly vnto him? could you ſalute him gentelly? could you ſhewe him anie token of loue? Haue you neuer reade in S. Iohn, that he that ſaieth, good morrowe, to wicked menne, is become partaker of their wickedneſſe? But you haue not onely ſpoken familiarly to this Martyr, but alſo commended him aboue the ſkies: and you haue ſaied, that

that

2. Ioan. i. c.

that same golden couple of olde men,
were brought into your Iland by the
prouidence of God, to shine ouer
you (which had alreadie the goodly
brightnesse of the newe sonne risen
emongest you) with a muche cleerer light.

Are you so sottish, M Haddon, that
you vnderstande not, howe muche
you haue disteined your estimation
by that countenaunce and shewe of
gentlenesse towardes him ? For what
can be more infamous, then to be fa-
miliare with a frātike and naughtie felowe ? But if you like his Doctrine also, then is it plaine, that you keepe not
the Sacramentes at al : for so much as
you haue vppon an vnsetled pange,
without al order, wisedome, or discre-
tion, taken awaie the greatest Sacrament, and that, that is of al other most
wonderfull. Whie then say you, that
you wonder, if there be any kind of
professours in diuinitie in the worlde,

that

that despiseth and setteth at naught the Sacramentes? But let vs now consider the description of your Church, the which you set before our eyes to behold, that we may vnderstand by it, that you haue had none other maister in Religion, but only the holy Ghost. You say thus.

First of all, bicause faith is by hearing, We sende downe into all partes of our realme teachers of the holie Scriptures, to instructe the people in all pointes of godlines, and to infourme them in the true woorshipping of God. Out of what fountaine sprang these Doctours? If they came out of the schoole of Luther, Bucer or Caluin : they can teach the people no godlines, being them selues open enemies to all godlinesse. It were therefore muche more tolerable, to haue no doctours at all, then to be infected with the most corrupt Doctrine of wicked menne. If they sprang out of any other heade, then
is it

is it manifeſt, that there is not emongeſt you any one and ſimple Doctrine, but diuerſe opinions fondly
iarring within them ſelues. It followeth.

Then haue we a common order of
praier out of the holie Scriptures, confir-
med by the authoritie of a Parlament,
(for ſo doe they terme the conſent of the
eſtates of our Realme) from the which
we ſuffer no man to depart. By what
order, lawe, or authoritie is this done:
that a Councel, or as you cal it, a Parlament, ſhould ſo impudently vſurpe
the office of the Catholike Churche,
to make orders for praiers, preſcribe
how religion ought to be vſed, and not
ſuffer any man to depart from the order which it hath decreed? For in holie thinges it is not lawfull for theſe
menne to geaue lawes, but to take
lawes. For otherwiſe they ſhall di-
ſturbe the common weale, if they wil
not content them ſelues with their
P iiij owne

owne vocation, but will thruſt them
ſelues into other mens doinges: and
they ſhal marre Religion, if they will
in matters apperteyninge to them
onely, that ſuſteine the perſonne of
the Churche, take vppon them to
meddle, and tranſpoſe the dignitie of
Prieſtes to them ſelues. You ſay afterwarde.

Prouiding both in the one and in
the other, ſo muche as we coulde, that
the commaundement of the holie ghoſt
be obeied, the whiche, willeth that ſuch
as ſpeake in the Churche, ſhould vſe
the word of God: and that there ſhould
be one common and agreable Doctrine
emongeſt them all. You doe verie wel
vndowbtedly. But wherehence riſeth
this ſo great debate and hourlie bour-
ly for Religion in your Churches?
Wherefore are the confeſsions and
Credes ſo often chopped and chaunged in places, where Luther hath had
a great name?

And

And we prouide, saie you, *that the Sacramentes be miniſtred verie neere vnto the preſcribed order of the holy ſcriptures, and according to the example of the old Church, in the whiche our Lorde Ieſus Chriſt firſt ordeined them himſelfe with his Apoſtles.* O valiant men, worthie to be commended aboue the heauens. O glorious attempte. O liuelie courage of luſtie blouddes, the which thought yt not ynoughe to approche neere vnto the holines of the olde Church, but they would preſſe euen at the verie hard heales of them. It followeth.

All theſe thinges are ſet out in our owne mother tongue, bicauſe it is a great madnes for a man to babble out before God, he can not tell what: and it is directely againſte the moſt wholeſome doctrine of S. Paule, and all the auncient examples of the Apoſtolike Churches. It is not you only, that teache ſuch as vnderſtand not the Latine, to praie in their

Praier in the vulgar tongue.

their owne tongue. For we alſo doe not ſuffer ſuch, as are ignorant in the Latine ſpeach, to ſerue God, but only in their own mother tongue: and there are manie bookes of praiers and holy ſcriptures writen, not by Parlament, as you call it, but by holie Prieſtes : the whiche (being firſte examined by the prelates of the church) are ſent abroad euerie where, and by them are children, women, and ſimple folkes trained in the knowledge of their dewtie towardes God. And the thinges that are thus written, they are not taken out of euerie mans fantaſie, but out of the holie Scriptures, and out of the writinges and examples of holie men. So that there lacketh not emongeſt vs anie diſcipline of manners, nor example of vertue, nor good bringing vp in true religion, to al ſuch, as coulde not imploie them ſelues to the ſtudie of learning. We haue alſo manie ſermós, by the whiche men are ſtirred vp to

the

the loue of godlines and religion. But
in preaching we vſe much diſcretion
and warines, that none of thoſe que-
ſtions be opened emongeſt women
and ignorant folkes, which are not verie neceſſarie vnto ſaluation, and yet
maie quickely intangle their mindes
with verie troubleſome dowbtes and
ſcruples. For as S. Gregorie of Nazianzene ſaieth verie wiſely: it is not conuenient to reaſon and diſpute of God,
neither to al men, neither in the preſence of all men, neither at all times,
neither of all matters, neither without
good diſcretiõ. For there is required to
the doing of this thinge a meruelous
cleanes of ſowl and body, a veri calme
and wel ſetled mind, good time, cõuenient oportunitie, earneſt zeale, much
fearfulnes and exceeding great modera-
rion. For ther is no man ſo ſimple, that
he can not vnderſtand the difficultie
of euery queſtion: but there are few ſo
witty, that they cã rid thẽ ſelues out of
the

Diſcretiõ
in prea-
ching.

Thinges
requiſite
in a
preacher.

the briers, when they are once fallen
in. And this is the caufe, whie manie
men are confounded in queftions, but
few efcape out of their fnares. Moreouer fuch is the arrogancie and pride
of certaine ignorāt felowes, that they
become intolerable, if they can atteine
neuer fo litle knowledge in any thing,
which they knew not before, fpecially
if it be in expownding the holy fcriptures. For they wil iudge fo prefump-
teoufly of the higheft pointes of Diuinitie (the which they vnderftand not)
as though they were called to be of
Gods priuie counfaile: the which rafhnes hath bred manie wicked and troublefome errours, and caufed much dif-
fenfion. But the end of the law, faieth
S. Paul, is not the vaunting of learning,
but charity from a pure hart, and good
confcience, and faith vnfained. He
therfore that can bring to paffe, that al
men maie be, linked the one to the
other in charitie, fournifhed with vertues,

1. *Tim.* 1. *b*

tues, established in true faith: although
he beate not into the heads of the vnlearned people a hundred questions
towching predestination, yet shal he
shew him to be a very good preacher.
Therfore for so much as this ought to
be our only intent, how to plant charitie, innocencie, and faith in the hartes
of men: and that maie very well be
taught without this translation of the
holy scriptures: what neded it, to take
the thinges that were côteined in the
latine tongue without perill, and to
translate them into the English tongue
with great daunger? Mary sir, say you,
it is against the most wholesome doctrine of S. Paul. How so I praie you?
If you marke well the meaning of S.
Paul, you shal see, that his wordes are
nothing contrarie to our pourpose.

But first of all it is to be knowen,
that in S. Paules time al Christian men
in a manner were endewed with such
vertues and qualities, as fewe men in

Not ne-
cessarie to
haue the
scriptures
in the
vulgar
tongue.

our

our daies can atteine vnto by ftudie and faith. Then it is alfo to be confide-red, that there were in thofe daies di-uers giftes and graces of the holy ghoft geauen vnto fuch men, as were infla-med with the loue of Chrifte. How-beit, although they were taught and fchooled of the holy Ghoft, yea and wel inftructed to be humble and mo-deft: yet were they in no fmall dauger of pride. The which is not to be won-dered at, for fo muche as S. Paul him felfe the maifter of heauelie wifedom, the perfecte example of humilitie and modeftie affirmeth, that the pricke of the flefhe was a thing neceffarie for him, left the knowledge of the fecrets of God might puffe vp his mind. Now as manie were puffed vp with thofe gyftes, fo were fuch, as had the gyfte of tongues, fomewhat more infolent then other men: and they would praife God in diuers tongues, whiche other men vnderftoode not, without any in-terpre-

1. Cor. 12.
b.

terpretour. There was alſo an other
great inconuenience, which was,that
he, that ſpake with vnknowē tonges,
would not tarie till an other man had
made an end of ſpeaking, but at one
time a great many together woulde
praiſe God in ſtraunge tongues. And
theſe three diſcōmodities were cauſed
in their aſſembles,for lacke of diſcretiō
in thoſe good men. The firſt was the
arrogant ſetting out of the gyftes of
God: the ſecōd was the diſquieting of
ſuch as would teach:the third was the
breaking of order,which of all thinges
becometh the Church of Chriſte beſt.

But S. Paule very wiſely remoueth
al theſe thinges.For to place humility,
he putteth al men in mind of that moſt
wretched ſtate in the which they had
liued before,when through the mociō
of the ennemie the diuell they went
ſuppliantly afterydols:that they might
the more eaſily gather by that, that ¹.Cor.12
thoſe gyftes ought to be referred, 4.
  not

not to their defertes, but to the infinite
mercie of God.

He teacheth them alfo , that other
mé were not to be difpifed, the which,
although they had not receiued thofe
gyftes, yet were they not vtterly void
of the gyftes of God: for fo much as no
man can confeffe our Lord Iefus from
his heart but by the benefite of the
holie Ghoft .

1.Cor.12.
4.

After that he declareth how that
the gyfte , which euerie man hath receiued, he hath receiued it , not for
him felfe only , but for all other : and
that it ought therfore to be imploied
to the profit of the vniuerfal Church.

Then he fheweth how emongeft al
the gyftes of God , charitie hath the
higheft roome and dignitie , that they
might thereby vnderftand, that it fkilleth not much , how manie tongues a
man knew , or ells how great miracles
he was able to worke, but with how
great zeale and diligence he furthered
                                    the

the Churche.

Laſt of al making a compariſon betwene the gyſte of tongues and prophecie, he deſpiſeth not tongues, but
perſerreth prophecying far before the
tongues. And theſe are the places, by
the which the Apoſtle brought the mē
of that time frō a certaine kind of lightnes, to the loue of grauity ād modeſty.

But that diſorder of talking together
and hindering one an other in ſuche
ſort, that the profitte of teaching was
thereby loſt, S. Paule tooke it awaie,
when he ſaied. But if any man ſpeake
with tongue, let it be done by two, or
at the moſt by three, and let one expounde. For you maie prophecie by
one and one, and you maie ſpeake by
one and one. And leſt anie man might
ſaie, that he was violently moued by
the ſpirite, in ſuch ſorte, that he could
not refraine him ſelfe from ſpeaking:
the Apoſtle ſaith, that the ſpirit of prophetes is ſubiecte vnto the Prophetes.

1.*Cor.*14
ſ.

Q   Wherin

Wherin he teacheth them, that it laie
in them, whiche were moued by the
holy Ghoſt , to moderate the gyſte of
the holy Ghoſt.

Finally he ſetteth an order, (of the
whiche he had ſaied much before) by
1.Cor. 14.
f.
theſe wordes. Endeuour your ſelues to
prophecie, and forbid no man to ſpeke
with tongues. But let al things be done
honeſtly and orderly. The Apoſtle forbiddeth not to vſe ſtraunge tongues :
but yet he preferreth before tongues
the gyſte of prophecie, that is to ſaie,
the declaration of the wil of God, and
the edifying of the Church: and he cō-
maūdeth, that al thinges be done with
verie good order.

Now there are two pointes to be
cōſidered in this place: the one is, that,
emongeſt many things, which maie be
done at one time at our pleaſure indif-
ferently , looke what thinges maie be
omitted without offence, are to be o-
mitted , when any daunger that maie
ther-

thervpon enſewe, and the time ſo requireth. And therfore, although in S.
Pauls time al myſteries might be com-
municated to al men: it foloweth not,
that they ſhold, in our daies(when ther
is no like capacity in al mē to cōceiue
them)be cōmitted to al men indifferētly without any reſpecte of perſonnes.

The other point is, that the meaning
of S.Paul in al that diſputation was, to
keepe downe pride, to ſet vp charitie,
and to cōmaund , that order ſhould be
kept. He therfore that geueth occaſiō
of pride, that ſlaketh loue and charity,
that diſtourbeth good order, although
he ſeeme to folowe the wordes of S.
Paule , yet goeth he directely againſt
the meaning of S.Paul.

Theſe thinges being thus determined , I wil aſke you a queſtion : what
came into your braines , to be ſo deſirous to take al the volumes of the holy
Scripture, and without anie neceſsity,
ye with no ſmal dáger of the vnlerned

Q ij   people,

people,to cōmit them to euerie iacke-
ſtraw to expounde? did you it , to re-
ſtreyne the pride of ſuch as are baſe ?
No : you haue rather puffed vp their
hartes incredibly , cauſing them to cōceiue a falſe opinion ot wiſedome in
them ſelues . Was it done to cauſe a
more feruent charitie emongeſt them?
No:you haue rather forced the weake
mindes to fall out within them ſelues,
through your diuers,yea and contrary
expoſitions of the law of God. Was it
done to ſet all thinges in good order?
No:you haue rather ouerthrowen all
good and aunciēt order.For now euery man is a prophete , euerie man is a
ſhepeheard,euery mā is a doctour,eue-
rie man will prate in euerie place very
vnſemely of matters of diuinitie,euery
mā wil babble what him liſteth of the
higheſt Myſteries , the loweſt pointe
whereof is farre aboue his capacitie.
This is by like your prouidence,wher-
by you haue taken quite awaie that ſilence

lenée which was vſed of olde time in
the churches: that baſhfulnes, whiche
became honeſt matrones merueloufly
wel:that modeſty, which kept the ſimple people verie wel in their dewtie.
And ſo it is come to paſſe, that wheras
you pretend to folow the wordes of
S.Paul, you bend your ſelues erneſtly
againſt his meaning.

What lacked there, I praie you, in
the olde time, that was neceſſarie to
keepe honeſt heartes in a ſobre diſci-
cipline? Were there not lerned Prieſts,
the which were able to chooſe out of
the holie myſteries ſo muche as was
needful to ſaluation, and ſo muche as
they might declare vnto the ignorant
people without dannger? Were there
none to ſupplie the place of the vnlerned man, and to anſwere Amen? Was
the ſownd and wordes of the Latine
tongue ſo ſtraunge, that no man vnderſtoode it in all your Churches?
Needed there the authoritie of the

Q iij   Apoſtle

Apoſtle to breake vp that diſordered confuſion of many tongues together, when there was heard, in the commõ praiers of the churches, but one kind of ſpeach only, and that by long cuſtome verie well knowen and commonly vſed?

If the vſe of one common tongue ioyneth the mindes of men in one, then was there nothing more agreable to the rule of Chriſt, then that the ſeruice of God ſhould be openly ſaied in one only tongue, the which was in all churches of the weſt part of the world learned in ſcholes, and practiſed in the dailie affaires: and nothing leſſe conuenient, then that the ſeruice is now ſaied in ſo manie tongues as there are nations, emongeſt whome men without learning, without witte, without religion take vpon them the office of expounding the holie Scriptures. Wherfore neither was our ſimplicity ſo vnprofitable, as you wiſe men
thought

thought it was: neither is your prouident warines so wholesome, as your maisters imagined it would haue ben. For out of it are risen errours, and disorders, and a false opiuiō of wisedome (whiche is the greatest madnes in the worlde) with manie other discommodities.

Then you goe forewarde in the declaration of the doctrine of your Church, saying. *We vse at the laying on of handes, the celebration of mariage, the churching of women after child bearing, the visiting of the sicke, and the burying of the dead, solemne and publike seruice set out according to the truth of the ghospell.* Al the rest you comprehend verie briefely in one sentence, perswading your selfe, that it is sufficiently declared, that you are not destitute, neither of Sacramentes, neither of anie other thinges apperteyning to religion.

You confesse plainely after that, that you haue shaken of from you,

the yoke of the high Bifhop or Pope:
bicaufe it was heauier, then that either
you or your fathers could beare it.
Your fathers and auncetours I know,
did beare it verie well and with great
commēdation: but you I graunt, were
not able to beare it. For how had it
ben lawful for you, to breake violently into the monafteries, to difanull the
rules of monkes, to deflower the holy
and chaft Virgins, to deface like vngodlie and furious men al orders of religion, to laie your greedy and violent
handes vpon the Churche goods appointed to holie vfes, to pul powne all
monumentes of vertue and godlines,
to ouerthrow the auncient Churche,
and to botch vp an other at your ple-
fure: if this yoke had not ben firft taken
of from your neckes? You bring in a
litle after.

Neither doe we acknowledge anie Bif-
fhop, but onlie our Lord Iefus Chrifte, to
whom the holy fcriptures appoint this pe-
culiar

culiar honour . O worthie saying , full
of wonderful godlines, and contey-
ning in it a most euidēt proufe of heauenlie life. What shal we doe to these
mē, which are so holie, so vtterly void
of al care of this present life , that for
the desire and loue of the presence of
Christ him selfe, they can not abide to
see any Vicare of Christ vpō the earth.
But lette vs see a litle . This name of
Christ, doth it import the dignitie and
office of a bishop only, or elles doth it
comprehende also the authoritie and
maiestie of a King? Surely it can not
be denied, that by the worde and meaning of Christ, in this name of Christ is
conteined the power both of a bishop
and of a King. Whie then doe you acknowledge any other king, beside our
Lord Iesus Christ ? Whie are you not
so free and earnest, to shake of this
yoke that remaineth? Whie suffer you
this freedome of your gospell to be
hindered through the power and au-
thori-

thoritie of a King? Whie doe you not
(as it hath ben already attempted in o-
ther places, whiche are infected with
the selfe same religiō) bend your selues
earnestly to make away the maiestie
of a King? for as you acknwolege one
only high bishop , so is it necessarie to
obei one only King . If you thinke it
mete to haue an other king in th'earth,
as Vicare of that high and almightie
king: what is the cause, whie you wold
not haue an other bishop as Vicare of
that most high and holy bishoppe? But
you wil say. We haue bishops, but we
wil haue no high bishop : Whie then,
it is not the name of a bishop , but of a
high bishoppe , that offendeth you.
Wherefore thinke you then , that the
authoritie of a Kinges power (whiche
dowbtles is the highest) is to be borne
in England? Are there not magistrates
emongest you? Is there not a publike
counsel ? Haue you not Princes and
Lordes? Then take awaie the controuersie

uersie of the name, and ther are in England a great many, (as there are also e-
mógest vs) the which haue the authority of kinges, although thei be not called by the name of Kinges . Ymagine
therfore, that they were certaine litle
kinges. What needed it then, being so
many kinges emongest you, that there
shuld be any one high or supreme king,
to restraine by his authority the other
inferiour kings? For if you thinke that
this word (high) mai not be born in the
dignitie of a bishop: why do you not in
like máner detest the name of highnes
in the Maiestie of a king? No, say you,
it was very wisely prouided, that al the
magistrats and Princes in Englád shuld
haue one supreme Prince, whom they
shuld al reueréce, and by whose power
ád autority they shuld be al restrained:
for otherwise, it cannot be chosen, but
that there would be stirred vp muche
trouble and discord, to the great peril
of the whole realme. I thinke you say
truly.

truly. And therefore I affirme in like
manner, that in the Churche, whiche
ought to be alwaies one, it is necessarie, that there be one supreme power
of a high bishop, whose authoritie all
other Bishops should reuerence. For
otherwise it must needes be, that there
arise much debate and manie pestilent
sectes, to the great ruine and decaie of
the Churche, and that the Church be
brought therby into verie great daunger. For if within the space of fourtie
yeares, sence a great peece of Germanie, and afterwardes England sel
from the Bishop of Rome, so many seditions haue risen emongest the Princes of your Religion, that they cã not
possibly agree, neither with other mé,
neither yet within them selues : what
ende, thinke you, wil ensew, in case al
Christendome (the which God forbid)
being thereunto procured and moued
by your diligence and vnreasonable
meanes, should rebel with the like outrage

rage and madnes? It remaineth therefore, that, as in England there is one
fupreme power, whiche comprehen-
deth al other Princes vnderneth it: fo
there be alfo in the Churche one fupreme authoritie, the whiche al other
inferiour powers muft willingly and
diligently obeie. For otherwife it
is not pofsible, that the crewel tem-
peftes rifen in the Churche fhould e-
uer be flaked, or the flames of difcord
quenched, or the ciuile warres ended.
Now, for fo much as Chrift is the authour of peace: Whofoeuer wil faie,
that they wil haue but one only bifhop
which is our Lord Iefus Chrifte, and
by the religious pretéce of this worde,
wil open a gap to fo manie opinions,
and to fo much peftilent diffenfió: thei
are lyers. No, they doe rather fight a-
gainft Chrift, and worfhippe Satan the
authour of debate and difcorde. But
contrariewife, fuch as honour and reuerence the bifhoppe of Rome as the
Vicare

Vicare of Chrift, for that refpect only, bicaufe he is the lieutenant of Chrift in the earth : they doe in deede acknowledge only Chrift to be the high Prieft.

And yet you faie, that, by this your rebellion and contempte, you doe not cut and mãgle the coate of Chrift, but only geue a touch at the Bifhop of Romes cloke. And by and by after you bring in thefe wordes. *Neither doe we laie open the waie, as you faie, to fedition, but we doe dãme vp the path, the which goeth downe, through his licentious lead, to the great decaie of good manners.* Of this lead, and of your notable reproch I haue fpokē before, with as much modeftie, as the matter would fuffer me. But of this your bafe, vile, and fhamelefle boldnes, when you fay, that you haue not rent and torne the coate of Chrift, but rather, that you haue, by this your moft wicked rebellion, made a goodlie prouifion, that good man-

ners

ners ſhould not decaie, I can not wel
tel what to ſay to you. Dare you, ſeing
euerie where , as you doe, that there
are ſo many diuiſions of peſtilēt ſectes,
with ſo much debate and diſcord: that
there is no certaine faith emõgeſt you,
no agreemēt in Religiõ: that your con-
feſsiõs are changed almoſt euerie day,
your beleeſes and Creedes corrected:
that the olde places of doctrine are diſanulled, and new ſet vp: that manifold
ſectes ariſeth daily, and the old Church
is diuided in many parts: howdare you,
I ſay, report that this your falling from
the Church hath not māgled the coate
of Chriſte ? When you ſee with your
eyes, that pride , arrogancie , diſobe-
dience, ſtubbernes, ſaucie talke, ſlaunderous report, fleſhlie pleaſure, naughtines, diſhoneſty , tumult and ſedition
goeth vp and downe freely and vncõ-
trolled, whereſouer your maiſters put
their foote : with what face dare you
ſay, that you haue after this rebellion
                                        ſet

set the manners of men in good and seemelie ordre? The thing it selfe speaketh, dailie examples declare, neither doe the open aisises, no neither secret parlars hold their peace.

But let vs now see, howe worshipfully you confute that my discourse as touching the Monarchie of the holie Church. You say. *In the best time of the Church, there was one God and one faith.* That is true. But now neither is there one God, nor one faith emongest the ministers of your gospel. For one offereth vp diuine honour to pleasure, an other to madnes: some to the bealie, and some to railing. Luther hath one faith, Bucer an other, Zwinglius hath one, and Caluin an other. And yet you say.

Peter had his Prouince, Paule had his, and Iames his, and other had other Prouinces. And yet did not this separation of their persons disioine the vnitie of their faith. What conclude you then? maie
it be

it be gathered by thefe things, that you faye, that Peter, when he was refident in one Prouince, had no preeminence ouer the reft of the Apoftles? That is not wel côcluded of thefe things, that you haue fpoken. For now euery Bif-fhoppe hath his Prouince, and the Bif-fhop of Rome hath his. And yet are we all fubiect vnto him by the lawe of God. It foloweth.

In proceſſe of time, many of the Biſhops of Rome, were Martyrs, and were facri-ficed vnto God by prophane and vngodlie Princes: but Crownes had they none, vn-leſſe it were the Crownes of Martyrdome. This extraordinarie foueraintie of Pope-dome, they knew not. Yes M. Haddon, it is wel knowen, that the moft bleffed Princes and foueraignes of the Church of Rome them felues, to witte, Cle-ment, and Euariftus, and Lucius, and Marcellus, and Pius, the which attey-ned the Croune of Martyrdome with very great glory, whom neither ambi-

R tion

tion, nor any other vnlauful defire moued to feke for that fupreme honoure:
do beare witnes againft you. For their
writinges declare plainely , that their
iudgement was , that the foueraintie
of the vniuerfal Churche, was euer in
the Church of Rome. What fhould I
here reherfe Ireneus, Auguftine, and al
other holy Fathers ? What fhoulde I
here vnfolde the memorie of al the antiquitie ? Of the new writers reade, if
it pleafeyou, Eckius, the B. of Roche-
fter, Cocleus, Pighius , and fuch other
moft excellét men both for vertue and
learning, and you fhall fee , how ignorant you are in this mater of the fupre-
macie. They difpute and contend, not
with reprochful wordes, not with lies,
not with impudécy : but with teftimonies of the holie Scriptures , but with
the authorities of the holy Fathers, but
with examples of the vnfpotted antiquitie: and they preffe their aduerfaries , and proue them to be not onely
wicked

wicked felowes, but alſo very mad and
frantike mē. But how is it poſsible, that
you ſhould vnderſtand theſe thinges?
What time could you ſpend in the ſtudie of Diuinitie, being a mā alwaies cōuerſant in the law court, and hindered
with many affaires? And ſo, me thinketh, that you are not ſo muche to be
blamed, as your maiſters, the whiche
haue nouſeled you in ſo mani errours.
How be it you are alſo to be blamed
for two points. The firſt is lightnes, for
that you haue ſo lightly geuen credite
to naughty mē. The other is impudēcy,
for that you haue ſo raſhly auouched
thinges, that you neuer read. Tel me, I
pray you, where haue you read, that
Gregorie did abandone this ſupreame
dignitie of the B. of Rome? And yet
you put it in your oratiō affirming it ful
ſtoutly, and are neuer a whit aſhamed
of your lying. At the length you conclude thus. *Wherfore if the beſt ſtate of*
the church, was without this Monarchy:

R ij   we

we may also lack it ful wel : yea we ought to lacke it, not only bicause it is expressely forbidden by the Gospel, but also bicause it standeth wel with reason. What a rashnes and impudencie is this in you, to conclude an Argument after this forte without al reason ? You must bring in your conclusion vpon thinges, that are true, knowen, and agreed vppon, not vppon thinges that are false and not graunted . If you be ignorant in this, you are a very dolt: if you know it, and yet will goe about to conclude your argument vpon false propositiõs, without any proufe going before : you are to be taken as a very shamelesse sophifter For emongest the guyles and subtilties, which the babling sophisters are wonte to vse, this is accounted for one of the firft, to goe aboute to conclude what them lifteth, vppon thinges, that are not true, neither graunted, neither agreed vppon . *If the best state of the Church,* faie you, *was without this Monarchie,*

narchie, we may also lacke it full well .
What, if the best state of the Churche
was neuer without this Monarchie,
may you then lacke it? I thinke not.
If it be then proued by writinges and
records, yea and by the ful agreement
of al the holy Fathers, that the best state
of the Church was neuer without this
Monarchie : if you are able, neither to
cōfute the authorities, neither to make
any good prouse for your selfe, neither
to bring any sure ground of antiquitie,
but only in bare wordes to saie, what
ye list : doe you not see, that all your
talke is fainte and weake, and that it is
pitifully shaken and battred of it selfe
without gónneshotte? And yet, as
though you had already contriued the
whol matter according to your hearts
desire, you say moreouer: *Yea we ought
to lacke it.* How proue you, that it is
of duétie? What fruict can you shew
of this your wicked rebellion? What
light haue you shewed to the worlde

by this your outrage and madneſſe ſo wonderfull, that you may wel ſay, that you haue diſcharged your duetie and office commendably.

Nowe, whereas you ſay, that the Goſpel forbiddeth it expreſly, you declare the verie true cauſe of all your doinges. For it ſeemeth, that you are minded to doe that onely, that the Goſpell of Chriſte forbiddeth you to doe. How be it you woulde not ſaie ſo, but rather that you do by the warrant of the Goſpel refuſe the authority of the B. of Rome. Suche is your eloquence, that you are not able manie times, to vtter your owne meaning. But by what teſtimonie of the Goſpel, by what authority haue you proued it? Bring foorth the place, preſſe vs with the wordes, cóuince vs with the commaundement, ſhew where the Goſpel hath forbidden, not darkely, but by expreſſe and plaine words, that we ſhuld not acknowledge any one man as the high Vicare of Chriſt in the earth.

You ſaie moreouer, that it ſtandeth
with reaſon : whereas you neuer ſhewed before, how reaſon and this your
lewdnes may ſtande together.   And
yet, as though you had moſte plainely
and inuincibly proued the matter: you
do not only cōclude veri much beſides
the purpoſe, but alſo vaūt your ſelf beyond al modeſtie. Some il hap come to
that felow your Schoolemaiſter, that
brought you vp ſo il. It is like, he toke
vpon him to make you eloquent : and
he made you not only a babe, but alſo
an vntoward and a ſhameleſſe felowe.
Wherfore I would geue you counſel,
to take an action agaīnſt him, to make
him repaie his waiges, that he tooke of
you. For you beſtowed your time very il with him, the which might haue
ben better ſpent in drawing out writes
and proceſſes in the Law.   But let vs
ſee, what reaſon you bring. You ſaie.
  Neither can the head ſo far frō the mē-
bers diſagree cōueniently. What are you
                    R iiij   yet

Conueniē-
ter diſſi-
dere.
are M.
Haddons
vvords in
Latine.

yet to learne to ſpeake Latine? What
meane you by this? What is to diſagree conuenientlie? For the thing that
is in it ſelfe conuenient, is nothing diſa-
greeable. Whereas you ſaie therfore,
that a thing doth diſagree conuenient-
ly, you ſpeake not pure and cleane Latine, but you vſe a monſtruouſe kinde
of Latine ſpeache. For this cauſe I am
not aſhamed to confeſſe ſo often, that
I doe not vnderſtand, what you ſaie.
I ſuſpect, you would ſaie in this place,
that it is not poſſible, that the heade
ſhould fitlie be ioyned vnto the members being ſo farre a ſunder. If you ſay
ſo, you are much deceiued, if you beleue that the cōiunction of the church
conſiſteth in the nighnes of places, and
not in the conſent of faith, and agreement in one Religion. But if you doe
compriſe vnder this diſordered kinde
of ſpeach, ſome other more ſecret myſterie: When you haue exponnded
your ſelf, then peraduenture I wil anſwere

fwere you. You fay afterward . *Efpe-*
cially for fomuch as this Monarchie or only
foueraintie, for the which you laboure fo
much, we haue it at hand at home with
vs in Englande , fo that we neede not to
feeke it abroad . It is not my part to rehearfe al your woordes after you, like a
childe . But I will afke you this one
thing, what only power or foucrainty
is that ? We haue, fay you, the abfolute authoritie of a Kinges Maieftie,
wherein is conteined fully and wholly
the Princelie eftate of our common
weale . What, would you alfo, that
the fupreme authoritie of the Church
fhould be fubiect vnto this Kingly Maieftie, as you faie ? For no man euer
faid, that your common weale ought
to be gouerned by the authoritie of the
Bifhop of Rome, in matters cocerning
the ftate of your ciuile affaires:but only, that the Churche of Englande can
not refufe by any means without great
offence the authority of the Bifhop of
Rome.

Rome. For this doe we contend and, as you saie, labour so earneftly. This is that, which you faie is nothing necef-farie : for fo much as the Kinges Maie-ftie hath an abfolute authoritie emon-geft you, and therefore you neede not feeke any other abroad. You fay ther-fore expreflely, that your Quene doth rightfully take vpon her the gouerne-ment of Englande in fpiritual matters. And the more hardelie to preffe me therewithal, you reafon with me after this forte. *But furely this feemeth vnto you, a thing not to be borne. And in this place you are fo chaufed, that you laie Sa-crilege vnto Princes charges, bicaufe thei wil rule the lawes of the Church; and vn-reuerently handle holy thinges.* Anon after, you counfell me like a fage and graue man, that I fhoulde tempre my choler, faying vnto mee. *O Maifter Ierome be not ouermuch difquieted. Such great choler and wrath is not feemely in a Philofopher.* In this place, M. Waul-ter,

ter, if you dally, you dally very ftalely.
If you fpeake in earneft , it is nothing
true that you faie . Neither was it angre (whiche is a fodaine rage ftirred
through the opinion conceiued of difhoneftie) that could haue moued me
to write thofe my letters, for fo muche
as I was neuer prouoked to difpleafure
with fo much as one rough worde of
any Englifh man: but it was the loue of
moft holy Religion, and the good wil I
beare towards the Quene, that moued
me to fend thofe letters, and to aduertife her to efchew the danger that han
ged ouer her and her Realme. Neither
is there any token of anger to be feene
in my talke, excepte you will cal a iuft
and lamentable complaint of the ftate
of our mofte vnhappie time, angre .
But that that foloweth, howe pretily
it was fpoken? *Take breath a little* .
As thoughe you had with this your
wonderfull force of talke fo difquieted
me, that I coulde not take my breath.
Then

Then that other saying of yours, what a pleasante grace it hath : *Come to your selfe againe.* This is a foule rebuke. For it seemeth to M. Haddon a wise man, whose iudgement was alwaies simple, pure, and vncorrupted , that I am out of my wittes . Or els he would neuer warne me, to come to my selfe againe. You saie afterwardes. *You shall see all that be wel.* That do I loke for in dede: how be it I am sore afraid, lest you being an eloquente man and wonderfull in perswading, may force me to beleue thinges , that are not proued vnto me. Yet I looke for your reason , by the which you wil proue, that it is lawfull for your Quene to meddle in Ecclesiasticall matters , and to laie suche lawes vpon Churches, as her listeth . What saie you Sir? *The Kinges Maiestie*, saie you , *maistereth al persones in England.* What els? So doth the French King the French men, and the Scottish King the Scottes. I commend your briefe-

nes

nes in reasoning. For you conclude al
in one worde, as often as you list , and
that meruelouse wittily. But yet you
take such thinges , as are neither true,
neither of force to conclude those
thinges, that you would proue . For
first of all , the gouernement of a King
is not violent, neither tyrannical : and
suche as he hath taken vppon him to
mainteine like a louing Father, he doth
not maister them like seruauts: neither
doth he imploye his regimente to his
owne commoditie, but to the safety of
his subiectes . It is therefore false, that
he doth maister them, except he wold
rather be accounted a tyranne, then a
King. Moreouer, admit it were true,
yet doth it not folow, that he doth gouerne them in al matters. That therefore, that you should haue proued, you
laie for a ground, as though it were al-
redy proued and graunted: the which is
one of the gretest faults, that mai be in
a disputer. Last of al, neither doth the
                                 French

french King gouerne the fiench men
in spiritual matters, neither the Scotish
Kinge the Scottes: and if he doe (the
which is nothig true) then doth he not
his owne office, but vsurpeth an other
mans. Yet you say. *But the Quene put-*
teth not her hand vnto holie thinges.
Why so, I pray you, M, Haddon? Is it
bicause she thinketh it not lawful? Or
els bicause she wil not? If she thinke,
that it is not lawfull, then doth shee
speake directely against you. If she be
occupied with other affairs, and therfore committeth holie thinges to men
of the basest sort, shee doth otherwise
then her estate requireth. For she thinketh, that there is some other thing to
be preferred before holie things. You
say. *The ciuile affaires are cõmitted te the*
ciuile magistrates, the Church matters to
the Bishops. What Bishops meane you?
Are they those Bishops, that you haue
violétly thrust out of their Bishopriks,
and cast into the iayles? or els are they
such

suche as you haue caught vppe in the
streates, and frō the alebéches, and haue
placed thē in the roome of those most
holi bishops? O what an honorable pre
sence of Bishops is that, for all subiects
to reuerence, and al il men to be afraid
of? But I would faine learne of you,
what goodly glosse of vertue was that,
that moued you to place those base
felowes in this roome and dignitie?
Was it their meruelouse and chast life,
which you can not abide? Was it the
knowledge of holie Scriptures, the
which thei had learned in tauernes, or
in scholes, where perhappes they had
ben Maisters? Was it their wonderful
eloquence, wherewith thei were able
to withdrawe the cōmon people from
licentious liuing to continency, which
they them selues abhorre? For it is to
be thought, that they that depriued
those godlie and learned Bishoppes of
al their dignities, would not haue done
such wrong vnto the vertuous men :
                                        vnlesse

vnlesse they had meant to set other in their places, that did very farre excede them in all godlines, learning and eloquence.

But I wold demaūd one thing of you: if they be so holi, so lerned, and so eloquēt, wherfore did you not cōmit vnto them aboue all other this care and charge to write against me? Wherfore would you betray to the worlde your owne ignoaāce and babishnesse? Was there suche a scarcity of learned Bisshops, that you must needes take vpon you a charge that was none of yours, no nor seemely for you to medle in? For, to mainteine Religion, apperteineth to a Bishop, not to a man, that is tourmoiled in the suites and questions of the ciuile Law. If they did not excel in such vertues and qualities as are to be required in Bishops, what a frowarde malice was that to thrust out the good Bishops, and to put such base felowes in their roomes and dignities?

You

You politike wise man, doe you not
see that that common weale is neere
to vtter ruine and decaie, wherin such
honours as are dewe to honestie and
vertue are geauen to base varlettes?
But be it, that they had ben promoted
to this honour for their excellent qualities (for I can not wel gesse the truth
of the matter : and it maie be that thei
were, before thei came to that dignitie, put to schoole to Bucere or els to
your Martyr:) but sir, I demaunde of
you, by what right or iustice was it
done? Howbeit as touching iustice
you haue already satisfied me, when
you affirmed, that within the cõpasse
of the Queenes Maiesties authoritie
is conteined, what so euer concerneth
God or man. But yet I pray you tell
me, with what ceremonie, with what
solemnitie, with what Religion was it
done? Who laied handes on them?
who cõsecrated them? I would know
what holines and puritie you vsed in

S   the

the doing of it. For it is like, that such fine and deintie felowes as you are, were offended with our ceremonies, (the which peraduéture might seeme vnto you very ftale and old) and therefore you deuifed other much trimmer then oures, the whyche you haue brought not neere, but, as you terme it, exceding neere to the very paterne of the gofpel.

You fay afterward, *that the Church matters are ordered by the bifhops : but when there is ought to be decreed, the diuines do determine it.* It is euident, that you cal thé diuines, who were brought vp vnder Bucer or Caluin. Why then haue you diminifhed the right of bif-fhops? for it perteineth to the bifhops to determine: the diuines haue no more to doe, but only to afsift the bifhoppes with their aduife. But you in geauing ouer the right of the bifhops to the diuines, declare, that your bifhops are no diuines. Your bifhops therfore are (as

the

the common report is)not only poore
ſcrapers and baſe felowes, but alſo vtterly ignorant in the holie Scriptures.
And menne ſay, that the principall
cauſe whie they are choſen, is, that
they muſte content them ſelues with
ſome ſcantling of their reuenewes, and
leaue the reſt to be rifled of you vnder
pretence of the Queenes eſcheker. If
this be not true, you muſte not blame
me, a man(as you ſay your ſelfe)vnac-
queinted in the affaires of Englād: but
the falſe report of your il willers. Yet,
this I warne you, that you and ſuch as
you are, doe ſuſteine the great dint
of this infamie. For when you chooſe
ſuche Biſhops, you make menne ſuſpecte, that you are greedie and coue-
teous.

You conclude at the length, that
both the adminiſtratiō of the biſhops,
and decrees of the diuines are autho-
riſed by the confirmation of the Quē-
nes Maieſtie. Whie then, if there

ſhalbe anie thing done by the biſhops,
or els determined by the diuines, that
is not for the Queenes profitte, that
ſhal not be ratified.

Here you ſpeake darkely, I can not
tel what, of the Kinges of Iſrael, as
though the Prieſtes in olde time had
done al thinges, that concerned religion, after the preſcribed ordre of kinges: the which is falſe. You ſay afterward. *Then the goſpel ſucceding and di-*
uiding theſe powers, in the firſt place it
ſetteth the authoritie of Kinges, and vn-
der it other powers by the authoritie of
Peter and Paule, whoſe names you abuſe
to ſet vp the kingdom of the ſea of Rome.

Flatterie. O. what a plague and deſtruction of
common weales, what a whirle wind
and tempeſt to your moſt flouriſhing
Ilãd, what an vtter ruine and decaie of
al kingdomes and peoples is this, that
is comprifed vnder the naughtines, au-
dacitie, crueltie, and coueteouſnes of
flatterers? What wild beaſt can anie
man

man deuiſe in the worlde more horrible and crewel, then it is ? For what
ſo euer the pleaſure of Kinges ſtandeth vnto, be it neuer ſo wicked, heinouſe and vngodly, be it not only hurtful to the common weale, but alſo cōtrarie to al good and godly ordre: it is
made forthwith by thoſe clawbackes,
whome thei cal to their counſel, to be
dewtiful, iuſt, commédable, religious,
moſt wholeſome to the cōmon weale,
and moſt acceptable to God. The
which thing is wel knowen to haue
chaunced vnto king Henry, who was
vntil that time both for his vertue, wit,
and deedes a moſte noble and renowmed Prince. For when as the king had
cōceiued an earneſt loue, and alſo an
earneſt diſpleaſure, and was deſirous
both to ſatisfie his loue, and alſo to re-
uége the diſpleaſure taken of the Pope
(who forbad the new mariage) he was
brought, by the perſuaſion and authoritie of a certaine wicked man, to be-
S iij   leeue,

leue, that he was suprem head of al the Churches that are within the realme of England . This thing was the vndoing of the bishop of Rochester, and More, and of other holie mé, that abid extreme punishments: if a most honorable death constantly suffed for the glory of Christ and establishing of religion may be called an vndoing. From hence as out of a flouldgate issued so many pestilent opiniós, such a broile of sectes and heresies, suche outrages of lewd felowes into the state of the Church of Englád, to the great decay of the auncient custome.

But what was the place, the which that most vile corrupter would abuse to proue it? Submit your selues, saith S. Peter, to euery wordly wight for gods sake , whether it be to the King, as to the more excellét personage, or els to the rulers, as sent fró God, for the punishment of malefactours, and cómendation of good men. what other thing doth

1. Pet. 2. c.

doth S. Peter in thefe words but only
cut of al occafion of difordre and outrage ? for he would not , that , by the
pretenfed name of the libertie of the
gofpel, the cōmon weale fhould be difordered, or the fociety of men by ciuil
policie gathered togetherbe diſſolued.
And therfore doth he bind al Chriſtiā
men to the lawes and ordinaunces of
menne, fo that they be not againſt the
lawe of God. He commaundeth ſeruantes to obey their maiſters, be they
neuer fo crewel: womē to obey their
huſbandes: huſbandes to honour their
wiues: children to obei their parentes:
parentes to loue their children, and to
prouide for their bringing vppe and
mayntenaunce . Finally the holie A-
poſtle commaundeth, that ordre both
in commaunding and obeying be kept
(whether it be publike or priuat) without any grudging or pretending of ex-
ceſſiue libertie. The which ordre was
to be kept of Chriſtian men with fo

S iiij   much

much the more diligence, as it was cóuenient, that their vertue fhould fhine more then the vertue of other menne. The felfe fame thing doth S. Paule, when he warneth vs to fubmitte our felues to the magiftrates, and to obey the lawful cómaundementes of Princes. He teacheth maifters and feruantes, parents and childré, houfbands and wiues the very fame leffons.

Ro.13.a.

I demaund now of you, what goodly pregnant wit is this of yours, or rather of them that brought you into fo great an errour: that they would picke fuch a meaning, as you fpeake of, out of thefe words of S. Peter? Did this word, More excellent, moue you to doe it? Surely that were a manifeft token of a verie great folie, and extreme madnes. For fo do we faie in common fpeach, that that man doth excell in nobilitie, or is More excellent, whiche is in deede verie noble, although he be not of all other mofte noble.　So
doe

doe we faie alfo , that a man excell-
leth, or is More excellent then other,
in vertue, or learning or authoritie, the
which paffeth other in thefe qualities,
although he paffe not al the worlde in
them. The felfe fame fignification and
meaning hath the Greeke word ὑπερί-
χων and fuch is the vfe of it. Moreouer
when we faie, that anie man excelleth
in fome one thing, we doe not by and
by in fo faying yeald , that he doth excel in al thinges: but in that thing only,
whereof we fpake . If mention were
made of the ciuile law, and we would
faie, that M. Waulter Haddon did excel in the knowledge of the ciuile law:
we did not in fo faying geaue him authoritie to expounde the holie Scriptures , wherein he is altogether ignorant.

I woulde now demaunde of you,
what matter was S. Peter about, when
he faid that the king was the more excellent perfonage ? Was he about the
gouerne-

gouernment of Churches, or thinges apperteining to religiõ? No doubtles, but abowte ciuile gouernement, the which he would not haue to be diſordered by anie ſedition.

What goeth S. Paul about, when he commaundeth vs to ſubmit our ſelues to all powers? The ſelfe ſame thing, that S. Peter doth. And to confirme that, he ſheweth that all power is ordeined and appointed by God. And to teache vs, that this is our bownden dewtie by the law of God, he ſaieth: Geaue therfore to al men their dewe. Tribute, to whome you owne tribute: cuſtume, to whom you owe cuſtume: feare, to whome feare is dewe: and honour, to whom honour apperteineth. It liketh not the Apoſtles to haue anie ſedition or broile in the cõmon weale, or anie thing that maie diſtourbe the peace and good order. And therfore, although Princes were at that time verie ill affected towardes the moſte

Rom.13.a

ᵇ

holie

holie ordinaũces of Chriſt: yet in matters apperteining to the ciuile gouernment, they cõmaund al Chriſtian men,
not only to obey their Princes, but alſo
to make their hũble praiers vnto God *1. Tim. 2·a*
for their good eſtate. S. Peter therfore
gaue not vnto the king, in calling him
more excellent, the ſupreme authoritie in the Church : (neither did anie
man euer dreame of that beſides you)
but he graunted vnto him the ſupreme
power in the ciuile gouernment .

Tel me, I praie you, who helde the
kingdome at that time, when S. Peter
wrote theſe thinges ? either it was Caius, or Claudius, or Nero. For Tiberius
(which was alſo a naughtie and vniuſt
man, as we maie coniecture) was dead
before. Is this your iudgement then M.
Haddon, that Peter and Paul did commaunde, that the Preſident of the
Churche ſhoulde doe nothing, but by
order of Caius, or Claudius, or Nero: that he ſhould retcine ſuch Prieſtes
onlie

onlie, as they wuld haue and put away
the reft, if it liked the emperour : that
he fhould, if there chaunced any difficultie or hard queftion in the Church,
referre it to Cefar:or that(to be fhort)
he fhould minifter all the ceremonies
and facramentes of our religion according to Nero his pleafure? If thefe
thinges be voied of al wit and reafon,
then is that your opinion, whervpon
thefe thinges doe neceffaliy folowe,
fuche, that if you would ftudie for it,
you can not deuife anie thing more
foolifh and vnreafonable.

But you will faie, that this fentence
of S. Peter perteineth not to fuche
Princes as are enemies to the faith of
Chrift, but only to Chriftian Princes.
If you faie fo, then are you of this
mind, that S.Peter gaue this cōmaun-
dement to the Chriftians, that, fo long
as fuch men reigned, as were not well
affected towardes the name of Chrift,
they fhoulde not acknowledge their
autho.

authority, they should not regard their officers and magistrates, they shoulde despise their lawes, they shoulde like rebelles disorder the peace and tranquillitie of the common weale. The which it were a verie great madnes to speake. For then to what pourpose should S. Peter bring in this sentence afterward. That you maie, saieth he, by well doing put the ignorance of foolish men to siléce. Doutlesse, if they had not obeied vngodlie Princes, no man would haue ben put to silence by them : but euerie man would haue set vpon them, (and that for their desert) as vpon peace breakers and enemies to al good order.

1. *Pet.2.of.*

If then neither the signification of the word requireth it, neither wil reason beare it, neither the comely diuision of the orders ecclesiasticall and temporal by anie meanes in the world suffer it, that kinges should beare anie swaie in the Church ; what a straunge kind

kind of flatterie was this in you, to yeld vnto kinges a full power and supreme authoritie in Churches? But what a shameles part is that in you, to affirme by the authoritie of S. Peter and Paul, that the authoritie of kinges is aboue al other authorities? I graunt you, that kinges are by the authoritie of S. Peter set ouer al rulers and gouerners in the ciuile gouernemēt: but not ouer things apperteining to religiō, not ouer the holi ordināces of the church, not ouer the sacramentes and seruice made to appease the wrath of God.

And whereas you saie, that we doe abuse th'authority of S. Peter and Paul to set vp the kingdome of the sea of Rome, it is false. For we leane to the wordes of Christ, when we defend the authoritie of the bishop of Rome: and who so euer doth violently wrest the most plaine woordes of Christe, we iudge him to be a presumptuous felow, we take him for an vnreasonable, naughtie

naughtie and wicked persone. But before I procede vnto other matters, I thinke it expedient briefely to signifie these thinges vnto you.

Dathan and Abiron, for vsing violence towardes the Priestes of God, were with a terrible noise and sodeine earthquake deuowred with all the cōpanie of their wicked complices. Core in like manner with the rest of his conspiracie, for taking vpō them impudētly and wickedly the office of Priestes, were cōsumed with sodeine fier. Oza, bycause he presumed a litle to staie vp with his hād the Ark of promise being like to fall, was sodeinly stryken dead. Ozias the king, bycause he wold haue vsurped the office of a Priest, was disfigured with the lepry. Balsesar the king of Babilō, bicause he tooke the vessels that were appointed to holie vses, and did vse them to riot ād bāket in, lost in one night his kingdome, his riches, and his life. But you, neither doe you feare

the

Laie men plagued of God for taking vpō them the office of Priests. Num, 16.a

2. Re.6.4.

2. Paral. 26.d. Daniel, 5. g.

the euerlasting goulse of hell, neither
doe you tremble at the thunder and
fier of Gods wrath, neither are you a-
fraied of any punishment dewe vnto
your rash presumpteousnes, neither do
you regard the leprie of perpetual infamie, neither doe you take anie care,
lest ye be robbed and spoiled of the riches of the euerlasting kingdome together with the losse of your wordlie
dignitie, and temporal life.

But all these thinges not withstanding, you leaue not to raile at the Popes dignitie. What (a mischiefe) hatred
is this towardes the Pope, so crewell
and so bitter, that you repete one thing
so often? You say thus. *But you contend
not only for the Popes sceptre, but also for
his holy ordinaunces and Decrees: (as
you esteeme them) by the decaie whereof
you thinke that all feare is vanished a-
waie out of mens hartes .* This is true.
For being once agreed that the authoritie of the Pope is good and godly: it
folow-

foloweth, that we muſt obey his ordinaunces and lawes. For as Kinges, to
whome God hath cõmitted the ciuile
gouernement in the common weale,
not contenting them ſelues with the
holie ſcriptures, ſuche as concerne the
ſtate of the cõmon weale (for ſo much
as al things that maie happen in diuers
kindes of cõmon weales, could not be
compriſed in them) haue made other
ſtatutes and lawes, the which all men
are bownd to obey by the law of God:
ſo the Biſhops of Rome, to whome is
committed the rule and gouernement
of the vniuerſal Church (although you
ſwel and burſt at it) doe make decrees,
not only by word, but alſo in writing,
as the times require: the which all we,
that beare the name of Chriſtian men,
are bownd to obſerue and keepe.

As for the feare, the whiche, I
ſaied, was taken quite awaie by you,
I doe impute it, not only to the decaie of the Canon lawe, but muche

T   more

more to the neclecting and defpifing
of the lawe of God . For I faie , that
thrugh the decrees of Luther the fear
of Goddes iudgement and euerlafting
damnation is vtterly quenched. *I haue*
heard, faie you , *that verie manie men*
haue ben by the Canons excedingly en-
ritched:but I haue not heard,that manie
haue ben inftructed in the feare of God.
What M.Haddon ? Such as folow the
ftudie of the ciuile lawe, are they al inftructed in the feare of God?No truly.
And yet you woulde not haue the
whole ciuile lawe to be burned for
that. For the ordinaunces of Princes
are not to be difanulled for the malice
and crafte of the interpretours:but the
lewdnes of fuch as turne all lawes to
their owne gaine and aduantage were
moft feuerely to be reftreined . And
yet you faie, that you doe obferue the
decrees of Popes,bicaufe they are not
a litle profitable . The whiche thing
truly

truly I meruaile muche at , for two
cawſes . Firſt , bicauſe in this pointe
yon diſſent from the moſt holie father Luther , who , as you ſaie , was
ſent from heauen . For he burned all
the Popes decrees in ſuche ſorte , that
he left not one of them . Then , bicauſe all your trade ſo dependeth of
heauen , that you eſteeme all wordlie
thinges no better woorth , but to be
caſt awaie.

Whereas you ſaie , that I doe accuſe your Doctours , bicauſe they
haue cawſed a certaine vnreſtreined
libertie in ſuche as they teache : I
graunt I am yet of that opinion , and
howe true it is , I will declare hereafter.

You complaine afterward , that I
mocke thoſe your holie men . Your
woordes are theſe . *I woulde haue you*
to remembre , what your great Maiſter
of eloquēce wrote ſometime verie wiſe-
ly : that it is an vngodlie coſtume to daly

T ij　　　　*againſt*

against the Gods, whether it be done in earneſt or inſport. You are to ſuperſti-tious, M. Haddon, and I ſee now, that Luther is a holie God with you, and that you praie, that Bucer wil be mer-cifull vnto you, and that you thinke, that you muſt appeaſe with ſacrifice the maieſtie of your Martyr alſo. For theſe men do you eſteeme as Goddes: and therefore I looke when you will erecte aulters vnto them. For els, what other Goddes did I euer ieſt at? Then by like theſe are the Goddes, of whoſe diſpleaſure you warne me to beware. But whereas you ſaie, that I do vſe ie-ſting wordes againſte Chriſte, in that point you folow your maiſters, which are in the myſterie of lying very hand-ſome crafteſmen.

You chalenge me to diſpute, a thing ful vnſeemelie for your perſone. For you vnderſtād not the ſcriptures, no, Luther him ſelfe could not, (being, as he was, altogether blinded in vice and wicked-

wickednes)diſcerne, what great light
was in them. And this is the cauſe why
he is caried to and fro, ſo diuerſly, ſo
dowbtfully, and ſo vncertanly, that to
this daie no man in the world is able to
ſaie for certaine: this was his opinion.
For at one time he affirmeth, that all
ſtandeth in only faith: and he bringeth
me in ſuch a faith, as, if it be once re-
ceued, al good works are put to flight.
At an other time being ouercome by
the very force of truth it ſelfe, and ad-
uertiſed by his frindes to auoid the enuie of men, he ſeeketh out the good
works againe. I would you wold read
ouer my bookes of Iuſtification: and I
iudge, you ſhould not neede to be to
ſeeke in anie point, concerning this
matter, which you now ſpeake of.

We beleeue, ſaie you, *the goſpel.* You
do wel. But the deuils beleeue alſo, and
quake for feare. But what ſaieth the
goſpel? *That there is no dāger*, ſaie you,
of damnation to them, that are graffed in Rom, 3, 4,
       T iij   *Chriſt:*

*Chriſt:that liue not according to the fleſh
but according to the ſpirit.* For I wil not
goe farre from the verie woordes of the
holie ſcriptures, leſt I maie ſeeme in ſome
point to deale not vprightly. That ſeemeth in deede, M. Haddon, to be the
propertie of a perfect lawier, to mainteine the writen word of the law, and
to goe ſometimes directely againſt the
meaning of the lawe. But, I praie you,
what words are thoſe, the which you

Ro.3.d might in no wiſe leaue out? *S. Paul*, ſay
you, *after a long and earneſt diſputation
concludeth, that he thought, that we are
iuſtified by faith without the woorkes of
the law.* What S. Paul hath concluded,
I know very wel: but what you wold
conclude, I doe not yet perfectely vnderſtand. *We muſt needes yeld,* ſaie you:
we are not able to diſcredite the goſpell.
But yet we muſt take that withal out of
the ſelfe ſame S. Paul: *faith that worketh*

Galat.5.a *by charitie.* If we doe keepe theſe thinges
ioyned together : you maie not ſeparate
them,

them, and so reason againste an errour,
whiche hath none other author besides
your owne selfe. By these your wordes I
doe coniecture, M. Haddon, that your
opiniõ is, wheras S. Paul saieth, that no
man is iustified by workes, and againe,
that we must kepe that faith that worketh by charity: (although these things
maie seeme to disagree the one with
the other) yet that we maie not in anie
wise depart from the verie wordes of
the gospel. And how so euer the ioyning together of these thinges maie
seeme to be a hard matter : yet for so
much as S. Paul is the authour of it, it
were a presumpteous acte to go about
to separate what S. Paul hath ioyned.

But I am of a cõtrary opiniõ, that this
only argumét is sufficient to proue, that
S. Paul neuer spake these thigs, bicause
they hãg not together. For what thing
standeth better together and is more
agreable, then the reasoning and doctrine of S. Paul ? And nothing is lesse

agreable then this : that iustice is not geauen without that faith, that woorketh by charitie: and, that no man can be iustified by works. Not the hearers of the law, saieth S. Paul, but the doers of the law, they shal be iustified. They therfore that doe the thing, that is cō-maunded in the law, by the authoritie of S. Paul are iust before God. If that be true, what is more cōtrary to the meaning of S. Paul, then to saie, that no mā is made iust by workes? You therfore knit those things together, that cānot be ioyned. But I would stand in it, and proue by this reason only, if I had none other, that S. Paul wold neuer speak it.

Whereas you saie, that I doe fight or contend against an errour, it soundeth to my commendacion. For what goodlier thing can I doe, them to plucke vp pestilent opinions by the roote?

But when you bring in vpō this, that of the selfe same errour, which I contēd against, ther is none other authour bisides

Onlie faith iustifieth not.

Rom. 2, b.

bifides myne owne felfe, we had nede
of Oedipus to expound it . You haue
a meruelous liking in darke fayinges.
Heard you it euer reported , that I
fhould fay , that the workes of holie
menne were defiled and fpotted with
fynne , and that for this caufe no man
could atteine iuftice by holy workes?
This is the errour whiche I doe ftand
againft. But you wil not once fay fo,
and yet you are fo babifh, that you can
not vtter , what you thinke . But the
fambling of your tongue we wil lette
paffe , and confider howe fowly you
are ouerfeene in weightie matters .

You faie , that woorkes are not a-
uaileable to iuftification, and yet, you
fay, that workes are not to be defpifed,
for fo much as we haue both thefe o-
pinions grounded vpon the authoritie
of S. Paul. The principal deuifours and
Archbuylders of your newe gofpell,
whome you worfhippe as Goddes, of
whome you learned thefe myfteries,
went

Luthers most dānable doctrine touching Workes.

went further then so, and said plainly, that al the workes, the which holy mē doe, are not only vnprofitable, but also vncleane and spotted through the contagion of originall synne. For they doe not beleeue, that originall or engraffed synne, the whiche we tooke from the spring, is quite blotted out in the baptisme of life: but that it groweth still, and casteth out such a deale of vncleane vice, that all the doinges of holy men, although thei be done by the mocion and instincte of the holie Ghost, yea and referred to the glorie of Christ, yet they are deadlie synnes, and deserue of iustice the punishment of euerlasting damnation, without the great goodnes and mercie of Christ. If it be but litle ciuilitie, as you saie, (and as yt pleaseth your great lawier to write also) to iudge of a lawe, vnlesse it be thoroughly weighed and considered: reade diligently the bookes of **Luther**, Melanchthon, Caluine, and other

other your learned men, and you fhall
fee, that this was their opinion, or rather that the whole fomme of the doctrine, whiche they profeffed, ftoode
vpon this opinion, that they condemned al workes as wicked and fynfull.

You fee here an extreme defpera-
tion of atteining vnto iuftice. For if no
man can be iuft, but he only that kee-
peth the law, as S. Paule faith: if not he *Rom.2.b.*
that faith Lord, Lord, fhal enter into *Mat.7.c.*
the kingdome of heauen, as our Lord
him felfe declareth plainely, but he
that doth the wil of the Father: if iuftice, as the Prophetes witneffe, is a
fhunning of all vices, and an earneft
defire to folowe vertue and honeftie:
if iuftice côfifteth in cleanes of life, in
innocencie, in good and feemelie ordre of the mind, in holy conuerfation,
in newnes of heauenly life, and in the
côtinual exercife of charity: and we be
able, neither to keepe the commaundementes of God, neither to forfake
vice,

vice, neither to folowe honeſtie, neither to doe the woorkes of charitie, if
it be ſo, that, (wil we, nil we) we muſt
needes beare the yoke of ſynne : by
what meanes in the worlde ſhall we
be able to aſſure our ſelues of the ſtate
of iuſtice, through the grace and mercie of Chriſte, if Chriſte hath not yet
broken the force of ſynne in vs by the
merite of his bloude , as your maiſters
ſay? You ſee here, after what ſort that
man, that was (as you ſay) ſent from
heauen, hath cut of by his deuiſes all
hope of atteining vnto iuſtice. But ſee
on the other ſide, how wittily he hath
deuiſed a remedie, and how al the reſt
haue folowed him.

He ſaieth , that no man hath anie
particular iuſtice through the grace of
Chriſt , but that the iuſtice of Chriſte
him ſelfe is applied to all beleeuers by
faith, in ſuch ſorte , that the iuſtice of
Chriſt is no leſſe accõpted and eſtee-
med in euerie faithfull man (be he ne-

uer so wicked)then if it were that mãs
owne iustice, that staieth vppon faith
onely. He sayth therefore,that it cometh to passe through this faith,by the
which euerie Christian man assureth
him selfe that he is in the fauour of
God,that the iustice of Christ is imputed to be the iustice of that man , that
beleeueth. You haue here the law of
Luther , so muche as concerneth this
present place,thoroughly scanned, so
that you can not iustly complaine of
any wrong done vnto Luther.

Nowe consider you on the other
side,what a meruelouse easie waie he
hath deuised to atteyne vnto iustice.
For to whome shal it not be a very easie matter(if he wil beleeue Luther)to
say thus with him selfe? This geare
goeth gaily wel with me. I am in high
fauour with God for my faithes sake.
It is so,that the iustice of Christ is become mine owne iustice. I am therefore as iuste as Paule, as Peter, yea as
the

the moſte bleſſed mother of God her
ſelfe:forſomuch as no man hath the cōmendation of any particulare iuſtice
through the grace of Chriſt: but there
is one only iuſtice applied indifferētly
to al ſuch as keepe the faith:the which
bicauſe it can not be higher or lo-
wer,greater or leſſer,it foloweth,that
I am ſo iuſte my ſelfe (although there
remaine ſynne in me)as he that is moſt
iuſt .

You ſee now,how by the diligence
of this excellent felow, all feare is put
to flight , preſumption ſet on tip toe,
boldhardineſſe confirmed in her full
ſtrēgth and force.For ſo much as therfore a man can not be earneſtly prouoked to doe any vertuouſe acte , being either in extreme deſpaire or elles
in extreme preſumption : and Luther
hath in parte cutte of all hope of iuſtice , and in parte hath brought his
diſciples into a moſte preſumpteous
affiaunce of atteyning vnto it , by deuiſing

uiſing an other iuſtice that was neuer
hearde of before : is it not euident,
although to eſchewe enuie he ſpake
ſometymes manie thinges concerning the woorkes of iuſtice , that he
quenched all loue and deſire of well
doing ? For , I praye you , by what
meanes wil you encourage a faint man
to doe anie honeſt thing , if he haue
learned before of ſome graue perſon,
that ſuch as endeuour them ſelues to
doe anie vertuouſe acte,doe but looſe
their labour ?

Agayne , howe will you driue the
feare of euerlaſting damnation into
them , that are altogether careleſſe,
and preſume ſo muche of their owne
iuſtice , that they beleeue , that no
man doth paſſe them in any excellencie of iuſtice ? Wherefore no man
in the worlde wil euer bend him ſelfe
to doe holie woorkes (if he hearken
to the Doctrine of Luther) for ſo
much as it is impoſsible , that any man,
being

being either in extreme despaire of
honestie, or elles in extreme presumption of saluation, should earnestly endeuour him selfe to folow godlines.

But, you wil say, that it may be, that
Luther did exhorte his countrey men
to good workes in his Bookes and sermons. I know that wel. So did Epicure
him selfe, when he had with Decrees
taken away al vertue, yet woulde he
dispute now and then of vertue very
notably. I consider not, what the light
felowe saith sometime, either through
the inclination of nature, or elles for
feare of enuie: but I see, what is most
agreeable to his decrees and doctrine.
This is most vndowbtedly true that,
when thinges are either vtterly des-
paired, or certainely assured, there is
no man, that wil take any great paines
in folowing of vertue. Therefore, for
so much as Luther hath shewed him
selfe to be the authour both of this extreme desperation, as also of that, extreme

treme preſumptiō: who doth not ſee, that, by him, al good and godly works hath ben quite ouerthrowen ? Wherfore this was in him a great fault, a cruel deede , a ſhameleſſe acte , a wicked crime, an intolerable villanie : but yet was that other muche more heynouſe and deteſtable , that he woulde wreſt the godlie and wiſe ſaying of S . Paule after his owne pleaſure , and abuſe the teſtimonie of the holy Apoſtle to confirme his ſhameles opiniō and doctrine.

But let vs now ſee , howe you will make Luther the defacer of all vertue, labour, diligence , and induſtrie : to agree with S. Paule, the high Schoolemaiſter of al holines, religion and vertue ? S.Paule, ſay you, ſaith, that there is nothing auailable to ſaluation , beſides faith that worketh by charitie . The ſelfe ſame Paul ſaith, that no man is iuſtified by woorkes. It is therefore euidēt, ſay you, that theſe two points are ioyned together.

V But

But I say on the other side, that, for so much as these things do disagree excedingly the one fró the other, it is impossible, that euer S. Paul should ioyne them together. But that it may be sene how il your maisters vnderstãd S. Paul: it is to be cósidered, what his meaning was, what he went about, what intention and purpose he had, as in al his Epistles, so especially in this, whiche he wrot to the Romains, out of the which you haue taken these testimonies corruptly vnderstood.

A sound and catholike doctrine touching vvorkes.

What was then the purpose of S. Paul in this Epistle? Doubtleisse this, to withdraw men from all affiaunce in worldly things to the faith of Christ. He teacheth therfore, that there was no sure staie of saluation, neither in nature, neither in the ordinaunces of the olde Law. For it was neither nature, neither the law, that toke away iniquity, and brought in iustice, in the which only stãdeth our saluation and honour.

For

For only iuftice procureth the fauour
of God towards mankind.

And firft that nature of it self holpe
nothing towardes iuftice, he proueth
by this argument: bicaufe all menne,
which ftaied vpō nature ōly, although
they were endewed with excellente
witte, yet they were fpotted with iniquitie, with vncleane luftes, malice,
couetoufnes, difhoneftie of life, crueltie, and with other vices vnfemely to
be named. As though he fhoulde faie
thus. If the excellencie of nature, if the
fharpeneffe of witte, if the force of the
mind and reafon had holpen any thing
towards iuftice: then had the Gentils,
which excelled in nature, in wit, and
in reafon, ben well appointed and fur-
nifhed for al helpes and ftaies of iuftice.
But the brightnes of iuftice fhone not
emongeft them: (for they were full
of iniquity and vices without number)
wherefore the excellencie of nature
holpe them nothing to liue iuftly.

Then turning him self to the Iewes, he vrgeth the selfe same argument, but more earnestly and with greater force. For he had entered into a most ernest cōflict with the Iews, as touching the ceremonies of the old Law: the which the Iewes, thought necessarie to kepe stil, beleuing that the soules were purged by them. Against whom S. Paule disputeth, declaring that al the ordinā-ces of the Law, which were but only shadowes of Iustice, vanished away at the coming of the true and perfect iustice : and that suche as referred the cause of iustice vnto those shadowes, appaired the honour of Christe. For they distrusted the power and merite of Christ. And therefore writing vn-

Gala.5.a. te the Galathians, he saith. If you be circumcided, Christe shal doe you no good. In like manner writing to the Hebrewes, he saieth, that the Lawe

Hebr.7.c. broughte nothinge to perfection, but that it stirred vp men with shadowes only

only and Images to the hope of the faluation to come. And those ceremonies and sacrifices ordeined by the law, the which in this place and in the epistle to the Galathians, he termeth the woorkes of the Lawe, writing to the Hebrewes, he calleth them the iustices of the flesh. S. Paul therefore speaketh of this part of the Lawe, whiche consisteth in shadowes of iustice, which conteineth the cleansing of the bodie, and reacheth not vnto the soule, whe̅ he saith, that no man is iustified by the woorkes of the Lawe. This was the meaning of S. Paule, and the conclusion of that so long and earnest disputation, which you speake of. As though he would saie thus. If Circumcision, if the sprinkeling of asshes, if the offering vppe of brute beastes, if the other cleansinges of the Law did make men iust, it should solow, that al the Iewes which obserued and kept orderly the holie ceremonies of the Lawe, attei-

Hebr.9.6.

V iij   ned

ned vnto iustice. But it is euident, that
al such Iewes as leaned and trusted vnto the lawe only, were naughty men,
vncleane liuers, backbiters, murderers,
and wicked persones. Wherefore they
receiued not the fruit of iustice by the
law. And so it remaineth, that no man
is iustified by the workes of the lawe.

If you haue any wit at al this reason
concluding so aptely maie teach you,
what workes S. Paule meant, when he
saied, that no man is iustified by the
works of the law. For otherwise what
could any man haue said more vnapt-
ly, woorse hanging together, and lesse
to the purpose? If S Paule had said, that
the Iewes had excelled in cleane liuig,
in godlines and innocētie, and yet that
such vertuos dedes had helped nothig
towardes iustice: if he had vpon these
thinges concluded, that they were not
iustified by the workes of the law: you
might well haue gessed, that by the
works of the law, he had vnderstoode
the

the deedes of vertue and godlines. But
S. Paul neuer ſpake any ſuch word. No,
he declareth plainly by the teſtimonie
of the law it ſelſe, that ſuch as beſtowed much diligéce and labour about the
ordináces of the law, wer very naugh
ty and wicked men: whereupon he có-
cludeth, that the works of the law did
not iuſtiſie. What then? Think you that
S. Paul doth cóclude his argumét vpon
things that are not proued and agreed
vpon, as you do? If you preſume to ſay
ſo, then ſhal you falſly charge the wiſedome of the holy man with the crime
of raſhnes and ſolie. The whiche thing
how far it is from S. Paul, is wel know-
en to al ſuche as ſtudie his writinges
with a pure intétion. For what can be
deuiſed more witty and better applied, fuller of wiſedome and more earneſtly endited, then the reaſoninge
and ſtyle of S. Paule? His Argu-
ments are al ſo wel linked within them
ſelues the one dependeth of an other
Works of
the lavve
do not iu-
ſtiſie.

V iiij   ſo apt-

so aptly, they are knit together so finely, the seconde cometh in vppon the
first, the last answereth vnto the mid-
delmost so necessarily, he chaineth all
the whole discourse in one, with such
an excellent order and cunning, that it
is not possible to finde any one pointe
in al his talke, that agreeth not wonderfully wel with his meaning expres-
sed in any other place before. It is
therfore gathered by the reason it self
of S. Paule, (which concludeth verie
aptly) what workes of the Law those
are, by the which, he saieth, no man is
made iust. They are those workes, the
which S. Paule pluckerh at euermore
in his disputatiõ, against the which he
contendeth moste earnestly, from the
affiance of the which he endeuoureth
to withdraw the Iewes : for the cause
of the which he was cruelly assaulted
of the Iewes, and oftentimes put in
great peril of his life.

Now if you desire to know, wherfore

fore these sacrifices of the Lawe, are
called the woorkes of the lawe : howe
those workes also, which are done by
the strength of reason only, (vnto the
which men leane and trust to muche,
and therefore require against al reason
a reward for them, not accordinge to
grace, but of duetie) are to be accounted emongest the workes of the Law:
how the workes of godlines, charitie,
humanitie and vertue are to be referred vnto the power and holinesse of
faith : in how great blindenes thei are,
the whiche not vnderstandinge these
places of S. Paule, and wresting them
from their true meaning, abuse them
to proue, that the workes of holy men
are not only vnprofitable, but also wic
ked : I haue declared these thinges
plainely ynough in my bookes writen
of iustice, which are now abroad: and
therfore I thinke it not nedefull to repete them againe in this place. I doe
not therefore pul in sunder such things
as

as are ioyned together by reaſon : but
the things, that are diſagreable and cōtrary the one to the other, I can not a-
bide to ſee them hudled vp together
without reaſon. For, ſeing that S Paule
doth moſt earneſtly exhorte vs to the
loue of vertue, innocēcy and charitie :
ſaying, that euery mã ſhalbe rewarded
according to his workes : ſeing that he
affirmeth, that al ſuch as are ioyned vn
to Chriſt, are waſhed and clenſed of al
vncleanes of ſyn , and are become holy : yea and that they are for cleannes
of life and brightnes of vertue compa-
rable to the ſterres : what thing in the
world could haue bē ſpoke more cōtrary to this ſaying, ſo oftē and ſo cōſtant-
ly repeted, then to affirme, that ſuche,
as the Apoſtle reporteth to be cleane,
holy, cleere, moſt excellētly beutified
with the brightnes of heauēly vertues,
are ſpotted with ſinnes, and that their
workes are not only nothing auailable
towards the heap and perfection of iuſtice, but alſo that thei are vnclene, ſin-

ful, and disteined with the contagious
infection of our corrupted nature ?

But let vs côsider the place of S. Paul
it selfe, which you alleage. *S. Paule*, say *Rom. 8.a*
you, *warāteth, that there is no danger of
dānation in such as are ēgraffed in Christ.
But we take that withal, that foloweth in
the same place: such as liue not accordig to
the flesh, but according to the spirit.* You
doe wel to take in that withal. But let
vs see, what are they, that walke, as S.
Paul saith, accordig to the flesh? Doutlesse thei are those, which are, as S. Paul *Gal. 5.c.*
writing to the Galathians saith, corrup
ted and defiled with auoutrie, with the
filthie pleasure of the bodie , with vncleanes of life, with cursed superstition, with hatred , with making debate
and strife betweene men , with stirring vppe troubles and discorde , with
pestilente sectes , with enuie , murder and creweltie , with drunkenes,
and glottonie , with these and other
the like vices , of the which saieth the
Apostle,

Apoſtle, I tel you now, as I haue alſo told you before, that who ſoeuer doth ſuch thinges, ſhal neuer poſſeſſe the inheritaunce of God. He excepteth no man, he ſaied not, vnleſſe they haue faith : for it is like that this light of the new Goſpell had not yet ſhined in his eyes. And what they are, that liue according to the Spirit, the Apoſtle declarerh, ſaying, that they are ſuche, as enioye the moſt ſweete and pleſaunt fruit of the Spirite. Nowe the fruit of the ſpirit, as he ſaith, is charity, gladnes, peace, conſtancie in vertue, gentlenes, bowntifulnes, faith (not meaning that ſlacke faith, but ſuch a faith, as is ioyned with obedience)mekenes, continencie, and other the like commendable vertues, againſt the whiche no man can procede by law. And yet a manne might doe it, in caſe they were ſpotted and defiled with any ſinne. S. Paule therfore doth in no wiſe promiſe the inheritance of the euerlaſting

kingdome

kingdom to them that leane to the only faith of Luther : but to suche as doe
good workes, and direct all the doings
of their life to the glorie of Christ.

Here wil you crie out againe, and
protest the faith of Gods and men, that
this is a notable slaunder, and not to be
borne : and that you did not put suche
affiaunce in onely Faith, but that you
determined withal, that good workes
were also necessarie vnto saluation.
I will not as now dispute, howe farre
from al reason it is, to put any hope or
affiaunce of saluation in a thing, that is
vncleane and wicked. And therfore,
if al workes, as Luther saith, are defiled with sinne: then are thei not to be
wrought diligetly, but to be neglected
and despised. But omitting this matter,
we wil consider, how these works, be
they neuer so euil, yet must thei nedes
be had of you : (for this pointe haue I
searched out with much diligéce.) Bicause, say they, they folow faith of necessitie :

ceſsitie : not for that, that workes doe make the way vnto ſaluation, (for as of them ſelues they came not into iudgement) but bicauſe there is in them a certaine fruit of Faith. For as a tree of it ſelf bringeth forth fruit by the ſtrēgth of nature , ſo dothe faith of neceſsitie bring forth workes. Theſe two points of doctrine do your maiſters teach: but both the one and the other is falſe .

For firſt of al, the works themſelues do deſerue either ſaluatiō or dānation : and the workes ſhalbe weied by them ſelues in the balāce of Gods iudgemēt. *Pſal. 61. d.* Otherwiſe Dauid woulde neuer haue ſaid, that God wil rēder vnto euery mā *Ro. 2. b.* according to his workes: S. Paul would neuer haue ſaid, that God wil rewarde euery man according to the qualitie of his worke good or il : he would neuer haue ſraied men with that threat, that *2. Cor. 5. b* we muſt all ſtand before the iudgemēt ſeat of Chriſt, to make account euery *Ro. 14. d.* man , of what ſo euer good or euill he

hath

hath cōmitted in this life: and that eue
ry mans own works shalbe most exactly tryed: to make short (for so much as
the testimonies, that may be alleaged,
are infinite) the most holy iudge himselfe would neuer haue said, that such
as haue done well, shal goe into life e- *Mat. 25.d*
uerlasting, and such as haue done euil,
into euerlasting fier.

Then that other point is also false,
that good workes do necessarilie arise
out of Luthers faith. I graunt you, that
good workes do folowe my faith, but
not yours, M. Haddon, if you beleeue
Luther. How so say you? Bicause faith *Ro. 10.C.*
cometh by hearsay, ād hearsay cometh
by the worde of Christ. For so much *The faith*
therfore as my faith, that is to say, the *of the chu*
faith of the holy Churche is grounded *che is fru-*
vpon the wordes of Christ, and Christ *ful.*
him selfsaith, that al such as do not repente, shall be condemned: that faith
and credit, which I geue to the words
of Christ, causeth me to do penaunce.

Againe

Io, 15.b. Againe when our Lorde saieth : you shalbe my friendes , if you will do the thinges ,that I commaunde you to do: if I belceue the wordes of Christe,and desire earnestly to be receiued into his frindship : I wil endeuour my selfe to the vttermost of my power,to do such thinges as are by him commaunded. And whereas Christ telleth vs before, that not he that calleth him Lorde,

Mat.7.c. shal come to haue the possession of the kingdome of heauen,but he that ordereth al his workes according to the wil of the euerlasting Father : If my faith be not faint , if it be liuelie and strong and inflamed with the desire of that kingdome:I am stirred vp by this faith to directe al my doinges according to the wil of God. See you not now,after what sort this faith conteineth holy workes within her wombe , which are engendred of the fruictefulnes of her.?

Now let vs see the faith of Luther, whe-

whether it be able to bring foorth any
fruicte, that is quicke. No without
doubt. First of all, bicause al workes
as he saieth, seeme they neuer so holy,
are disteined with synne. And no man
maketh any account or estimation of
a thing that is vncleane and spotted
with synne. Moreouer bicause (as he
mainteineth) the force and strength of
inordinate lust is so great, that he thinketh it impossible to withstand it by
any meanes in the world. Seing then
it is impossible for any man to endeuour him selfe to doe any good workes, vnlesse he doe firste destroie the
kingdome of synne: and the kingdome
of synne can not possibly be destroied,
if it be true that Luther saith: it remaineth, that no man can possibly do any
holy workes. For who is so mad, that
he wil bestowe his labour in any thing
in vaine and without fruicte? Last of
al bicause Luther hath determined
such a kind of iustice, as needeth not

X the

Luthers faith fruitles.

the healpe of any doing or worke. For
if I perfuade my felfe, that the iuftice of
Chrift is applied vnto me by faith, no
leffe then if it were mine own iuftice:
and that I haue atteined vnto that
mofte high and perfecte iuftice of
Chrift, although I lyue and continue
in fyn: with what defire, care, or hoo-
fulnes fhould I be pricked forewarde
to doe any good worke ? Forfomuche
therefore as Luther both defpifeth holy works, and cutteth of al hope of honeftie and holineffe: and by this faith,
which he hath deuifed, taketh away al
feare of punifhment : is it not euident,
that he is the ouerthrower of holy
workes, the deftroier of honeftie and
godlines? although he pretéded fometime to ftirre vppe his difciples to the
loue of vertue? Wherefore it is manifeftly feene, that this man of God, whó
you cómend aboue the heauens, what
with bringing good workes into contempt, and what with caufing men to
def.

despaire of honestie, and by teaching a vaine affiaunce in his newly deuiled iustice, hath quite taken away al desire of doing and working.

Let vs now come to your other cõplait, in the which you say, that I make no end of babling, while I lament the vnsensiblenes of Luther, which tyed vp the wil of man with necessitie of destenie. *Truly*, say you, *I am not wonte to be moued with angre, and yet now I can hold my selfe no longer.* It is my great fault. M. Haddon, that I haue by this my babling as you terme it, caused you (being so gentle and soft by nature as you are) to rage like a mad man. Wel let vs then heare the talke of this felow which is iustly prouoked to plaie the bedlome. What saie you sir?

This slaunder, say you, is not only blockish and ignorant, but also blasphemous: and suche, as the verie stoones them selues, whiche you speake of, if they could speake, would not tourne it against

X ij   *our*

our men. I know, M. Haddon, that that place of Rhetorik is wel applied to this vehement kind of speach, whiche you now vse. And therfore I looke, when you wil bring in those stones, and make them to speake. You say afterwarde.

But haue you an eye vnto the Scriptures a litle while, and repent yeu. Truly I haue a diligent eye vnto them : but I haue not as yet gone to schoole with doctour Walter . Now therefore I am attétiue, if I may, by your good instructions come to a cleerer vnderstáding of the secrets of God. I wuld ye would vtter vnto vs this wonderful stuffe of your high wisedome. Well: what say you then?

Predesti-
nation.

God the Father hath chosen vs in Christe , before the foundations of the world were laied , to the ende that we should be holie and vnreproueable before him. How knowe you, M. Walter, I pray you, that you are one of the chosen? Againe which be they, that are holie

ly and vnreprooueable before God?
Doubteles they are such, as are void of
al synne. But by Luthers doctrine, you
can not be without sinne. For he saith,
that sin is not al put out, but that a certaine steime of vice breaketh out of it,
as it were out of a burning fornace, the
which deuoureth and consumeth all
thinges round about it: whereupon it
foloweth, that no man is vnreprooueable. But if you peraduenture will
say, that you speake not of your selfe,
but of al mankinde : if no man in the
worlde be deliuered from al synne (as
Luther teacheth) then doth it followe, that no man can be vnreproueable.

You heare, say you , *the election or
choise of God out of the gospell, the which
you so muche detest in your talke : and
you heare the tyme also*. Doe I detest
the election of God? With what face
dare you saie so? In what place? in
what woordes? before whome? who
X iiij   is your

is your witnesse? who was made priuie? in which of all my writinges can
you conuince me to haue sp:ken any
such word? Haue you such a pleasure,
to babble out, what so euer cometh
vpon your tongues end?

Neither is this necessitie of Gods ele-
ctiō say you, an occasion whie we should
yeald our selues wholly to felowe the plea-
sures of the bodie and vncleane vices (as
it pleaseth you full vngodly to sport) but
that we should be holie and vnreproue-
able before God through charitie: as it is
declared by the expresse woordes of the
gospell. Although I vnderstande you
not verie wel, yet I thinke you make
with me. For I saie the verie same
thing, that we are not compelled by
any necessitie to doe euil: for so much
as God hath geauen vs (as it is manifestly prooued by many places of the
Scripture) a free choise of life and
death. Wherefore we are free, and
not tied with any fatal necessitie.

Free Wil.

But

But here again forgetting what you
saidbefore,you alleage certaine places
out of S.Paule, by the which as I imagine , you intende to take from vs our
freedome of will.

It is God , faie you , *that woorketh in*
vs both to will and to doe.S. Paul in thefe   Phil. 2. b.
woordes hath tyed vppe our wil, and re-
ftreined our power. Neither did S.Paul
euer thinke it , neither did your maifters vnderftande the meaninge of S.
Paule. Muche leffe is it to be thought
that you, being farre inferior to them,
fhould be able to atteine to the Apoftles meaning in this matter.We graũt
this to be true, that our thoughtes and
works(fuch as are wel begon and ended)ought to be referred vnto god,by
whofe power thei are don.For except
Godhad called me backe,when I rãne
into all mifchiefe : excepte he had ad-
uertifed me by the inftincte of his fpi-
rit,that I fhuldnot caft my felfe head-
lõg into euerlafting thraldome:except
                    X iiij   he had

he had with his wholesome grace and
sure aide so strengthened me, that I
might be able to doe the godly worke
which he commaunded me to doe : I
could neither haue done, neither yet
haue thought any good thing: but what
so euer studie or diligence I had emploied either in deuising, or els in doing any good worke, it had benne all
in vaine. Yet this much we say, that
we may, not yeald our assent to the in-
spiration of God, that we may, not regard his liberalitie, that we maie, refuse his gentle offer, yea and leese,
thorough synne and wickednesse, the
grace, that is alreadie goten. I, saith
our Lorde, doe stand at the doore and
knocke. He saith not, I doe breake o-
pen the doores, or I doe pul them out
of the hinges, or I doe breake in by
violence: but only, I doe knocke: that
is to say, I doe warne: I doe declare
the peril that may ensewe : I do shew
the hope of saluation; I doe promise
healpe:

Apoc.3.d.

healpe : and I doe allure men vnto me
by benefites. Yet you faie.

*What then? Is there no difference be-
twene vs and a ftone ?* He muft needes
be more vnfenfible then a ftone , that
wold gather after that fort. As though
I had gathered this, M. Waulter, out of
the fobre meaning of S. Paul , and not
out of the dronken dreming of Luther:
as it fhal appeere hereafter.

The felfe fame S.Paul, faie you , *calleth vs the coadiutours of God , and
commaundeth vs to woorke our faluation
in feare and trembling.* See you
not then , by he verie woordes of S.
Paul, that the freedome of will is buyl-
ded vpon his authoritie , the whiche
Luther goeth about to ouerthrowe?
For wherefore fhoulde he haue faied,
that we are the coadiutours of God, if
a man coulde doe nothing towardes
the woorke , that God woorketh in
vs? Wherfore fhould he haue warned
vs to woorke our faluation , if it were
                                        not

not in our power to doe it ? But you,
euen as in that ioyning of faith that
woorketh by charitie, and of woorkes
thatare vnprofitable,laboured in vaine
to glew together by the teſtimonie of
S.Paul ſuch things, as can not poſsibly
be ioyned : in like manner you would
bring to paſſe , by this your ſingular
wit , the which we ſimple idiotes can
not reache vnto , that freedome and
bondage ſhould be knit together with
a moſt faſt knot of frindſhip , and that
by the ſayings and meaning of S.Paul.
And therfore at one time you alleage
certaine places of S.Paul,that maketh
for freedome : at an other time you
bring other teſtimonies, the which,as
you thinke, confirmeth bondage. But
I might proue by this argument alone,
that you could neuer ſo muche asſuſ-
pecte, what great wiſedome was in S.
Paul:(as in whoſe heart reſted the ſpirite of Chriſt) bicauſe you labour to
prooue, that he ſpake ſuch thinges , as
                                             are

are verie contrarie.

And yet you saie, that I doe abhorre the Gospel. In deede I do abhorre Luthers Gospell : and when I name Luther, I meane Melanchthon also, and Bucer and Caluine, and the reste of your Bassaes. For although they be diuers channels of waters, yet came thei al out of one fountaine. But whereas you abuse the testimonies of S. Paul to auowch your vngodlines, me thinketh it is a thing not to be borne. You saie afterward.

You shall know by three wordes of S. Paul. What shall I know ? *I am able to doe al thinges in Christe, whiche strengtheneth me.* And S. *Augustine comprised the selfe same sentence in other wordes verie finely: God, saieth he, crowneth his owne woorkes in vs.* Verie well. But to what purpose bring you these thinges ? Be we of them, thinke you, that take parte with Pelagius ? Did we euer saie, that we coulde doe anie

Philip. 4.

anie good and commendable woorke
by our owne ſtrength and diligence?
No truly. And yet you in this place, as
though you had wonne the field, begynne to vaunt your ſelfe without all
modeſtie, and ſaie.

What is it? See you not how the proui-
dence of God is fortified by the authoritie
of the holy ſcriptures? And yet you vn-
derſtande, that it is not the mother of
ſynne, but the nourſe of all vertue. O M.
Haddon, what agew fitte is this that
holdeth you? What damned ſprites
are theſe that vexe you? What plagues
of ſynne are theſe that folow you vp
and downe? Where haue you heard
or read, that I doe denie the prouidence of God, or that I doe affirme,
that out of it there ſhoulde ariſe anie
euil in the worlde? Is this no furie? Is
this no madnes? Is this no impudencie?
You coulde neuer gather anie ſuche
thing out of my writinges: vnleſſe you
thinke perhaps, that the prouidence of
God

God can not ſtand by anie meanes, except the freedome of mans will be taken quite awaie. If you thinke ſo , you are worſe then mad. If you thinke not ſo, and yet wil charge me falſely withall: you are paſt al ſhame. And yet you ſaie.

But let vs goe vnto the fountaines themſelues , out of the which although there flowe moſt ſweete honey , yet hath your moſt corrupted mind ſucked out of them verie peſtilent poiſon. O M. Waulter, how much it eaſeth your ſtomake, to vomite out this railing poiſon, with the whiche you are glotted ? S. Paul writing to the Galathians ſaied: would God they might be cut of that trouble you. In like manner doe I praie vnto Chriſt my God, the authour and geauer of vncorrupted and vpright life : that all ſuch as come to hādle the holy ſcriptures , with an vncleane minde, with fowle eyes, with an vngodlie intent , maie at the length repent them ſelues: *Gala.5.ſ.*

felues : or els, if they wil not, that they
maie be put to moft fharp punifhment
and horrible death , raither then to
bring fo much mifchiefe into the common weale of the Church .

In this place, (good Chrift) what a
ftirre you keepe ? how wonderfully
you laie about you ? how you vaunt
your felfe in wordes like a conque-
rour? You doe, in your owne conceit,
not only beate backe the hornes , as
you faied before , but alfo ouerthrow
and difcomfite a whole armie . You
bring diuers places of S. Paule , which
are nothing neceffarie, to prooue that
there is a prouidence. After that you
laie out againft me with open mowth,
as though I fhould cóclude that by the
prouidence of God, if there were any,
a man were bereft of his fenfes. The
which is in deede a verie fhameles lie.
For you neuer read anie fuch word in
my oratió. Neither doth it folow, that
a man fhould be like a blocke, of gods
pro-

prouidence, but of Luthers madnes, by
the which, cõtrarie to gods prouidéce,
he taketh awaie the freedome of the
will. But you peraduéture thinke, that
the lewdnes of Luther is ſo ioyned
with this prouidence, that who ſo euer
ſpeketh erneſtly againſt Luthers madnes, he muſt needes appaire Gods prouidence. But I am of a contrarie mind,
that who ſo euer foloweth the lewdnes of Luther, doth ſo much as in him lieth, ouerthrow the prouidéce of God.

But what meaneth this ? Wherfore
declare you not in plaine words, what
you wold haue? wherfore vſe you ſuch
darke parables ? wherfore forſake you
the name of Babilonical bondage, and
take vp violétli the name of prouidéce?
Luther ſaied, that free wil was either a
thing of a title only, or els a title without a thing. He ſaith, that mã doth ſuffer, and not doe: that he is drawen, and
doth not deliberat: that he is onli an in-
ſtrumét, the which God turneth, as him
liſteth:

lifteth:that God driueth him foreward
and pulleth him backeward as his ple-
fure is:and that he vfeth him as a fawe
or a hatchet:and that man hath no power or ftrength in the worlde to doe
either good or euyl.But he correcteth
him felfe afterward in this manner. I
did il, faith he, to faie that free wil before grace is a thing of a title only : I
ought rather to haue faied fimply,that
free wil is a feined deuife in thinges,or
els a title without a thing.For fo much
as it is in no mâs power once to thinke
anie good or euil (as it is in the article
of Wicleffe condemned at Conftâce)
but all thinges doe come to paffe of a
mere and abfolute necefsitie. He am-
plifieth thefe things afterwardes with
manie wordes, and ftreineth him felfe
verie fore , to prooue that the mind is
alwaies tied, the wil bownd, the power to doe taken awaie , yea in fuche
fort,that we can not pofsibly not only
doe , but alfo not fo much as thinke
                                    vpon

vpon anie thing good or bad. Thefe
thinges taught Melanchthon alfo, and
fo did Caluine with great copie of
woordes, and other, whome I here
omit. To be fhort, the fomme of this
doctrine was, that ther is no difference
betwene vs and anie other woorking
toole. Thefe are the thinges, whiche
your Doctours teach openly.

But I faie, (and al good men, al holy
men, all men endewed with godlines
and vertue auowch my faying to be
true) that to teach this your doctrine
is a heinoufe offence, a defperat boldnes, a deteftable owtrage, a courfed
acte. For graunt me this doctrine to be
true, and I faie, that lawes are taken
quite awaie, counfells put to filence,
honeft craftes ouerthrowen, learning
defaced, ciuile gouernement difordered, the determination of right and
wrong confounded. I faie moreouer
(for it foloweth of necefsitie) that man
is bereft of his fenfes, fpoiled of counfel,

Y   depri-

depriued of reſon, and brought to that paſſe, that there is no difference betwene him and a ſtone caſt out of the hand. I ſaie alſo, that the warninges of the lawe of God, the commaundementes, counſells, exhortations, and threatninges, the rewardes aſsigned vnto vertue, and the puniſhmentes appointed for ſinne and wickednes, were to no purpoſe enregeſtred in the holie ſcriptures for the perpetuall remembraunce of them. All theſe inconueniences folow vpõ the doctrine of Luther neceſſarily. There foloweth alſo an other incõuenience, the which, (to conceiue it only in heart) is the moſt horrible blaſphemie, that euer could be ſpoken or ymagined, that God the moſt holy and vpright iudge, in whom no iniquitie can poſsibly reſt, doth vniuſtli puniſh that offence, of the which him ſelfe was (as Luther ſaieth) a perſwader, a forcible mouer, yea the doer. For euẽ as, when a murder is cõmitted, not the ſweard, but he that committed

the murder with the fwerd is arained :
fo, right and reafon would, that not I,
which was forced to doe a mifchiefe
by a certaine fatal violence,the which
I could not withftand,but he that vfed
fuche forcible meanes towardes me,
fhuld beare the blame of it. I faie therfore,that this point, out of the whiche
foloweth fo many and fuche horrible
mõfters,is fo heinoufe and wicked,that
if al the reft were gathered together,
in cõparifon of this, they might feeme
to be very light.For it doth both ouerthrow quite the focietie and good order emongeft men : and it doth falfly
charge that our moft holie Lord and
bowntiful father with the crime of vniuftice and creweltie.This therfore do
I faie,iudge,define, determine, taught
by infinite teftimonies of the holy fcripture,moued therũto bi the monumẽts
of al holy mẽ that euer wrote either of
old time or in our daies , inftructed by
many difputatiõs of the moft excellẽt

philofophers, endewed alfo with vpright reafon, the whiche was wont to
be called the lawe of nature and God:
that this abfolute or fatale necefsitie,
with the which Luther tied vp all the
doinges and thoughtes of men, without exception, can neither ftand, nor
enter into the mind of anie reafonable
man: and that, who fo euer deuifed it
firft, was of al men, that euer liued vpon the earth, moft vile and wicked.

This is that, which I faied. This I
would haue you to confute, and to declare, either that Luther neuer fpake
it, or els if he did, to prooue that he did
it vpon good cófideration. The which
thing of like you doe not (peraduéture
for feare of enuie) and therefore you
fhifte your felfe into a difputation of
Gods election, and you goe about to
prooue by the teftimonie of S. Paul,
that there is a prouidence: as though I
had difputed againft the prouidence of
God, and not againft the madnes of
Luther.

Luther. Can anie man in the worlde deuife a more fond or foolifh order of difputation and cófutation, then this is?

You are ouer bold and rafh to abufe the epiftle of S. Paul to the Romaines, being, as you are, altogether ignorant in it. And yet, as though you had with this your leadden fweard killed God haue mercie on his fowle, when you had brought in that example out of S. Paul of the children that were yet vnborne, you ranne vpon me like a mad man. This is the language, that you vfed.

What faie you good fir? Behold the election once againe, and that according to the pourpofe of God. Behold the time of the election which was, before the children were borne. What fhall we then faie? that there is anie vniuftice in God? S. Paul detefteth that faying, but Ierome Oforius dowbteth not to auowch it. O M. Haddon, what madnes is this that vexeth you? What faie you? What

Y iij   thinke

thinke you ? What a shamelesse lust of lying is this? When saied I so? in what wordes ? Shew the place : reprooue me by witnesses: conuince me by good proofe. Before you doe this, why rage you? Whie take you on like a mad man ? Thinke you, that Luther, that mad felowe and filthie varlet, and the heauenlie doctrine of S. Paul are so neere ioyned together, that who so euer is against Luther, must needes be against the most holie ordinaunces of S. Paul also ? *Oh* (saie you) *it is the voice of God to Moyses. I will haue mercie on whome so euer I haue mercie, and I will haue compassion, on whom so euer I haue compassion. S. Paul bringeth in vpon this: that it is not in him that will, neither in him that runneth, but in God that taketh mercie.* After this you recite the example of Pharao, but you shew not plainely, to what ende you alleage it. And then ; as though you had

Rom. 9. c.

had alreadie declared by the testimonie of S . Paule, that the freedome of mans wil was taken awaie , you conclude after this sort.

What saieth Ierome Osorius? For sooth he saieth: if manes reason be tied vppe , if freedome of deliberation be taken awaie , if the will be fettered with euerlasting bandes : that it must needes folowe , that man is altogether bereft of his iudgement and senses, that there is no difference betwene him and a stone , yea that God is made to be the authour of euill .

And that it standeth not with reason , that we shoulde be punished for that offence , whiche we committed , not with our will. That is true , M. Haddon , neither haue you confuted my argumentes , neither haue you brought anie testimonie of S . Paule, the which might cause me to chaunge my minde . And yet as though you had determined the matter all at

Y iiij   pleasure,

pleasure, you rowse your selfe, and en-
tring into a more earnest vaine of
speach, you bring those woordes, that
folowe, out of the innermost corner of
your cunning. You saie thus.

Doe I make anie thing of my selfe? doe
I alter or chaunge anie thing? do you not
acknowledge your owne wordes, whiche
are partly false, and partly wicked? These
things while you declaimed them like
a fine Rethorician, and vaunted your
selfe somewhat insolently with a certaine lustie kind of talke: you make
that same glistering glosse of wordes to
shine a great deale the brighter by putting in (as your manner is) a taunt or reproch. Your wordes are these.

Of like you are that prowd reasoner,
whose haughtines S. Paul rebuketh very
sharply. Will you being an earthen vessel,
made of dyrt and claie, demaund of the
potter, to what vse he hath so made
you? These and the like tauntes you
caste out against me, and you warne
me

me withall, that I doe not ouerthrow, thorough this my intolerable
pride, such as leane vppon the prouidence of God. These are the thinges,
which you vtter in exceeding great
choler.

O goodly golden veſſel, made by the
excellent woorkemanſhip of Bucer, I
pray you diſdaine not the poore earthen veſſels: for it is in them, to become golden veſſels. In a great houſe,
ſaith S.Paule, there are veſſels, not only of gold and ſiluer, but alſo of wood 2.*Tim.2.c*
and earth. And ſome are made for ho-
nour, and ſome for reproch. If any
man therefore will pourge him ſelfe
from theſe, he ſhalbe a veſſel for honour, made holy and meete for our
Lord, and prepared to all good worke.
You ſee how S.Paule declareth, that
it is a very eaſie matter for vs, if we
wil, to be chaunged out of woodden
and earthen veſſels, into veſſels of gold
and ſiluer. And by what meanes this
thing

thing may be brought to passe, he declareth plainly, when he saieth : If he wil pourge him selfe from these. From whom? From them doubtlesse, which as he said a litle before, had ouerthrowen the faith of certaine men. But that you may vnderstande, howe ill your maisters haue expounded those testimonies of S. Paule, whiche you haue hudled vppe together, I thinke it necessarie to set out at large the meaning of S. Paule. The which thing, that it may the better be done, it is to be considered, to what ende S. Paule brought al those argumentes.

A learned expositiõ of S. Pauls Wordes.

When he had therefore described in moste ample manner the blessfull state of those menne, the whiche despising the pride of mans nature, and forsaking the ordinaunces of the law, whiche was now disanulled, betooke them selues wholly to the seruice of Christ : yea and so gaue them selues thereunto, that they walked, not according-

cording to the flefhe, but according
to the fpirite : that is to faie : they put
away all filthineffe of vncleane life
and naughtineffe, they cutte of the
verie ftringes of carnalitie, and followed the woorkes of vertue, godlineffe, and iuftice with an earneft defire : when he recorded after this fort
in his mind the graces and gyftes, with
the which the mindes of thofe menne
were adourned and bewtified, that
were receiued into the protection of
Chrift, and ordered by the guydaunce
of the holy ghoft : he reioyfed incredibly. But the greater this ioye was, the
more grieuoufly did he forow at the
remembraunce of the moft bitter chaunce
and fal of his owne countrie menne,
whiche had for their crewel treache-
rie and horrible blindnes of heart loft
fuch great richeffe. But for fo much as
many men tooke occafion by this fall
of the Iewes, to appaire the eftimatio
of Gods truth and faithfulnes : faying,
that

that it could not ſtand with the conſtancie of Gods truth, that that nation,
which was foſtered in great expectation of libertie and felicitie., whiche
was called by Gods owne promiſes to
the hope of the heauenly and euerlaſting kingdome, ſhould be tourned out
of al good thinges, and left in moſt horrible darkeneſſe : and that it might be
gathered by this , that either the light
was not yet brought into the worlde
by Chriſt, or that God was not ſure of
his promiſe : for ſo much therefore as
certaine raſh and vndiſcrete felowes
vſing theſe argumentes went abowte
therby moſt vnworthely and ſlaunde-
rouſly to diſteine the glorie of God: S.
Paule diſputeth earneſtly for the glory
of God, and proueth by very good and
grounded reaſons , that God was ſure
of his worde, and that he had perfourmed al ſuche thinges , as were promiſed, abundantly . And ſo much doth
he ſignifie, when he ſaith . Not, that
the

the worde of God is fallen. Nowe the Rom.9.b proufe of this defence he taketh out of fower places.

The firft place is the defcription of a true Ifraelite, to th'intent that, when it was vnderftoode, that the Gentiles gathered together vnto Chrifte were nombred in the ftocke of Ifrael, it might appeare, that God had in their faluation and honour excedingly well fulfilled his promifes.

The fecond place was that, in the which he declared, that manie, euen of them that came of the very ftocke of Ifrael, were faued. For in that great fhipwracke, certaine remnantes efcaped through faith, out of that moft crewell tempeft and waues of infidelitie.

In the third place he teacheth, that ther was no ftay in god, but that al the Iewes might haue come to faluation. For God had his treafures and richeffe alwaies in readines to beftowe them, and

and allured them with often calling vpon them to repaire towardes him, and to receiue the fruicte of his bountifulnes : but they being through the affiaûce of their law brought into a pride, and through pride into verie madnes, with harts vnkind and obstinatly ben̄t to liue in synne , refused the liberalitie and gentle calling of God.

Rom.11.c.   Last of all he foretelleth , that the time shal come, when the ful multitude of the gētiles are come in, that al Israel shalbe saued . And with these argumentes, (whiche he handleth at large) the Apostle declareth very plainely, howe fast and sure God hath alwaies continued in his faithful promise . Of the which we wil touch those pointes onely , that apperteine to this present disputation.

First therfore he ioyneth the description of a true Israelite with the declaration of equitie and iustice: and declareth, that the nobilitie of a true Israelit consi-

consisteth, not in the communitie of bloud, but in the propagation of faith: and that he is the true sonne of Abrahā, that is borne according to the promise of God, the whiche faith beholdeth : and not he that is borne according to the flesh, in the which earthie men do glorie. Not they, saith S. Paule, *Rom. 9. c.* that are the sonnes of the flesh, but thei that are the sonnes of promise, are coūted in the seede. And this is a word of promise: I wil come about this tyme, and Sara shal haue a sonne.

But left it might be said, that Isaac was therfore preferred before Ismael, bicause he was begotten of a free mother, he bringeth in like manner an other example of twoo twinnes. For Iacob and Esau were begotten and borne both of one father, of one Mother, and in one hower : and yet was Iacob placed in the inheritaunce of his Father, out of the whiche Esau was caste by the prouidence

uidence of God. If you will respecte the condicion of their birth, it seemeth, that Esau should haue benne preferred, bicause he came first into the worlde. If you consider the merites of woorkes, it was determined in Gods secret counsel, before thei were borne, and before they had done anie thing good or euyl, that Iacob should haue the preeminence. S. Paule setting this similitude before our eyes, confirmeth, that this nobilitie of Israel is to be ascribed, neither to any stocke of man, neither to auncetrie, neither to any merite going before: but to the grace of God, the whiche according to election goeth before al merites of vertue and godlinesse. For Iacob represented such, as stay them selues vppon faith, and looke for the grace and mercie of God: but Esau resembled them, the which haue no respect vnto the grace of God, but are puffed vppe with an affiaunce, whiche they haue

in

in mannes woorkes.

This lesson therefore we gather out A sounde and Catholike conclusion. of this place of S. Paule : that it is not the stocke or Petegree of manne, nor woorke, nor the Lawe, that maketh true Israelites, but the election, calling, and grace of God.

But let vs see. This so notable a mercie of God, which is bestowed vppon vs without any desert or merit of ours, is it geauen without any choise ? No truly. For then were there chaunce and vnaduisednes in the iudgement of God, the whiche no man can once thinke without great offence. S. Paule therefore to put awaye that damnable opinion, saith. To the end that the determination of God might stand according to election : it was saied not by workes, but by the caller, that the elder should serue the yonger. *Rom. 9. c.*

This woorde Election, importeth Election. some oddes or difference wisely considered with counsel ; and it declareth

Z   that

that there was somewhat in the thing chosen, which was not in the thing refused. For the purpose of God is a preuented iudgement, in the which God according to election and foreknowledge of thinges, which he seeth shall come to passe, some he apointeth mercifully vnto glorie, and other he adiudgeth to euerlasting damnatiõ. Neither is the wisedome of God, which comprehēdeth in his endlesse knowlege al things, that hath ben, that are nowe, or shalbe hereafter, cõpelled to looke for the euent of things, when he wil geue iudgement.

What was that then, whiche God chose before? Was it any worke, or merite that was woorthy of the grace of God? No truely. For, if it were so, grace were no grace. It is certaine, that through the mere mercy of God al only, we were diliuered frõ the darkenes of syn, and set in the possession of iustice. For he was nothing in our debt.

But

But rather for the hatred towards the law of God engraffed in the nature of the body (which was after synne made subiect vnto the tyrannie of inordinate lust) we were al most worthy of euerlasting punishment.

Moreouer although that most high and euerlasting bountie woulde, as S. Paul saith, that al men should be saued: yet the order of iustice wil not beare, that such as vnkindly refuse the benefites of God, and continue in that wickednes to the end, shuld receiue them. They therfore are most iustly excluded from the benefites of God, whiche are at defiance with the bouty of God, and will not in any wise be receiued into his fauour. Now wheras God knew before the beginninge of the worlde, that it should come thus to passe, of his mercie he chose them, which he sawe woulde not at the ende stubbornelie refuse his so greate benefites. And thus it cometh to passe, that some

1.Tim.2,4

Z ij   are

are by his iust iudgemente refused, and
other are by his great mercie called to
enioye his euerlasting riches.

But you wil saie peraduenture: what
Sir? Saie you that any merite of man
goeth before the grace of God? No
forsooth. For the very yelding of my
minde, by the which I geue my assent
vnto the warninges and inspirations of
God, and do not refuse his benefites, is
to be referred to the grace and mercie
of him, that called me, and bowed my
mind: and in the receiuing of my saluation and dignitie there is no merite of
mine. For if I be a poore needie man,
and oppressed with extreme necessity,
what merite is mine, if I be susteined,
and enriched by the liberalitie of some
bountiful Prince, which ought me nothing? What doth the Physition owe
me, the which of his own accord hath
healed my wounds, bicause I haue suffered my selfe to be healed of him?
Againe what is he in my debt, whiche
                                    seeing

seeing me beset on euerie syde with theeues, deliuered me from present death? Nothing at al. So therfore it cometh to passe, that such as be receiued into the fauour and grace of God, are saued by mercy: and such as be excluded from the grace of God, are repelled by his most iust iudgement.

Rom.9.si

It foloweth in the text of S. Paule, What shall we then saie? Is there any vnrighteousnes in God? God forbid. For he saith vnto Moyses, I wil haue mercie on whom I haue mercie: and I wil haue compassion on whom I haue compassion. S. Paule geueth a reason, wherfore no man can possibly laie any vniustice to God. For the defence of Gods iustice standeth altogether in his mercie. For that often repetition of Gods mercie signifieth his great constacie in geauing mercie. And the mercy of God quiteth his iustice of al slaunder. As though oure Lorde him selfe should saie: I am by nature so merciful,

Z iij that

that I pleasure in no thing more, then in pardoning of syns, and in keeping a most constant and euerlasting mercie to mainteine them, whome I haue receiued into my protection. It may therefore be sene very wel, when I do punnish syn, that such as are codemned, do perish through their owne default. For if thei would come to good order, thei might obtein the like mercy and be saued. But forsomuch as of their own accord, thei estemed more darkenes then light, bondage then freedom, pouertie then riches, death then life: it was iust, that they shoulde be throwen downe headlog into bitter paine and torment. And so by this place which S. Paul allegeth after a heueli sort, of the assured nes of Gods mercie, we see his iustice vtterly discharged of al slander. Wherfore in the calamity of the Iews no mã could finde any lacke of truth in God, but he might well blame the vnfaithsulnes and wicked stubbornes of them, that would not be saued by the mercie

of God. Then to cõfirme this saying, ãd
to teach vs that al hope of saluatiõ is to
be referred to the merci of God, which
is so freely offred to al mẽ:he saith. It is *Rom. 9.c.*
not therfore in hĩ that willeth, neither
in him that rũneth, but in God that taketh mercy. Wil importeth a desire:
rũning signifieth an earnest endeuour
to honestie: the which both are com-
prehẽded in the benefit of God. For it
is he the which with often calling vpõ
me causeth me to wil: it is he also, the
which geueth a cheeresulnes vnto my
wil. Howbeit, neither my desire, neyther my cherfulnes, shal haue ani good
successe, vnlesse he of his mercie shall
bring both my wil and my earnest endeuour to perfection. For our strength
is appaired, our hopes vanish al to nothing, so often as the mercie of God
for our vnkindnes of heart, departeth
from vs. When I therefore doe any
good woorke, it is to be ascribed neither to mans will as being naturallie

       Z iiij   incli-

inclined to honesty, neither to my earnest endeuour: but only to the mercy of God. But that it might appeare yet more plainely, that the Iewes fell not through the vniustice of God, as vngodlie men reported, but through their owne vnfaithfulnesse and wilfull sinne, he reherseth the like example of naughtines and lacke of beleefe. For God vsed the like meanes in callinge Pharao to honestie, and fraying him from vnbeleefe. But he of a pride and stubbornes, which was in him, would abuse the mercie of God, to his farre greater punishmente and damnation. Vppon this, S. Paule bringeth in these *Exod.9.d.* wordes. For the Scripture saith vnto Pharao: for this haue I stirred thee vp, that I maie shewe my power in thee, and that my name may be declared in al the earth. In the which place, two thinges are to be noted.

The first is, that Pharao was not driuen to suche outrage by any violence

or

or force of Gods behalfe, as S. Paule declareth him self anon after. The other point is, that the wickednes of Pharao was therfore tolerated a great while of God, the most wise and bountiful Lord of al things, (which out of euil thinges draweth euermore some good, and bringeth thinges disordered into good order) that by shewing one example of seueritie, he might kepe a great many men in wel doing. And this may appeare much better, if we will trie the wordes at the Hebrew fountaine, for this sentence might very well be translated after this sorte. For this cause haue I suffred thee to stand, that I may shewe my power to thee, and that my name may be honoured in al the earth. He sayeth not, I haue taken away thy wittes from thee, and I haue caused thee to be madde, that thou shouldest continually rebell against mee : but I haue suffred thee a greate while, and haue differred thy due punnishmente,

that

that I mighte referue it to the greater
fetting out of my glorie, and the faluation of many men.

He called Pharao both to faith and
alfo to honeftie. But for fo much as
Pharao regarded not the goodneffe of
God, but ranne on like a wild colt vpon an vnbridled affection: it ftode verie wel, not onely with Goddes iuftice, but alfo with his mercie, that
many menne fhould by the moft iuft
example of Pharao be put in feare,
and fo brought to good ordre. For as
the gouernours of common weales
doe vfe to cut of with conftant feueritie, fuch as they can not redreffe by
lighter punifhmentes, to the ende that
they may by the terrour of that punifhment keepe the reft of the citizins
in ordre: euen fo doth that moft high
gouernour fhew fometimes an exaple
of feueritie vpon them, that wil not be
refourmed, but wil vpo finne wickedly
comitted heape a fhameleffe defence:
that

that he maie by the deathe of thofe
lewd perfons benefite the whole, and
that he may, in punifhing the wicked,
fhew many points of his high mercie.

What is the caufe then, that we fee
that word fo often repeted: And God
hardened the heart of Pharao. To har-
dē is, to geue vnto wicked men, which
do abufe good thigs vnto malice, fome
matter with the which they may en-
creace their fyn and ftubbornes. Kno-
weft thou not, faith S. Paule, that the
goodnes of God mooueth the to pe-
nāce? But thou, according to thy hardnes and vnrepentaunt hart, doeft trea-
fure vp to thy felf difpleafure. In like
maner therefore God caufed not that
hardnes in Pharao: but Pharao refufed
the mercie of God, and of a certaine
hardnes and frowardnes, that was rooted in him, abufed the clemēcy of God
vnto greater fyn, and fo encreafed the
heape of Gods wrathe towardes him
euery day more and more.

Now

Now marke how wonderfully the Apostle linketh together his argumēts. First of al he declareth, that to be a true Israelite cometh not of mans nature, but of the grace of God. Then he confirmeth the iustice of God, by the greatnes of his grace, which is offred freely to al men, that wil vse it. For by that mercie it is euidently seene, that such as perished, perished through theyr owne default: and this doth he declare more plainly by the example of Pharao, the whiche refused the mercie of God, and was willingly forlorne: that it might be gathered by this, that the Iewes fell in like manner through their owne wilful blindnes, bicause their hearte was to obstinatly bent and hardened in wickednes: and that their dānation is not to be imputed vnto God, which called them to saluation, but vnto their owne naughtines and stubbornes, whiche refused the goodnes of God. Vpon this the Apostle bringeth

in

in these wordes. Wherefore he taketh *Rom.9.6.*
mercie on whome he wil, and harde-
neth whom he wil. The which is not
so to be taken, as though the thing that
God willeth, he willeth it without
great good reason. For the wil of his
euerlasting wisedome can not be sundered from vnderstanding, reason, and
aduisement. And his will is to rewarde
the faith of the chosen, not as of dewtie, but according to grace. His wil
is also to withdraw his helpe and aide,
from such, as refuse it, ād to suffer them
to be of a corrupt iudgement. Hereup-
pon S.Paule sayeth: Then you wil say *Ibidem.*
vnto me: Wherefore doth he yet complaine? For who shal withstand his wil?
In these wordes S. Paule bringeth in
the person of a presumpteous man, the
which iudged rashly of the counsel of
God, and vnderstandeth this sentence
of the scripture naughtily: and he maketh him to speake very vngodly, that
he may the better stop the mowth of
vn-

vngodlines it felfe. If this be true,
faith euery wicked perfon, that God ta
keth mercy on whom he wil, and whō
him lifteth, he refufeth him, and hard-
neth his hart, and no man can refift his
wil: then he that fynneth, finneth of necefsity. If he do fyn of necefsity, wherfore doth God fo often cōplaine of the
hardenes and crueltie of wicked men?

This fynful and prefumpteous talke
S. Paule cōfuteth two waies. Firft of al,
he fheweth, that it is a prefumpteous
act, to iudge of the iugemēt of god. For
euen for this caufe only, that a thing is
don bi god, although we vnderftād not
the reafon of it, yet muft we affuredly
thinke, that it was done, not without
great reafon. Then he declareth the
counfel of God, by the which he hard-
neth, that is to faie, beareth long time
with the wicked, and at the length lea-
ueth them deftitute of his aide and
healpe, that he may fuffer them to pe-
Rom. 9. d. rifh to the profite of manie. O man,
faieth the Apoftle, who art thou, that

reaſoneſt with God? Doth the thing,
which is fourmed, ſaie vnto him that
fourmed it, why haſt thou made me ſo?
May not the potter make of one lump
of claie one veſſel to honour, and an o-
ther to diſhonour? In which place you
may cōſidre by the name of a pot, that
it is not a worke which is determined
without reaſon, but ſuch a thinge, as is
done by workemāſhip. Wherin he geueth you to vnderſtand this much. If
the potter, as a potter, doth what ſo e-
uer he doth, by art: much more doth
God al things, by art, reſon, and coūſel.
S.Paul therfore ſpeaketh after this ſort.
O man wilt thou not loke circūſpectly
about thee? wilt thou not acknowlege
the frailtie of thy nature? wilt thou not
cōſidre the wiſdom and power of god?
Wilt thou not dreade his Maieſtie? If
there were any ſenſe in earthen veſſels: ſurely ſuche veſſels were not to
be borne withall, as woulde diſpute
with the potter, whiche made them,

of

of the workemanship wherwith they were made. Much lesse is the presumpteousnes of a seelie man to be borne, the which improueth the iudgemente of that most excellent gouernour, and in an endlesse and incomprehensible wisedom findeth lacke of cunning and skill. Art thou at that point in deede? The thing, the cause and reason wherof thou art not able to atteine vnto by wit, wilt thou by and by stand vnto it, that it is void of al reason? The potter maketh by arte one vessel for honour, an other for dishonour: and loke what is made by arte, no man may wel finde fault withal. And wilt thou saie, that the thing, which is made of that most high and perfecto wisedome, (in the which neither rashnesse, neither vniustice may rest) is made vndiscretely and vniustly? By these wordes S. Paul intendeth only to put vs to vnderstād, that it is a very grieuouse offence, to trie the iudgements of God by the balance
lance

lance of mans reason, and to doubt of
his iuftice. He doth therefore onely
keepe downe vnreafonable prefump-
teoufnes, and fraieth rafh and prowde
menne, by denouncing vnto them the
iudgement of god.

After that he declareth, what is to
be holden as touching this queftion.
Thefe are his words. If fo be, that God Rom.9.s.
willing to fhew his wrath, and to make
his power knowen, hath fuffered the
veffels of wrath with much patience,
which were fhaped to deftructió, that
he might fhew the ritches of his glory
towardes the veffels of mercie, the
which he hath prepared to glorie. It
is an vnperfecte fpeach, the whiche
manner of fpeaking S. Paule vfeth ofté
tymes. There lacketh either this, or
fome other thing like to this. And yet
wilt thou reprooue the wife and iuft
counfel of god?

Now in thefe wordes, firft of al it
is to be noted, that God framed not the

A A   vef-

veſſels of wrath . Truth it is, that God
made nature vnto the veſſels , but nct
ſynne, not vngodlines , not the reſt of
vices, which deſerueth to be puniſhed
moſt ſharply by the ſeueritie of Gods
iudgement , (whiche the holie Scripture calleth wrath).For it cometh to
paſſe by the wil of euery wicked man,
that he is made the veſſel of wrath,
which would not be made the veſſel
of mercie. The whiche thing S.Paule
meanig to ſet forth more plainly, ſaith:
He ſuffered. And being not ſatisfied
with that word he ſaith moreouer:He
ſuffred in much patience the veſſels of
wrath . What is this ? What griefe is
that ſo great? What torment is that ſo
crewel, that, to the bearing of it, God
neded patiéce, yea and that no meane,
but exceding great patience ? Doubtles it is that, which is(if God were ſub-
iect to any griefe)of al griefes, that may
be deuiſed, the greateſt to wit, it is vicious liuing, wickednes, and an obſti-
nate

nate wil to cõtinue in synne. For there
is nothing els, that disagreeth with his
vertue, goodnes, and wisedome: there
is nothing els, that is directely against
his most holy ordinaunces and lawes:
to be shorte, there is nothing elles,
that God doth moste extremely hate
and detest. So that, it is no wonder,
if a verie great patience were (to
speake of God as of a man) needefull,
to beare such a bitter torment. God
therefore caused not this hardnesse of
heart in Pharao, but he suffred with
a certaine great patience the wilfull
stubbornes of that most wicked man,
whiche grieued his heart. The which
thing to expresse the beter, S. Paule
saith: Vessels made to destruction. He
saith not: The vessels which God him
selfe hath made to destruction: as he
saieth a litle after of the vessels of
mercie, the whiche God him selfe
hath prepared to glorie: that you may
vnderstande, that Godlie menne are

appointed vnto glorie by the wil and mercie of God, and that wicked men are thrust out violetly into euerlasting tormentes, through euerie mans owne wilful synne: as Esaie saith. Goe into the fier, whiche you haue kendled for your owne selues. But to what ende, I praie you, did that most high Lord suffer so long time and with suche great patience the vessels of reproch? To shewe, saith the Apostle, his wrath: that is to say, to shewe the seueritie of his most holie iudgement, and the power of his maiestie. Againe, I aske you: to what pourpose was it, to desire to declare that vnto menne? To shewe, saieth he, the ritches of his glorie towardes the vessels of mercie, the which he hath prepared to glorie. For he doth al thinges for the chosens sake.

Esai. 50. d

Rom. 9. c.

Now it remaineth, that we doe cōsider, what fruict doe the chosen take by setting the iudgemente of god, before

fore their eyes? Very great without
doubt. For firſt of al, while the choſen ſee the wicked puniſhed according
to their deſertes, it putteth a certaine
feare of Gods iuſtice into their hartes,
whiche cauſeth them to abſteine from
euil doinges. For the foundation of *Prou.1.4:*
true wiſedoth is laied vpon the feare
of God. Moreouer the vertue of the
good being aſſaulted both by the priuy
awaites, as alſo by the forcible attéptes
of wicked perſonnes ſhineth a great
deale the brighter. For vertue maketh
a great ſhew of her ſelfe, when it is
neither corrupted by the example of
vicious menne, neither tourned away
from the exerciſe of godlines through
naughtie counſell, neither drawen
from the loue of moſt holie Religion
by threatninges or tormentes. Againe
when they conſider by the fal of the
wicked, ourc f howe great thraldome
they are delyuered by the mercie of
God, they embrace their parent and
AA iij redee-

redeemer with a much more feruent
defire and earneft loue. Laft of al the
very holines it felfe of the euerlafting
lawe; and the ordre of Gods iuftice
being fet before the eyes and fight of
good menne, bringeth them to a cleerer vnderftanding of God, and caufeth
the mercy of God vfed towardes holy
men to be the better knowen : and fo
increafeth their ioye. To the intēt therfore that the good might take fo great
and fo manifold fruicts by the dānation
of the wicked: god would not vfe any
fuch violence towardes the wicked,
that they fhould cōmit finne as being
driuen vnto it of necefsitie:but he fuffred mofte patiently their wilful frowardnes and ftubborne obftinacy, that
he might in the end tourne altogether
to the glory of his chofen.

If you haue not vtterly loft al fenfe
of a fobre man, you may fee plainely,
that free wil is not by the faying of S.
Paule taken away, but rather verie
furely

surely eſtabliſhed . Theſe thinges the
Apoſtle proſecuteth afterwarde more
at large, and declareth at the length,
howe the Iewes fell from God thorough their pride , arrogancie , vn-
faithfulneſſe , and obſtinacie . For
they were ſo puffed vp with a vaine
affiaunce of a ſhadowed iuſtice, which
ſtoode vpon the woorkes of the lawe,
that they deſpiſed very ſtubbornly and
wickedlye the true iuſtice , whiche
conſiſteth in cleannes of life , in holi-
neſſe , in charitie , in peace , in ioye,
and in other the like fourniture of heauenly vertues whiche by the holie
ghoſt are planted in the mindes of godly men.

Now for ſo much as this is the ſaying and meaning of S. Paul, what rage
was that, that came into that mad mãs
brain, the which wēt about by the air-
tority of S.Paul to perſuade ſuch an o-
pinion, as both ouerthrew good order
emongeſt men, and falſly charged God

with vniuftice ? For what right is it,
that wicked men fhould be punifhed
for a wicked acte, whiche they comitted, not willingly, but being violently
driuen vnto it by an euerlafting and
external power.

Luther fay you, fet out a Booke, in the
whiche he fpake earneftly againft the
hurly burlies in Germanie. What if fome
one of them, whom he rebuked, fhould
haue faid vnto him euē then: ô Luther,
why doft thou blame vs innocēt men?
whie keepeft thou fuch a ftirre ? whie
plaieft thou the madde man ? we haue
learned of the, that it is not in vs to do
any thing good or euil: in fo much that
we are not free, fo much as to thinke
fuch thinges, as we would . For God
worketh al things in vs, as you fay : and
we are only certaine working tooles,
the which god thrufteth out with his
hand, whether fo euer him lifteth, and
wrécheth vs foreward and backeward
at his pleafure. Thefe tourmoiles therfore

fore ād feditiō, for the which you blame
vs, God al only, as you teach, hath ſtirred vppe. For ſo much as therfore, that
moſt mighty Lord, whoſe power can
not be hindered by any ſtrēgth of man,
is the mouer, the deuiſer, yea the doer
of this ſtirre, whie blame you vs for it?
Whie reuile you vs? Whie labour you
vainly to withdraw vs from this ſedition? If anie man, I ſaie, of that multitude, whiche Luther tooke vp with
ſuche ſharpe woordes, had ſaied thus
much vnto him: I praie you, what anſwere woulde he haue made? With
what honeſt ſhifte woulde he bothe
maintaine his doctrine, and defend the
iuſtice of God?

But to let Luther paſſe: what ſaie
you ſir Luthers aduocate, which ſaie,
that he was ſent from God: how maie
you(if you approoue his doctrine and
rules) puniſh malefactours? If there be
no freedome, if mans will be tied, if al
power be taken awaie, if the verie
thoughtes

thoughtes be fettered, if al things, both
greateft, and leaft, and middlemoft, be
bownd with an euerlaft necefsitie , if
God be the authour and doer of all
things both good an euyl: vndowbtedly thofe feelie wretches, which you (as
I take it) commaunde to be had awaie
to execution , haue done nothing. By
what right doe you punifh the innocent men ? What reafon haue you to
put gyltleffe perfones to death ? who
made this lawe , that the doers of fel-
lony fhould be acquited, and the tooles
or inftrumentes of fellons codemned ?
with what kind of fpeach, are you able
(if you minde to maintaine this doctrine) to rid that moft high Iudge of
the infamie of vniuftice. Is this no villanie? Is this no madnes? Is this no prefumpteous part of a rafh and an vnbridled mind? And yet wheras Luther doth
at one time both diftourbe the order
of mans life, and lay vnto gods charg,
(like a moft fhameles varlet) the crime
of

of vniuſtice : he is not afraied to ſaie,
that he ſtandeth in defence of Gods
glorie, whiche he goeth about to deface and ouerthrow.

You ſaie, that I doe condemne the
firſt ſownders of this doctrine, as no
leſſe wicked and vngodlie, then if they
were like vnto Protagoras or Diagoras : I am not ſo blunt, that I woulde
ſaie ſo. I thinke them not onlie com-
parable with Diagoras in wickednes,
but alſo incoparably worſe then euer
he was. For I take it to be more tolerable, to thinke that there is no God,
then to thinke that God is a maleſa-
ctour and vniuſt.

Protag.
and Diag.
thought
there vvas
no God.

Now as towching prouidence (that
I maie once coclude this matter) I ſaie
no more but this. If the prouidence of
God be a counſell determined by the
foreknowledge of thinges, if the word
of election, if the purpoſe of God, that
is to ſaie, the preueted iudgement and
euerlaſting decree do import a reaſon
and

Prouidece

and meaning : then doth he confesse
the prouidence of God, which beleeueth, that there was nothing apointed
and ordeined of God from before the
begynning of the worlde without verie great counsell , iustice and reason.
And contrarie wise, thei that saie, that
God hath sorted out of the common
lumpe of mankind such as he woulde
directe vnto euerlasting glorie , and
such as he would apoint vnto euerlasting dánation, vpó none other reason
or cósideration, but bicause him lifted
so to doe: how so euer they maintaine
the prouidence of God in word, they
denie it in deede . For he that taketh
awaie the meaning and reason, taketh
awaie prouidence.

Protestáts
denie
Gods pro-
uidence.

But will you see, how like a babler
you prosecut the rest of your matters?
Your woordes are these. *At the length*
when you haue scholded your fill, you be-
gynne to conclude somewhat, making a
totall somme of all suche thinges , as you
*   com-*

complaine haue ben ouerthrowen by our men : and you aske what thing hath suc-ceded in their roome. O M. Haddon I haue iust cause to complaine. For I see none other thing set vp in the steede of them , but only that woorshipfull acte of yours, in the which you glorie so muche , and therfore you repete it verie often. *For the superstitious ydlenes of lurking hypocrites , saie you, we haue set vp the necessarie busines of Christian profession : for wandering pleasures, most honourable marriage : for the dreames of mens inuentions. , the holie Scriptures of God the Father, and of our Lorde Iesus Christ.* The wast and hauoke of holie thinges I see : but what you haue re-stored in their roome I see nothing, as I told you before, except it be, for most godlie quietnes, most wicked stirring : for the loue of chast life , filthie and incesteouse ribaudrie : for the puritie of most holie doctrine , most pestilent errours of desperate selowes.

Would

Would God, saie you, ye had here bro-
ken of your most reprochful epistle: Of like
you are not ashamed of your tauntes,
which you haue gathered together with-
out anie cawse in the world. I assure you,
I am wearie of the rehersal of them. To
what purpose is it, to repeate so often,
without argumet, without comely grace,
without any likely hod of truth, those your
so shameles and vnreasonable errours, in
the eares of the Quenes maiestie, yea in
the eares of al Christendome? How stãdeth this geare together, M. Haddon?
Saied you not before, that I was an excellent framer of wordes and sentences? Confessed you not, that you liked
wel my kind of vtteraunce? Haue you
not called me often times in this your
booke Cicero his scholer? Wherfore
then saie you now, that my epistle was
written without anie argument (as for
the comelie and pleasaunt grace I wil
saie nothing?) Bylike, when you commended mine eloquence, you spake
not

not in earneſt and as you thought.
You dalied with me, Sir pleaſaunce,
you dalied: and the ladie Venus, in the
honour of whome you haue prophaned and vnhalowed the téples of chaſtitie, hath beſprinkled you with her
comelie and pleaſaunt graces. Howbeit I thinke this very much to be miſ-
liked in this your pleaſauntnes, that it
can not be well perceiued, when you
ſpeake in earneſt, and when you ſport.
But peraduenture you thinke it a cómendation of a ſharpe witte, to ſpeake
darkly, and therefore you vſe it in diſputation alſo. But howe often you
caſte me in the teeth with the name
of Cicero? As though I ſhoulde be
aſhamed of hym, or els thought my
ſelfe hable to expreſſe in my writinges anie parte of his witte, vehe-
mencie, and copie: as though I had
ſtudied Cicero only, and had not ſpent
verie muche time in other the higheſt pointes of learning. But you like
a foxie

a foxie lawier and wilie proctour, haue
made a verie good prouiso, that no
man maie well laie the name of Cicero
to your charge. For you speake nothing in cleane speach, nothing plainly, nothing distinctely, nothing orderly, nothing grauely, nothing eloquently. What so euer liketh you, you put it
in : and then you prooue it, not by argument and reason, but by railing and
shameles talke. At the length as though
you had wonne the field, you pricke
me with the bristles of your reprocheful tongue, you presse me with a numbre of apish questions, you triumph like
a noddie before the victorie. Whervpon you saie thus?

What saie you good sir ? And then ? *S.*
Paul detesteth it : *Ierome Osorius is not*
afraied to auouch it. As though I affirmed that thing, whiche you there denied, or els meaned to dispute with S.
Paul, and not with Luther. And again.
What saieth, Ierome Osorius? And again.

Doe

*Doe I make anie thing? Doe I chaunge
anie thing?* And with these woordes
forsooth, you would haue seemed to
be a vehement speaker. Learne this of
me, M. Haddon, if you can (bicause
your euyl lucke was to chaunce vpon
such a maister, which brought you vp
so foolishly and so ignorátly) that these
questions are then both graue and vehement in deede, when the aduersarie
is cóuinced by some firme and sure argument. For otherwise they are verie
folish and to be laughed at: for so much
as they haue no vehemécie or strength
in the worlde, but only a declaration of
a certaine pitifull pang or heat of the
stomake. So God healpe me, as I could
not sometime (although your talke
seemed vnto me verie much to be pi-
tied) hold my selfe fró laughing. And so
I am fully discharged of my promise,
whiche I made you, that, in case you
could driue me either by grownded
reasons, or els by true exáples to geaue

my affent vnto you, I would not refufe
it. For neither haue you brought anie
argument, neither alleaged any example, that was to the pourpofe : and
yet, as though you had borne your felf
like a pretie man, you rage and reuel in
wordes, and keepe a meruelous pitifull
and frantique ftirre. I can not deuife,
what wicked fprite it fhould be, that
put you in mind to take this charge of
writing vpon you. Yet I meane not,
but that you maie doe, as you thinke
good: neither wil I limite you in fuche
forte, that you maie not in writing
fhew your felfe to be as foolifh, as you
lift. And to put you in good comfort,
take this of my worde, that no man,
which is of anie iudgement, wil
find fault with you, for being to much a Cice-
ronian.

THE

THE THIRD
BOOKE.

IT foloweth now, that we make anſwere vnto your other complaint, in the whiche you ſeme to take that part of myne epiſtle very grieuouſly, wherin I reckened vp the impudencie, the robberies, poyſoninges, conſpiracies and other deteſtable vices, ſo manie, that my maiſter Cicero, as you ſaie, neuer heaped vp moe againſt Verres, with the whiche I ſhoulde ſaie, that England was atteinted. Wherin you ſhew verie plainly, that you read thoſe my letters with litle heede. For it was neuer my meaning, to condemne all Englande of ſuche vices. For I knowe, there are in that Iland verie manie godlie and religious men,

BB ij whiche

which neuer fel from the holy church, but would gladly yeald their liues for the glorie of Chriſt, if neede ſo required. Yea manie haue alreadie by their moſt honourable death ſet out their faith excedingly : manie haue abiden impriſonement, reprochful woordes, with diuers other incōmodities:manie being loth to ſee ſuche a decaie of religion, wander from place to place of their owne accord like baniſhed men and outcaſtes, and haue lieſer to keepe a continual combat with miſerie and needines, then to beholde with their eies ſo heauy a ſight. The which thing verie manie other men would do alſo, if you would ſuffer them. Moreouer and this I heare that ther are certaine places within that Ilād, vnto the which the infectiō of this morreine is not yet come: and it is reported, that there are manie noble men alſo , which are vntowched : A frind of myne, an honeſt and credible perſon, which hath ſome

doinges

doinges in England, tolde me this for
certaine, that there are moe in the
realme, that continue in their faith stil,
then there are of such as haue forsaken
it : howbeit they dare not professe it
openly, for feare of them, that are in
authoritie. For it is lawful for them, so
long as they are not required to professe their faith openly, to keepe it to
them selues, vntill such time, as, they
must either maintaine their religiõ by
suffring death, (if they be put vnto it)
or els reserue them selues to a better
worlde, to the ende that all good men
decaie not at once . And as for them,
whose heartes are not blinded with
pride, which are caried awaie, not so
much of malice and naughtines, as of
simplicity of mind(of the which there
are verie manie) maie verie easily be
brought home againe. Wherefore I
saied not, that al the Iland was geuen
to suche vices, neither haue I laied
downe al hope of the recouerie of the

whole : no , I truſt to ſee within theſe few daies ſuch an alteration of things, that the verie remembrance of this moſt peſtilent plague ſhalbe vtterlie aboliſhed.

Furthermore I meant not in thoſe my letters (as I tolde you before) to make anie enditement or accuſation, but to aduertiſe your Prince , that ſhe ſhould not ſuffer her ſelf to be infected with the peſtilent ſectes of deſperate felowes: the which thing that I might doe it the better , I declared certaine tokēs, by the which true religiō might be diſcerned from falſe religiō, and true Prophetes frō falſe Prophetes . In the doing wherof if I lacked diſcretion, we ſhal ſee anon. Thus much haue I ſpokē concerning my letters, the which you ſaie were writen without good argument, and without anie comely grace. Wherin I find a great lacke of grauitie in you : for it is not the part of a graue mã, to be moued with a talke, which is

void

void of all good argumēt. And yet you
(as a man maie wel cōiecture by your
writinges) after you had read my letters, fell into such a pelting chafe, such
a rage and madnes, that you betraied
your griefe by reprochfull and railing
talke: yea you went so farre in it, that
you were not ashamed to bewraie to
the worlde the verie stammering and
stuttering of your tongue.

You confesse also, that my letters
were caried vp and down throughout
al Christendome, the whiche shoulde
not haue ben done, if they had ben
written without anie good grownd.

But let vs see, how you, which saie
that I had no argument to staie vpon,
will answere that myne argument,
by the whiche I prooued, that the
puritie of the Gospel was not restored
by your maisters, for so much as emongest the disciples of your Gospel there
raigneth a numbre of most detestable
vices. *Tushe*, saie you, *it is all false,*

that you report of the dishonestie of the men of our side. Such is your impudécy, M. Haddon, that you will denie the thing, which is knowen and commóly bruted, yea which is sealed and cófirmed by the testimoniall of the whole worlde. Doe you not cófesse the broiles and tumultes of Germany? See you not with your eyes, how volupteousnes flieth to and fro auancing her selfe? how licentious liuing getteth vp and down vncótrolled? how the churches of religious men are prophaned with bloudshead? how al places of deuotió are rifled and robbed how treason and wilie practises are wrought againste Princes by your sectaries? how al places, where so euer your maisters set vp schoole, are distourbed with hurly burlies? How then dare you saie, that that thing was neuer done, which you not only heare of other men, but also see it done daily with your owne eyes?

Admit

Admit, say you, *that this were true:
yet could it neuer com of this cause which
you gather.* I would faine learne of you,
how it should not come of this cause.
There was alwaies, say you, *darnel so-
wen emongest the good corne. There was
alwaies seedes of diuerse kindes, of the
which some were choked in the thornes,
and some were dried vp by the heate of
the sonne.* The false Prophettes did alwaies bende them selues against the true
Prophets: our Lord Iesus Christ fownde
Caiphasses; the Apostles found Nerons:
the Martyrs, that folowed them, founde
Decies. But to omit these thinges as o-
uerstale, I wil bring you home to your
owne doores. In your Churche is there
not synne committed openly? Do not men
offend in the sight of the worlde? You deny it not. Wel then, throwe away your argument, the whiche either it is of no
force, or els, if it be, it is against your
owne selfe firste, and against your Churche.

By

By this talke you thinke, that you
haue tourned the eadge of our dag-
ger. But you fee not, howe manie
faultes there are in it. Firfte of all I
deny not, that it was euer fo (as I faid
plainely in my letters) that there
were manie vices in euerie common
weale, and that the feades of naughtines were fowen emongeft the good
corne. But I required (and that inftat-
ly)to vnderftand,how thefe menne of
god had difcharged their duetie,which
tooke vpon them to purge the corne,
and to plucke vppe al fuch weedes are
were noifome to the corne. The
which thing when I faw they perfor-
med not,yea,when I faw that through
their diligence vice came vp a great
deale ranker then it did before, I gathered by that,that their doctrine was
nothing wholefome. That the true
Prophetes fufteined the enmitie of
falfe Prophetes, Chrifte of Caiphas,
the Apoftles of Nerons, the Martyrs
of

of Decies, I graunt you : but that maketh much more for the confirmation of myne argument . For vertue was euer enuied of the wicked, hatefull to viciouse, assaulted by the vnfaithful . And yet was it alwaies of suche puyssaunce, that it preuailed against al crafte and policie, against all subtile practises and priuie awaites, against the force of wickednesse and vice, and brought to the world a goodly and wholesome ordre . For they that gaue eare to the Prophetes, that folowed Christ, that kept the faith of the Apostles, that reuerenced the constancie of the Martyrs, were not presumpteouse, wicked, disordered, and vicious: but they were wise, modest, getle, courteous, decked and beutified with diuerse and sundry vertues. For the vertue of holy me, the more it was assaulted, the greater and goodlier increase it yealded of godlie fruict . But your doctours whiche were sent, as

you

Vertue euer assaulted, and yet preuaileth.

you say, from heauen into the worlde, hauing the aide of great Princes, being garded by the common people, yealded no fruicte of honeftie, chaftitie. or meekeneffe to fuch as folowed them.

I fpeake not of your aduerfaries, by whom you wil complanie peraduenture, that your brethren haue benne wrongfully withftoode, euen as the Martyrs were fome tyme by the Decies: but I fpeake euen of them, that loue Luther, Bucer, Zwinglius, and your Martyr, that praife and reueréce them, yea that efteeme them as gods: I fay, that they them felues, whiche procured to haue thefe wife men to be their fchoolemaifters, prooued neuer a whit the better: whereby it is concluded, that their doctrine was nothing wholefome, euen to fuche as did not only not difalowe it, but alfo efteemed it very highly.

Now whereas you demaund of me of our Church (for fo you fpeke) whether

ther

ther-it be voide of al synne: I haue alreadie lamented the synful life of our
men very oft. There raigneth, I graũt
you euen at this day emongeft vs both
coueteoufnes and ambition in manie:
neither is volupteoufnes grubbed vp
by the rootes.

Why then, say you, the argument,
which I vfed, may eafily be tourned
againft our own felues. How fo I pray
you? If there fhould arife fome great
prophet emõgft vs, which would take
fo great a charge vpon him, as to purge
and fine the gofpel to reftore the aun-
ciẽt difcipline, to proppe vp the Churche, which tendeth to ruine, with heauenly doctrine, to bring his difciples to
liue like Apoftles : if we fhould folow
hĩ, and yet that notwithftãding liue in
vice as we did before, then were this
a good argumẽt, both againft our prophete, as alfo againft our owne felues.
But the brightneffe of this fo cleere
light hath not yet fhined vppon vs:
whero-

wherefore it is no wonder, if we continue stil in our accustomed synnes. But to you, whome the sprite hath replenished with a certaine new light, which might very easily haue ben instructed in heauenly thinges, by suche men, as were sent frō heauen for your saluation, whiche are by the goodnes of God already deliuered from superstition and hypocrisie, which despise al wordly thinges, and wil suffer nothing to be mingled with the puritie of your Doctrine, vnlesse it be drawen out of heauen: to you, I say, it were nothing seemely to haue any daungerouse disease or cracke of vncleane vice. For, if you haue : your doctours, whome you commende aboue the skies, you shame them for euer, and their Doctrine you declare by your doinges to be not only vnprofitable, but also hurtfull and pestilent. But for so much as you desire to vnderstande the state of our Churche, I will declare it vnto you to you, so briefly as is possible.

Firste of all, we doe moste constantly hold and mainteyne the Gospel, not of Luther, Melanchthon, Ca-
roloftadius, Zwinglius, Caluine or
Bucer, but of Matthew, Marke, Luke
and Iohn: and we keepe one faith,
not this newly deuised faith, whiche
is ioyned with a rash and vayne presumption: but that faith, which was
taught by the Apostles, and is not corrupted through the naughtines of outragious and mad men.

In lyke manner we are inclosed
within one Churche, whithe was
fownded by Chrift, inftructed by the
Apostles, fortified by the aide of the
Martyrs, fette out by the Doctrine
of holie menne, defended and kepte
alwaies inuincible by the power of
the holy Ghofte in spite of the maliciouse and violent attemptes of all Heretiques: and without this Churche,
we beleeue assuredlye, that there
is no

is no hope of ſaluation.

This Church we acknwolege to be ſo linked in one meaning, in one ſpirite, in the agreeable conteſſion of one faith, yea to be faſt glewed together with ſuch agreemḗt in religiṓ, that no man can poſſibly by deuiſing new opinions (ſuch as may concerne the principal points of religion) rend and teare it into a numbre of ſectes iarring and ſquaring the one with the other without al reaſon and ordre.

And bicauſe we know by the goſpel, by the teſtimonie of Martyrs, by the faithful and agreable report of holie menne, by reaſon and common experience of thinges, that it is not poſſible, that the Churche ſhould be one, excepte it haue one ſupreme Gouernour the Vicar of Chriſte, whiche may by his inuiolable authoritie ioyne together thinges ſeparated, knitte vppe thinges looſed, and keepe all menne in one faith and

vni-

vnifourme order: we do most willinglie obeie the Bifhop of Rome, which as
Chriftes deputy exerciseth this so great
office in the earth, and what so euer is
cõmaunded vs by him , we do it without any refufal. And the very experience of thinges maketh vs to do it the
more willinglie, bicaufe we fee , that,
where fo euer this authoritie is taken
awaye , there breaketh out by and by
many peftilent and troublefome fects.
That this power is builded not vppon
any decree of man, but vpon the ordinaunce of Chrifte him felfe, it is mofte
euidently proued , not only by the authoritie of the holie Scripture, but alfo
by the teftimonie of all the antiquitie,
(wherein we are not ignorant).

We refufe not the authoritie of any
lawfull power. For we beleeue, as S.
Paul teacheth vs, that al lawful power **Rom. 13.a**
is ordeined by God : fo that, who fo
euer refifteth a lawfull power, is to
be taken as though he didde refifte

CC   not

not men, but God him selfe. For this cause we beleue, that not only the decrees of Popes, but also the ordinances of Kings (such as are not cōtrary to the law of God) are most diligently to be obserued and kept. Emongest the ordinances of mē this choise we make. Al such as cause a slackenes in the keping of the law of God, we reiect, as the deuises of men: but al such as prouoke vs to be more earnest in the obseruation thereof, we iudge to haue ben ordeined, not without the instinct of the holy Ghost. For Christ saied: He that is not against you, is for you. For this cause, we thinke that the rules of Basile the great, of Benet, Bernard, Brunus, Frauncis, Dominike, and other the like singular good and holie men, suche as tende to the perfection of a Christian lyfe, are not to be sette at naughte. For they are all written to this ende, that suche as binde them selues vnto them, may the more willingly

Mar.9.f.

lingly keepe the chaſtitie of body, and cleanes of heart (the which two things are conteined in the counſelles of the Goſpell) and may with a great deale more freedome and cheerelineſſe ſing and prayſe God daie and night, and ſo with the more facilitie folow the lyfe of Angels here in earth.

If we ſee any decaie in their manners through looſenes or negligence, we thinke it expedient to prouide out of hand, that it may be ſtreightly boũd vp by the rigour of the olde diſcipline, and not to ouerthrow the place, where men may liue ſo godly and ſo wonderfull a life. And bicauſe we can not be weaned from the acqueintaunce of the bodie ſo much as it were to be wiſſhed we coulde : bicauſe we vnderſtande, that the beginning of mans miſerie procedeth of negligence and forgetfulnes, what ſo euer thing mai bring vs to remember the bowntifulnes and mercy of God, we vſe it very diligẽtly.

CC ij   There-

Crosses.

Therfore euen as we make the signe of the Crosse vpon our forehead (the which manner S. Basile reterreth to a tradition of the Apostles) so doe we set vp Crosses not onely in Churches, but also in our howses and highwaies, to the end, that the remembraunce of so great a benefite should neuer depart out of our minde. For if God, when he deliuered the peple of Israel by the diligence of Moyses out of the weake dominion of Pharao, gaue order vnto them, that they shoulde alwaies haue, before their eyes, in their handes, and in such places of their howses as were in sight, some monument of that bene-fit : how much more diligently ought we to doe it, which are redeemed, not by the meane of Moyses, but hy the benefite of that most bountifull Lord, which was offred vp for vs, from euer-lasting darkenes and damnation, into euerlasting light, libertie, and glorie?

For the same cause were the Images

ges of holy men set vp of olde time (as it is declared before) that men behol-ding them, should be moued the ofte-ner to bend their mindes to thinke vp-pon those men, whiche walked more feruently in the steppes of Christ, and to dispose them selues the soner to fo-low their godlines and vertue. For in holie men, we doe not so much reue-rence the men them selues, as the ma-iestie of Christe, whiche dwelleth in their heartes. For they are the sonnes of God, the brothers of Christe, the heires of the euerlasting and heauenlie kingdome : the whiche state all suche haue atteined by the benefit of Christ, as haue so nailed their senses vpon the Crosse, that there liueth none other thing in them, but only the spirit, will, and pleasure of Christ : as S.Paule said: *Gal. 2. d.* I liue, now not I, but Christ liueth in me. And so we honour in holy men a most excellent gift of God, a verie ex-presse Image of God, yea (after a ma-

C C iij ner

ner of spech) certain Gods, in the bright
nes of whome we extol and praise for
euermore the moste high and euerlasting benefite of God.

The Catho
like faith. Now the faith, in the which we liue,
is such, that it doth neither minish our
hope in attempting any good woorke,
neither wipe away quite all feare or
doubt of saluation : but it bringeth the
wel disposed mindes in hope of godlines and vertue , and it driueth withall
now and then a certaine feare into all
such, as think vpon the rigour of Gods
iudgementes. For Christe , which by
his bloud hath drowned synne (as it is
writen) into the deapth , and hath furnished all suche , as are come vnto him
with a liuely and true faith , with the
giftes of holines , puritie and iustice,
hath appointed euerlasting damnation
to them, that refuse to obeie his com-
maundemente . For he was made the
Heb.5.c. cause of euerlastinge saluation, not to
euerie man, that boasteth of faith , but
to such

to suche as obeie him (as Sainct Paule saieth) .

Wherefore we beleeue, that the Workes woorkes of holie menne are not disteyned with anie vncleanes of synne (for that were a derogation and dishonour to Christe, for so muche as they are donne by his grace and power) and we knowe for certaine, that suche as thinke not , that the lyfe of manne is to be spente in doing holie woorkes, (if they continue in that lewde opinion) shalbe tormēted in hel for euermore.

We confesse, that men being destitute of the aide and grace of Christe, can neither doe, nor endeuour, no nor thinke any thing , that is auaileable to euerlasting saluation : and therfore we beleeue, that all hope of saluation , all the meane to atteine vnto true honour , all the staie of lyfe euerlasting resteth in the mercie of God . And Freevvill. yet we beleeue this assuredlie , that it

CC iiij lieth

lieth in vs, either to refuse, or els to ac-
cept thankefully this benefite, when it
is offered vnto vs. And as we doe not
deface, neither the signes of the holie
Crosse, neither the Images of Christe,
neither the monumentes of holy men:
so do we thinke, that the reuerent or-
Ceremo- dre of al ceremonies, and the religious
nies. vsage of holie Sacramentes (I meane
not any newefourmed ordre, deuised
and trimmed by the witte of fine M̂.
Haddon, but that most old and auncient vsage , whiche was approoued by
the ful agreement of the holy Fathers,
as it may easily appeare by their writinges) is moste reuerently and inuio-
lably to be obserued and kept.

Penance. When we fall, we thinke it expedient foorthwith to haue recourse to the
Churche, and to the iudgement of the
Confessiō. Priest. There is made a due examination of the sinne , and it is seene howe
great the deformitie of it was : whervpon the mind, which is now ashamed
of

of such vncleanes, doth the more earnestlie hate and detest the offence cōmitted, and asketh pardon humbly, and is absolued by the sentēce of the Priest, whiche representeth the personne of Christ: but yet so, that he must discretly submit him selfe to such order as the Priest will inioyne him. He that heareth you, saith our SauiourChrist, heareth me, and he that despiseth you, despiseth me.

Mat.18.d. Luc. 10.c. 10.13.c.

After this we come with feare and trembling, and with a good affiance of the mercie of God, vnto that most holy and dreadful Sacrament of the body and bloud of Christ, in the which banket we are so refreshed and strengthened, that we doe withstand the tyrannie of bodily lustes with a greater force and courage. And bicause it were a daungerouse matter to leaue all this to the wil and discretiō of euery man (for there are many sicke men, which will not be healed: and the life of the common

Our Lords Supper.

mon

mon forte is not fo well gouerned by
will, as by lawe and difcipline) it hath
ben ordeined vpon great confiderati-
ons, that all Chriftian men fhould be
conftreined to laie this fo foueraigne a
falue to their wounds at the leaft once
euerie yeare. There are many, which
come vnto this Sacramente oftentimes: but yet fo, that they examine
them felues before diligently, as Sainct
Paule teacheth, and endeuoure them
felues to wafſh out all the fpottes of
fynne by the merite of Chrift, which
they may moft eafilie obteine, if they
will confeffe and forfake their fore-
mer lyfe.   It is a wonder to fee, what
a multitude of menne is fedde euerie
Sonnedaie and Holie daie in the yeare,
with this Diuine and heauenly foode,
and howe by the helpe of it they are
ftirred more earneftlie to feeke after
heauenly richeffe. For we fee in them,
that are oftentimes refrefhed with the
mofte holy bodie of Chrifte, that the
darkenes

darkenes of sinne is driuen away, the light of heauen riseth, vertue and godlinesse are planted in them, the moste goodlie fruictes of iustice are powred vpon them abundantly.

Bishops, such as are able to preach, The office (the which hath ben litle regarded of ofbishope some to the greate hinderaunce of the Church) do preach oftétimes. Such as are not able to discharge it themselues, appoint certain religious and wise persons, men wel learned, not in the rules of Bucer or your Martyr, but in the holy scripture, and in the bokes of the holy Fathers, to instruct the people with chast, pure, and religious doctrine. And as we see it come to passe, especially in such as are bleare eyed, that, if they be either put into an extreme dark place, or els loke ouer steddily vpő the sonne beames, thei leese their sight : euen so, if mé either be altogether turned away sró the light of God, or els wil looke to intentiuely vppon it, before the blea-

rednes

rednes of their minde be healed, they
are ftriken ftone blinde. Wherefore it
is very wifely and warily prouided of
vs,that we neither fuffer the common
people to lacke the light of Gods word
any time,neither do we dafel their eies
fo muche with the brightneffe thereof
(which they are not able to abide)that
they may be therewithall miferablie
blinded. We bring therfore none other
thing in our fermons, but that, which
we iudge effectual to bring men to the
loue of godlines and folowing of charitie, to the hatred of finne and forfa-
king of vncleanes of lyfe. And for this
caufe doe we fet before their eyes oftentimes, the crowne of euerlaftinge
glorie, and the paine of the euerlafting
torment. But the daungerous queftions of darke and fecret matters we do
for good confideration leaue vntowched in fuch fermons as are made vnto
the people. The authoritie of Bifhops
is great : in fo much that, it is not very
hard

hard for them to reftreine the vnbride-
led luft of difordered perfons, and to
remoue them, that be obftinate in fin,
from the Communion of the Church.
Neither are fuch menne chofen to be
Bifhops, as may be either for bafeneffe
defpifed, or for folifhnes fet at naught,
or for notorioufe vices reprehended,
and fo do much hurt by their example.

The times of the yeare are fo con-
fecrated and diuided with ordinarie
and folemne ceremonies, that at all
tymes there is fomewhat done in the
Church, which may renew in vs the
remembrance of Gods graces and benefites.

The times of the yere

And, to beginne at the Moneth of
Decembre, we are then ftyrred vp to
remembre that time, in the which the
holy Fathers of the olde time loked for
the coming of the Sonne of God into
the earth, and befought him with continuall prayers to haften it, and had a
moft earneft defire to fee it : that we
might

Aduent.

might the better vnderstande, howe muche we are bound and endebted to God, which hath graunted vs the ioyfull fruition of that moste excellent fruit, which the old Fathers, very holy men, and of God intierly beloued, so griedily lusted and longed after.

Christmas　When the daie of Christes birth is come, we keepe watches, aud singe hymnes and Psalmes by note : our organs also and others instruments sound euery where to the honour and praise of God:euery thing doth then stirre vs vp to beholde the Sonne of almightie God, the most excellēt Lord and maker of al the world, lying naked and crying in a mangier in the weake sourme of a sucking babe. We heare then with the eares of our heartes the voices of Angels bringers of that glad tydinges:and we endeuour by faith to doe our homage with the sheapeherdes vnto the King that is borne vnto vs : and fixing our selues in the contēplation of him,

we

wee receiue the fruicte of incredible
ioye.

The first day of Ianuarie, the Chur- Nevvyeres daie.
che putteth vs in minde, to beholde
the wound, which our Sauiour receiued that daie, and the Mysterie of circumcision, and the moste dreadefull
name of Ihesus, which is the pleadge
of our saluation, and the lesson, which
was then geuen vs, of that most perfect obedience: and so by the strength
and signification of this moste holie
name, we labour muche more cheere-
fully to atteine to the saluation, which
is promised vs.

What should I here saie of the most Tvvelfe daie.
bright starre, which appeared to the
Gentiles in the furthermost partes of
the East?

How might I expresse the incredi- Cādelm.
ble ioy and pleasure of the holie man
Simeon, when he bare the child in his
armes? What should I here rehearse
the exceeding gladnesse and cumfort,

the

the which Anna the widowe conceiued, or els the godli prophecies which
shee pronounced, when shee behelde
the Child ? All these thinges hath the
Churche set before our eyes with solemne pompe, and procession, and can-
dels burning, to the intent, they should
sincke the deeper into our heartes .

Lent.

Now when the time of fasting draweth nere, we behold how Christ was
baptised by Iohn in the floud Iordane:
we here the voice of the Father : we
consider the fast , wherwith the sonne
of God punished his owne bodie : we
record the tentations and wilie practises of Satan against him: we endeuour
our selues , as muche as we can, to set
out the victorie of Christ : we call to
minde the homage of Angels , which
brought him meate and serued him .
By this exãple of Christ we are taught,
that we ought to kepe stil that puritie
and cleanes , whiche we receiued in
the holie fount of Baptisme : that we
should

should receiue the voice of the father commaunding vs to obeye him, with heart and minde: that we should subdewe the body with fasting, and encounter with our old enemie the diuel: to the end that, at the length, the battaile being fought, and the victorie by the mightie protection of God atchieued, we might be refreshed with heauenly foode and comforted by the ministerie of Angels.

When the time approcheth, in the which we mind to celebrate the supper of our Lord, to do so holy a worke with the greater deuotion, we prepare our selues much more diligently then at other tymes: and we doe it with gladnes and feare together. Then doe we consecrate the holy Oiles, by the which are signified diuers gyftes and graces of the holy Ghost, according as S. Denyse and other holy Father write: and we minister the body of our Lord to al such as are readie to

The holy Weeke.

D D   receiue

receyue it : and we wash the feete of
poore men , not only with water, but
alſo with many teares ſometimes : and
by this example we cauſe ſuche , as
looke on , to powre out teares abon-
dantly . But when we behold atten-
tiuely Chriſt hanging on the Croſſe:
when we conſider, how he was ſcorned , reuiled , tormented and put to
death: when we pray for the ſaluation
of all menne : when we come ˏbare-
footed to worſhip Chriſt in his Image:
when we bring in God him ſelfe com-
plaining of our miſliuing : when we
craue pardon for our ſynnes in moſte
humble and lowly wiſe : what man,
thinke you , is then in the Churche,
which is not foorthwith ſtirred vp to
forſake ſynne, and to folow a better ordre of life ?

　　But when Eaſter day is come , we
vſe ſuche honour and pompe, we ſing
ſuche Hymnes and Pſalmes , to aduaunce the victorie and triumph of
Chriſt

Eaſter.

Chrift raifed from death, to fet out the fácke and fpoile of his enemies, to magnifie his euerlafting kingdome and empire, that we may feeme for verie ioye and gladneffe to be befides our felues.

His afcenfion alfo we recorde in *Afcenfion* fuch fort, that we thinke it our part, to bend our felues, as much as we can, to clymme vp together with Chrift into thofe goodlie dwelling places of heauen.

What may be faide of that ineftimable benefit, wherin the holy ghoft *Witfontide.* enkendled the Difciples of Chrifte with the loue of God, and enflamed them with fyerie tongues, to the end that they fhould go throughout al the world, and wrap vp that heauenly fyer in the bowells of faithfull men ? With howe great ioye and gladneffe is that feaft alfo obferued and kept in all the Church ?

Moreouer whē we keepe the memo- *The feafts of Sainēts*

rie of

rie of holy men, in whose heartes the maiestie of Christ dwelled, with dew reuerence: (for it is not lawful to separate them from the companie of Christ, whom he him selfe taketh vnto him as felowes and comparteners of al his goods) we are stirred vp to a hope of a certaine diuinitie, when we cast with our selues, how they, that are of the selfe same nature that we be of, for the likenesse which they had with God in vertue, haue most happily atteyned the state euen of Goddes.

The feasts of our Ladie.

And as we doe most highly prayse the holines of other (as it becometh vs to do) so do we especially honour, reuerence, and worship that singular paterne of cleanes, virginitie, and godlines, that heauely and meruelous téple of the holy ghoste, that most holy and immortal tabernacle of the euerlasting promise, out of the which riseth the sonne of iustice, to put away with the brightnes of his beames the darkenes of

of the whole worlde : and wee doe
with right good affiaunce cal for the
helpe of the fayd moſt bleſſed Virgin
in our diſtreſſe and neceſsitie, and
wee finde, that her prayers doe vs
muche good often tymes before her
Sonne.

The feruice of the Church is ſo ordered, that, the yeare tourning about,
there is no benefite of God, the remēbraunce whereof the holy Churche
wil ſuffer to be forgotten. And the
Churche doth repreſent the memorie of al theſe benefites in ſuch ſorte,
that it ſeemeth, that they are not ſo
much declared in words, as expreſſed
in doinges. For as the excellent Poete
ſaith:

The thinges we heare, do not ſo ſoone
     prouoke the mind to riſe,
As doe the thinges, that vewed are,
     with true and faithful eyes.

Al theſe thinges, which I haue here
declared, with manie other of lyke

forte, whiche I haue omitted (for I thinke it not neceſſarie, to rehearſe particularly euery point) are not (I graunt you) matters of perfection. They are certayne introductions and neceſſarie helpes for vs, whiche haue ſome what to doe as yeat with this mortall condicion, as we feele by experience. For ſo often as theſe ordinaunces of the Churche are litle Regarded, the minde waxeth dul, diligence fainteth, the loue of religion ſlaketh, and ſo by litle there creapeth into our heartes a certayne forgetfulnes of vertue and godlineſſe. Agayne, when we bende our mindes earneſtly to ſette vppe agayne thoſe godlie ordres, we feele, that the loue of religion and godlineſſe is ſtirred and enkendled in vs. And no meruaile. For why, the brightneſſe of that light, which hath ſo wonderfully lightened your mindes, is not yet riſen vnto vs: neither are we ſo weaned from the

ac-

acqueintaunce of the body, that we may be without all these outward signes of heauenly thinges any tyme without greate daunger. This is the ordre of the Churche, which is holy, simple, and one: this is the rule and Discipline, by the whiche all wee, whiche haue not yet atteyned vnto the highest degree of wisedome, are instructed.

Now I haue declared these thinges, it remayneth, that I tourne my talke vnto those your heauenly felowes, and men of God, the which being not contented with this beaten and common discipline, haue taught their disciples a newe trade and doctrine which is more wonderful then this. Geue me leaue therefore to talke with them after this sort.

It is a great matter (right woonderfull Sirs) and a harde enterprise, whiche you haue taken in hande: a thinge of so greate importaunce in deede, as none of al those holy Fathers, whose vertue and witte we esteeme very much did euer attempt the lyke in all their life : to cure an old forgrowen disease with a new kind of medicine. When you sawe that the old discipline was fallen, that manners were decaied, that vnlauful lust raged vp and downe without restraint, that the Church tended to ruine : you did, (as it became holy men sent from heauen) take it verie heauily. Wherein I can not blame you. For it was a matter worthie of many teares and much bitter weeping. But you rested not so : bicause it were a token of a feint heart and weake stomake, to pitie the fal and ruine, and not to procure any other remedie for suche a mischiefe, but onely a fewe teares. You did not therefore, as we are woont to doe, sorowe and lament so great a mishap, and powre out teares vnto God for it: but you thought it good to prouide

by

by your labour , ſtudie , and wakeſull
diligence, that the Church ſhould not
be quite ouerthrowen. And who can
denie, but that this is a token of an honourable hart and a valiaunt cowrage.
But let vs ſee, after what ſort you haue
perfourmed this ſo great, ſo weightie,
and ſo worthie an enterpriſe.

I muſt therfore repete a ſentence,
whiche I vſed in my letters , for the
whiche M. Haddon, a man brought vp
in your rules and doctrine , quarelled
with me verie ſharply. What : haue
you thought it expedient to heale the
woundes, which the Chriſtian cōmon
weale hath taken , by ſuch meanes , as
the moſt holy Fathers vſed of old time
in propping vp the Churche , when it
was like to decaie ? No, ſaie you : for
they were the deuiſes of men : and ſo
great a miſchiefe coulde not be reme-
died by mans healpe, but only by the
ſtaie and mightie power of God. And
therfore you determined to forſake all
wordlie

wordlie healpes, and to ſticke only to the word of God. Verie wel . For that is it in deede, which healeth the mind, fortifieth the ſtrength, geaueth light to the ſoule, and bringeth it to euerlaſting glorie. Wherfore I long to ſee ſome worke of this your word of god (wherin you glorie ſo much) which maie be ſo notable and ſo vndoutedly wrought by God, that it mai appere to the world by it , that you did not without good cauſe ſet all other remedies at naught, and lay all the hope of your ſaluation vpō the only ſtaie of this your goſpel. But for ſo much as the kingdom of god that is to ſaie, the goſpel and power of the word of God cōſiſteth, not in the vaunt of woordes, but in a meruelous vertue: and this vertue ſtandeth, not in vndiſcret and ſawcy talke, not in filthy and licentious liuing, not in bitter hatred and flamboldnes, but in modeſtie, cōtinencie, and charitie, in the workes of iuſtice, and loue of godlines: my deſire

fire is to furueie narrowely this your
wōderful gentlenes, courtefie, foftnes,
patience, continencie, charitie, holines
of life , and other the like vertues,
which maie witneffe that the Church
hath ben preferued by you . But this
can not be , faie you , before all fuche
thinges , as hinder this our great and
godlie pourpofe, be taken quite away.
For it is the office and dewtie of the
worde of God, to pul downe the olde
howfe, before the fowndacions of the
new howfe be laied. I take this alfo to
be verie well and wifely fpoken. For
euen as a medicine pourgeth choler
or other noifome humours, which do
moleft the body, before it doth repaire
nature being feeble and brought low:
fo was it expedient for you , to expell
pride , coueteoufnes , leacherie , and
other diffeafes of the fowle , be -
fore the Churche coulde receiue the
comfortable nourifhment of vertue
and godlines . This deuife of yours I
                                    like

like verie well. But now I defire to
know , how thefe hurtfull and peftilét
humours haue ben pourged by you.
Oh, faie you, ther was nothing in the
world fo much againft godlines, as fuperftition: wherfore our principal care
was, to take awaie al fuperftition. You
are not to be blamed for that : for in
deede there is nothing fo muche contrarie to true vertue, as is falfe and
counterfeicte vertue. Wel now, I will
not demaund of you , howe you haue
taken awaie fuperftition : for that is
verie euident. You haue defaced the
authoritie of the Bifhop of Rome: you
haue ouerthrowen the howfes of
Monkes and Nunnes : you haue laied
hand on fuch goods, as were apointed
to holie vfes: you haue rifled churches:
you haue beftowed the goods of them
vpon whome you lifted: you haue mi-
niſhed the reuerence of the auncient
ceremonies: you haue defiled the religious vfage of Sacramentes: you haue
                                    throwen

throwen downe Images, monumétes,
Croſſes, and aulters : you haue condéned the deuout teares and good works
of holie men as naught and vngodlie:
you haue diſanulled the holie decrees,
lawes, and ordinances of the Church:
you haue cut of all hope of true vertue and honeſtie, by a certaine tyrannical eſtate or inuincible kingdome of
ſynne, which you haue ful clerkely by
your doctrine ſet vp. Neither were
you cótented with this waſt and ſpoile
of thinges, but you haue alſo taken
quite away the freedome of mans wil:
and contrarie to nature and reaſon, có-
trarie to the equity and iuſtice of gods
lawe, you haue tied vp all the doinges
and thoughtes of men, good and bad,
wholeſome and vnwholeſome with a
certaine fatall neceſsitie. Theſe are the
thinges (with marie other of like ſort)
whiche, I ſee, are by you, as the lettes
and ſtaies of wholeſome doctrine,
pulled downe, defaced, deſtroied,
man-

mangled and minced in peeces.

I doe not now bewaile the decaie and waſt of holie thinges. For if the health of the church could not otherwiſe be recouered, if the Goſpel could not otherwiſe be brought to his olde brightnes and dignitie, I could eaſily beare this loſſe, and it woulde not grieue me to ſee thoſe thinges, that ſtande whole, the whiche you haue not yet deſtroied, to be vtterly raſed withall.

Wherfore if you haue left anie thing vntowched, ſette vppon it alſo, if it like you, ſhake it, pull it, hourle it downe vpon the grownde, ſo that you reſtore vs that auncient ſeruencie of godlines, that loue of iuſtice and equitie, that ampleneſſe of charitie, that contempte of wordlie thinges, that earneſt deſire of heauenlie life, with the whiche the Churche was inflamed of old time in the Apoſtles daies. This is the puritie of the Goſpel,

pel, this is the excellent worke of the
worde of God , in this ſtandeth the
whole perfourmaunce of your promiſe . You can not diſcharge your
dewtie and bande with anie meane
vertue. For when I ſee the ſacke and
ſpoile , whiche you haue made , to be
ſo great , howe might I thinke it to
ſtande with right or reaſon , that
you ſhoulde recompence it with anie
meane commoditie ? Wherfore I will
aske you once againe , although M.
Haddon be offended withall , I will
earneſtly demaunde , yea I will moſt
inſtantly require of you , what thing
is reſtored by you in the ſteede of
all thoſe thinges , whiche you haue
pulled downe ? I will repete the ſelfe
ſame woordes, that I vſed in thoſe my
letters, whiche M. Haddon ſo muche
reuiled.

What is ouerthrowen I ſee, but
what is ſet vp, I ſee not : what is grubbed vp by the roote I perceiue , but
what

what is planted I perceiue not. Tell me, I praie you, what it is, to repaire the doctrine of the Gospell when it tendeth to decaie? What it is, to bring al thinges verie neere, as M. Haddon your disciple saieth, to the rules of Christian godlines vnto the most holie doctrine of the Apostles? what it is, to driue awaie with a newe light and brightnes the darkenes of errours, and mist of synne, in the which men liued? I think it be, to bring to passe, that men maie haue no wil to looke down vnto the earth, that they may be desirous to looke vp to heauenward, to become modeste and humble, to be inflamed with the loue of holines and chastitie, to be decked and beawtified with the comendable vertues of meekenes, patience, grauitie, and constancie, to be verie obedient to the Rulers of the Churche, to yeald verie great honour and loue to the gouernours in the comon weale, to emploie their whole life,

life, deuiſes and practiſes to a common
profitte, to be zelouſly bent towardes
godlines and Religion, finally to make
and prepare the way to heaue by godly vertues.

I demaund of you therefore, whether there be anie one man amongeſt
al thoſe, that ſo much eſteeme and reuerence you, yea that ſette you vp as
Goddes, endewed with ſuch a feruent
loue of heauenly thinges, with ſuche
chaſtitie and cleannes of life, that he
wil not ſuffer him ſelfe to be diſteined
with any ſpot of diſhoneſtie: with ſuch
patience and gentlenes, that, although
he be prouoked with railing and di-
ſpiteful language, he wil not only not
offende in worde, ſuche as wronged
him, but alſo wiſh them al good things
and proſperitie : with ſuche louingnes
and charitie, that he wil beſtowe all
his ſubſtance to the common profitte:
with ſuche grauitie and conſtancie,
that he wyll neuer be diſordered :
with

with suche a burning loue of euerlasting life and glorie, that he wil forsake
all the light and vaine pleasures of the
worlde, that he will pitch downe his
Crosse, and dash against it all his vnlawfull lustes: that he wil thinke vpon
Christ only, and sit downe at his feete:
that he wil loue God ernestly, and be,
as it were, violently caried vp to heauen in mind and thought. With al these
vertues did the Churche sometimes
flourish: with these fier brades of godlie loue were men of olde time inflamed: from this most feruent loue of
godlines coulde they not possibly be
brought by anie terrour or tormentes.
And this tooke you vppon you, to
pourge the gospell thoroughly, to put
to flight superstition vtterly, and to en-
kendle againe the light of the anciet
Church, which was put out.

Be therfore as good as your word,
perfourme your promise, discharge
your debt, into the whiche you are in-
curred.

curred. Reſtore that puritie of mind,
reſtore that chaſtitie of bodie, reſtore
that feruencie of godlines, reſtore that
continencie, and gentlenes, that peace
and concord, that band of charitie and
frindſhip, bringe your countreimen
againe to that ſtate, from the whiche
we are al fallen: that you maie by ſuch
a wonderful alteration of thinges, and
heauenlie example of vertue put vs to
ſilence, to whome this new fanglednes
is both ſuſpected and hateful. As for vs,
it is no meruaile, if we haue not as yet
atteined this great and high perfectió
in vertue. For you haue not yet ſet
out this goodlie light to vs. I aske this
queſtion therfore of ſuch only, as take
your part, how holily, how vprightly, how religiouſly they liue. For reaſon would, as I ſaied before, that we
ſhould looke for no meane matters at
your handes. For you haue taken
vpon you a charge of ſo great honour,
magnificencie, and profite to the

worlde, as possibly there can not be
deuised a greater. Wherefore vnlesse your adherentes and disciples
doe so much excell in vertue and honestie al other men, that are vertuous
and godlie, (and yet be not of your
schoole) that they maie dymme the
light of their vertue, and put them
out of conceite: you haue not fulfilled your promise. For if the selfe same
degree of honestie might haue ben
kept and mainteined by vs, without
the losse and ruine of those thinges,
vpon the whiche you haue laied your
violent and griedie handes: if the vertue of your brethren doe not verie
much passe the vertue of our men: shal
it not appeare to the worlde, that you
wise men haue taken a great deale of
paines in defacing of those thinges,
which you haue ouerthrowen, to no
pourpose or profite? Shall it not be
seene, that those thinges were not the
lettes or staies vnto you, for the which
you

coulde not exercise iustice and godlines?

What if your Disciples are not only neuer the better by defacing those
thinges, but rather much more disode-
red and outragious, muche more wicked and vicious? What, if licentious liuing be now lesse punished, if mischieuous hardines be now greater, if more
debate and greater broyles haue bene
stirred vp, sence you haue set your selues to be teachers of men? What, if
moe robberies and shamefuller actes
are now comitted emongest you in e-
uery parte of the realme (if it be true,
that is reported)? What, if there be
wrought more traiterous practises a-
gainst the maiestie of Princes, euen by
such as haue geauen them selues fully
and wholly to your doctrine?

But I wil let your maisters goe, and
will vrge you, M. Haddo, once againe?
What can you alleage? What example can you bringe of that auncient

vertue ? How can you mainteine and
defend this newfanglednes? And yet
you will auowch, that your Churche
differeth nothing at al from the order
and difcipline of the Apoftles . You
faie manie things in deede: but no mã,
which is in his right wit, will euer beleeue you. It is not ynough to affirme,
what fo euer you lift, in wordes. I loke
for the examples of this heauenly vertue, and not for vaine woordes. If you
fee vnlawful luft fet at libertie, difor-
der flinging vppe and downe without
checke , the highe waies befet with
theeues and murderers, tumultes ftirred vp, cõfpiracies wrought, and daungerous practifes deuifed againft common weales euerie where : if all thefe
mifchiefes be not only not taken awày
after the time that the doctrin of thefe
felowes, whom you fo highly commend, tooke place, but rather muche
more increafed: with what face dare
you faie, that this your newe doctrine
                                    differ-

differreth nothing from the doctrine of the Apostles?

You faie, that I require a perfection which can not be had in this life. It is like ynough fir, that i doe fpeake of light offences, fuch as continent and honeft men may fal into euery houre, and not of moft vile, filthie, and infamous crimes, fuch as haue cawfed all holie things to be wafted, fpoiled, and cófumed with fyer, without any fruict of godlines and Religion, the whiche thinges thefe felowes promifed to reftore.

You require of me, that our church as you cal it, and yours maie be fet together and compared, that it maie appeare at the length, whether of them both is more eftablifhed by the authoritie and doctrine of the Apostles. Your requeft is not reafonable. For I faie not, that there is no fpot of vncleanes at all emongeft vs. But I faie and affirme, that it is verie ill done of

EE iiij   you,

you , that thofe fpottes are not taken
awaie emongeft you by the diligence
of your Apoftles . We haue promifed nothing, we haue not pleadged
our faith and truth , that all thinges
fhould be brought againe to the olde
perfection by our diligence : no man
can call vs into the court, and chargo
vs , that we haue not ftoode to our
promife. But thefe men, who, as you
faie, were fent from heauen, haue také
this much vpon them : to reftore the
puritie of the Gofpell, to bring againe
charitie, holines, cótinencie, with that
moft earneft longyng after the euerlafting glorie, to bring al other fuch vertues, as ar cóteined in the word of god,
to light, which were before buried in
darkenes , and to fet vp once againe a
heauenly cómon weale vpó the earth.

But that you maie fee, what courtefie and fauour I wil fhew you in this
conflicte, I will not require of you to
examine and trie your manners by
the

the ftreight difcipline of the Apoftles,
and by that exacte rule of moft holie
and perfect religion : but to compare
the ftate of this your Church with the
grauitie, vertue, religion, and worfhip-
ful behauiour of your auncetours: the
which thing if I can intreat you to do,
you fhall vnderftand that there is fo
great oddes betwene your gofpellifhe
doctrine, and the honorable religion of
olde England, as can not be expreffed
in wordes. Why then fir, what a thing
is this ? If you were neuer able , after the tyme that you gaue your felues to thefe newe and vngodly opinions, to reach to any part of the honour of your auncetours : by what
meanes , I praye you , fhall you be
able to atteyne to that auncient perfection of the Churche, whiche flou-
rifhed in the Apoftles dayes to the
great wonder of the world? Are you
fo voide of all witte and reafon, that
you thinke it ynough to fay, that your
                                    Church

Churche differreth nothing from the Apostles doctrine, as though mē were bound by and by to beleeue you ? No sir, that muſt be ſhewed and prooued, not by braggyng and light behauiour, not by boaſting and reprochfull wordes, but by wonderful examples of iuſtice, innocencie, chaſtitie, cleanes, religion, and charitie, by a moſt holy life, a moſt vertuouſe conuerſation, and a moſt feruent loue of godlineſſe. Yea, M. Haddon, I tell you once againe, that it is not ſufficient for them, that haue promiſed to bring the looſe manners of our tyme to that moſt floriſhing ſtate of the primitiue Church, to be meanly vertuous: they muſt excell, they muſt be wonderfull. The whiche thing bicauſe they do it not, but rather, wherſoeuer they put their foote, they leaue the grownde embrewed with muche naughtineſſe and vice: it is very euident and plaine, that they could not perſourme ſo much, as
they

they had promised. For they haue brought into the common weale, for the cleannes of the Gospell, fowle vices: for peace and loue, debate: for modestie, pride: for religion, wickednes: for liberty, bondage: for good ordre, licentious liuing: for pleasaunt calmenes, a most crewel storme. And yet you like a godly man lay before me the iudgement of God, to make me afraied: in the whiche you say, that I poore wretch(for so it pleaseth you to terme me)shal yeald an accōpt of this so heinouse and wicked offence before the iudgement seat of Christ, bicause I haue presumed to rebuke those holie, continent and religious persons.

In deede there is good cause, why I should feare. For M. Haddon a wise man, and such a one as hath familiar cōference with God at al tymes, wold neuer haue said it, vnlesse it had bē declared vnto him before, by some heauenly reuelation. Reason would therfore,

fore, that I fhould tremble and quake for feare of that iudgement, the which you your felfe feare neuer a deale, and yet you threaten me very feuerely withal.

You fay, that I doe not only laugh at your Gofpell, and deface your Doctours, (whiche are very heauenlie menne) but alfo violently wreft Hieremie. The which thing how falfe it is, I wil declare hereafter.

You fay afterwarde, that all that teftimonie of Hieremie concerning falfe Prophetes perteyneth vnto vs. Howe fo fir? Hearde you euer fay, that there was any newe Prophete e-mongeft vs, that went about to tourne vs away from the auncient Religion? That warranted vs of peace and ioy-litie, as though he had had commiffion from Chrifte fo to doe? That taught the people, that fynne fhould efcape vnpunifhed? You retourne once a-gayne to fpeake your pleafure by the holy

holy Church, the ordre wherof I haue alreadie declared : in the whiche although there be some diseases, yet they are suche as may be cured. For we refuse not the medicine, the which without the Church can not be found els where.

After that you commend your own Church highly. *The publike sermons, say you, you commit to certaine seely friers: and they declaime after their owne fashion, in other matters they are dome.* As touching preaching, I haue said already, that this charge is in no wise to be neglected of the Bishoppes : neither doth the holy Churche beare with such negligence : but rather exhorteth and chargeth al Bishops most streightly, to folow the office of preaching and teaching with all diligence. And it is no reason, that the negligéce of a fewe men snould be imputed to the whole Church, the which is so careful to take good and wholesome ordre

dre with euery particular man, that
he should doe his dewtie. Moreouer,
there are, as I sayd before, many Bisshops emongest vs, the which preach
oftentymes, and stirre vppe their subiectes to the loue of godlines. But admitte it were alwaies so, that the sermons were made by Monkes: doubtlesse it is more tolerable, that godly and
religious persones should be appointed by the Bishops to doe that office,
then that base fellowes, and suche as
are poisoned with most pestilent and
erroneous doctrine, should be made
rulers ouer Churches.

Whereas you say, that at our sermons the audiéce is brought a sleepe,
I graũt it must needes happen so sometimes, when he, that preacheth, can
not be so eloquent and fine, as you are.
What then? Bicause some man nap-
peth a litle sometime, therefore shall
not the rest awake them selues, and
geaue diligent eare to the sermon?
shal no

ſhall no preacher be able to moue and
exhort his hearers to ſerue God with
greater loue and feruency?

    In the miniſtring of Sacramentes,
ſay you, *the Prieſtes only are doers, the*
reſt are but lookers on. Of lyke you are
not pleaſed with that. You haue no
liking in modeſt and ſeemely ordre.
You would peraduenture, that there
ſhould be made a diſordre and confuſion of offices, and that al men ſhould
take vppon them the office of prieſt-
hood. But we thinke, that that comely ordre was ordeyned by God, that
Prieſtes only ſhould miniſter the Sa-
craments, and that the reſt ſhould take
the profit of them with ſilence, and
not medle them ſelues with the diuine
ſeruice.

    As concerning the vnknowen ton-
gue, in the which the ſeruice is ſaide, I
haue ſpokē ſufficiently already: wherfore, bicauſe I wil not repete one thing
oftē tymes, I referre you to thoſe
                    thinges,

thinges, that are said before.

Let vs now enter, say you, *into the maſſes, in the which you would haue the very marow of religion to be powred out.* That is very true. For they conteine in them a moſt feruent lifting vppe of the heart vnto God, moſte holy and deuout prayers, the monumentes and remembraunces of Chriſte, whiche repreſent vnto vs his life, his paſsion, his death, and meritos, the ordre and woorking of our ſaluation, and the appeaſing of the diſpleaſure of God. And (that I may ſay nothing elles) in them is offered vppe the moſte holie bodie of Chriſt, the ſelfe ſame Sacrifice, that taketh away the vncleane ſpottes of ſynnes, that yealdeth vppe thankes to our moſt mighty Lord and bountiful parent, that enkendleth godly mindes, and inflameth deuout hearts with the loue of euerlaſting life and glorie.

You ſay moreouer, that no mā entermedleth

medleth with the Gospell emongest
vs. You say wel in that. For we can
not abide, that euery man should be a
Reader, euery man a Doctour, euerie
man a Prophet. But we thinke it expedient to prouide, that al thinges may
be done honestly and orderly.

Where you saie, that all exhortations out of the Gospell are whisshed
emongest vs: that is false. For we haue
continuall preaching, and there is expounded, what so euer cócerneth sal-
ualtion, (not vnlearnedly, nor yet vn-
sauerly, as you imagine:) and the hearers keepe silence after a very modest
and comely forte.

You come, saie you, *to the Lordes
Table once peraduenture euery yeare, and
that more for a solemne ceremonie, then
for a contrite heart.* This gesse of yours
is very vaine also. Truthe it is, that al
men are bownde by lawe and order to
come vnto our Lordes Table once in
the yeare: but such as doe it but once

FF   in

in the yere, are not wont to be cómen-
ded . And emongeſt vs there are of
ſuch as feaſte them ſelues at this heauenlie banket very often, an exceding
great number . Whereas you ſay, that
it is done for a ſolemne ceremonie onlie, and not for a contrite heart, you
doe but geſſe as your manner it . And
for ſo muche as your geſſe prooueth
falſe, it ſeemeth, that you may woor-
thilie be numbred emongeſt the falſe
Prophetes . When you ſaie, that in
this ſupper the ſupper of our Lorde is
not remembred of vs, you ſpeake with
out the booke, euen as you didde before .   Howe be it, as touching the
Supper of our Lorde, I can not wel
tell, what to ſaie to you . For as yet
I am not perfectlie infourmed, whether you folowe the wicked opinion of your Martyr, or no . If you doe
folowe him, with what reuerence or
trembling can you come to the Sacrament of the Aulter, ſeeing that you beleue

leue, that there is none other thing in it, but onely a naked and bare remembrance of the death, which Chrift fuffred vppon the Croffe for vs? If you folow him not, wherefore do you not abhorre and deteft the naughtie and wicked felowe?

You find fault with vs alfo, bicaufe we haue no publike or open confeffion of our fynnes emongeft vs. I woulde faine learne of you, how that fynne, which is committed fecretely, is to be confeffed in the face of the worlde.

I haue, faie you, *declared your vfage.* You blamed me, bicaufe being vnacquainted with the affaires of England, I declared fuche thinges, as are notoriouselie knowen and caried by letters, by talke, by mofte conftante reporte of all menne, into all Countreis and Coaftes, euen to the furthermoft partes of the world, to the great griefe of all fuch as heare them: and

FF ij yet

yet you speake rashly of our matters, whiche you haue neither seene, nor vnderstoode, (and therefore you vse this word, *peraduenture*)and as though you knew very exactly, al those thinges, which you haue spoken, you saie boldlie, that you haue declared oure vsage, and that very plainely.

After that you tourne againe to the commendation of your Church. You speake much of your continuall preaching, of the despising of mans traditions, of your Psalmes, and Hymnes, and Lawdes, with the which you honour the Lord. Anon after you saie thus. *Then foloweth the holy table of the Lord, which is occupied euery holie daie. The minister of God calleth vp all such as haue prepared them selues to that so heauenly a banket.* Do you call that a heauenlie bāket, the which your Martyr, whom you set out with heauely praises, went about to bereafe of al heauenlinesse? Furthermore you tel vs not, how sober

they

they are, when they eome to this fup-
per, how wel they are clad with their
mariage garment, with what examination, with what feruencie and wakeful
diligence they prepare them felues vnto it. And of your Minifter you faie
neuer a worde, by what meanes, with
what ceremouie, after what ordre of
Religion, by whome he came to that
dignitie.

You talke muche of the puritie of
your fermons, whereas in deede there
can not pofsibly be any puritie in fuch
a corrupt and peftilent doctrine.

Laft of al you declare not, what
fruite this your religion bringeth. For
you fhew vs not your wonderful chaftitie, your puritie and holines of life,
your meruelous woorkes of godlines
and charitie. And yet you faie thus.
I might in this place make an oppofition
or cōparifon, left I lacked wordes, where-
with I might, if I would, trimme it and
fet it out. I would be glad to fee you

doe it, M. Haddon. Howe greate a praise had that bene vnto you, if you had laied together diuers examples of hothe sydes, and shewed, howe this churche whiche you set foorth so solemly, is most like vnto that auncient and primitiue Church, which was dedicated by the bloud of Christ, and instructed in the doctrine of th'Apostles, in vpright and heauenly conuersation, in innocentie, vertue, constancie, lowlinesse, pacience, chastitie, in modest and seemelie behauiour. If you had don this, you had dispatched the whol matter. Wherfore did you not brauelie set out that opposition or comparison, which you speak of? Wherfore did you not set out to the world the worthie actes and holie woorkes of your maisters? Wherfore did you not clere that point, in the which consisted the very groūd and pith of the whol matter? I assure you, you had had the daie of vs, if you had declared, how much these

thefe newe Prophettes dooe paffe in
heauenlie vertues, and had fhewed
withall that there is no difference betweene them and the olde Difciples
of Chrift. What, could a man offuch
a wonderfull witte and fingular eloquence, as you are of, lacke wordes, in
the defence of fo true and fo honeft a
caufe as this is?

But that conclufion of yours liketh
me mcrueloufly wel. You faie thus.
A man may fee more forowing and figh-
inge in one holye Supper of the Lorde,
Which our men doe reforte vnto, then in
fixe hundred of your folemne Maffes.
Firft of al if you thinke, that al Sacramentes are to be miniftred with teares
and fighes, you are fowly ouerfeene.
For there is a time of forow, and a time
of gladnes, as Salomon faith. Then it
cometh to paffe oftetimes that we may
think of heauely things more earneftly
ãd more attetiueli without forow then
with forow. Laft of all I would faine

learne of you, what these your sighes doe meane. Doe thei signifie a desire and longing after the olde Religion againe? Or els serue they for a cloke to couer your new disguised Religion? Or els is there no suche matter at all? For Erasmus and certaine other learned men, haue geuen this marke vnto your Religion, that none of you al wil once sigh, no not vppon such daies as are to be kept with teares and sorow. And Luther him selfe, the foreman of all this rable, he neuer wept nor sorowed, at the remembrance of the bitter paines and tormentes, whiche Christ suffered for vs vppon the Crosse. For he was a man fortified with incredible hardnes, and a deadly enemie to weeping and teares.

As for the diuerse expositions of our Doctors, which you speake of, thei are altogether impertinent to our matter. For there is no disagreeing emongest vs in suche matters as concerne the

grownd

grownde of our faith and Religion.

But to what end tend al thefe thinges,
M. Waulter, to what purpofe do you
bring them? Be it, that thefe your fo-
lemnities be kept of you with fo great
pompe and ceremony, as you wil your
felues: yet can I not fee hitherto, that
you haue by thefe your folemne facramentes newly deuifed by the goodlie
witte of you and your companions, by
this Religion fet vp with fuch diligéce
and prouident carefulnes, by thefe dailie fermons, by this fighing and forowing, brought the Churche to fuche a
ftate, as your Maifters promifed you
to doe. Wherefore you muft pardon
me, if I require one thing of you many
times, if I be to importunate in afking
it. Reftore, I faie once againe, reftore
vnto vs the puritie of the Gofpell, laie
abroad thofe goodly wares of heauenly vertues, fet out to the world the notable leffons of this worthy Religion,
that, when we fee by your wonderful
workes

workes and honourable dedes, that the mightie power of the holy Ghoste is within you, we may be astonished seing your miracles, and confesse, that those Prophetes, whiche taught you, were sent from God.

Marke diligently, I pray you, what our Lorde hath saied as concerning a false Prophete. The Prophete, saith God, the whiche being seduced with pride, shall presume to speake in my name, the thinge which I commaunded him not to speake, or elles shall speake in the name of other Goddes, shall be put to death. If so be, that thou shalt thinke in thy hearte, howe may I vnderstande the woorde which our Lorde hath spoken? Thou shalte haue this token. The thing, which that Prophet foretolde in the name of our Lorde, if it come not so to passe, our Lord spake it not: but the Prophet deuised it of a pride of his own heart, and therfore thou shalt not feare him.

What

Deut.18.d. (margin)

A mark to discerne a false Prophete by. (margin)

What thinge can be more euident and plaine, then this signe? What more prouidently spoken for our saluation? Being now warned and instructed by God, I geue no eare to wordes, but I tourne mine eye to workes: I loke to see, howe faithfully these Prophetes haue fulfilled their promise. It remaineth therefore, that wee consider, what Luther, Melanchthon, Bucere, Caluine and the rest of your Champions haue promised and taken vppon them, what hope they haue brought their adherentes into by their goodlie wordes. Doubtlesse thei caused men to conceiue this hope, that thei would bringe the doctrine of the Gospell to the olde perfection, that they woulde set Religion vp againe, as it was at the first, that they woulde staie vppe the Church, which tended to decaie.

Now this puritie of the Gospel, this holinesse of Religion, this sure staie of the Churche, by what power and

strength

ſtrength is it mainteined? By ſayth, gentlenes, chaſtitie, peace, concord, lowlineſſe, obedience, charitie, godlines, and the great loue of God. But they haue brought into the world, for faith and religion, Church robbing: for gentlenes, crueltie: for chaſtity, looſe liuing: for peace, whourlibourlie: for concord, ciuile diſcord: for lowlines, pride: for obedience, contempte of lawfull authoritie: for charitie, bitter hatred towardes all good menne: for godlines, wicked impietie: for godlie loue, the vtter decaie of all ſuch holie thinges as ſtirred vs vp to the loue of God. They are therefore ſo muche ſhorte of the perfourmaunce of thoſe thinges, which they haue in large and ample manner promiſed, that they haue rather by their laboure and diligence ſo woorſhipfullye employed, lefte all thinges, whiche they tooke vppon them to reſourme and bringe to the olde perfection, in much worſe

caſe

cafe, yea mucho more depraued and diſordered, then euer they were before. Wherefore theſe men were not ſente from God. And ſo it is concluded by the Lawe of God him ſelfe, that they deſerue no ſuch commendations, as you geaue them, but rather euerlaſting damnation.

I demaunde of you once againe. The vertue and puritie of the Goſpell, doth it conſiſt in good woorkes thinke you, or elles in woordes? Doubtleſſe if we beleeue our Lorde him ſelfe, we muſt ſaie, that it ſtandeth rather in woorkes, then in a goodlie ſhewe of woordes. For ſo muche therefore as theſe your Maiſters haue confirmed this new Goſpel, not by good workes, not by woorking of miracles, not by continencie of lyfe, not by vprighte couerſation, not by feruencie of mind, not by burninge deſire, and longinge after heauenlie things, but by boaſting and bragging woordes: is it not manifeſt,

fest, that they are not partakers of the kingdome of heauen? Is it not cleere, that they were not sent from God? Is it not verie euident, that they were false Prophetes?

But let vs retourne vnto Ieremie. And first of all, where you saie, that I would, for a certaine pride, which is in me intolerable, be esteemed as one of Gods priuie counsel, I would faine learne of you, whereof you gather that. Heard you euer saie, that I preached anie newe Gospell? that I professed anie newe doctrine, the which in the olde time was neuer heard of? that I withdrew the people from the olde faith and auncient order with goodlie promises? that I mainteined anie opinion deuised by myne owne selfe so constantly, as though it had proceeded from God him selfe? No truly. What reason moueth you then to saie, that I take this so great a name vpon me, whereas in deede you see no

token

token of such intolerable pride in me?
You saie afterward.

*You molest Ieremie againe, and will
not suffer the reuerende Prophete, to
take his breath.* If I haue molested
the holie Prophete, I haue committed no small offence against my selfe.
But let vs see, how you will prooue
it. You procede thus. *You alleage
these woordes of the Prophete. If they
had stoode in my cownsell, and had openly declared my woordes vnto the people, truly they had tourned them from
their euyll waie, and from their naughtie deuises.* The wordes of the Prophete are verie cleere. I can not tell
therfore how you goe about by your
woordes to make them darke. It foloweth.

*Let vs take our beginning out of Ie-
remie, whiche was a worthie Prophete.*
You can saie none other. If you could
M. Haddon, I doubt you would doe
it. You goe forewarde.

Did

Did he fraie al the Iewes from vice? Did
he bend them al to vertue? Marke wel
the whole ordre and proceffe of his pro-
phecie, confidre the wailing that he ma-
keth, which is in deede very lamentable.
Hitherto you reafon, not againft me,
but againft the moft godlie Prophete,
to prooue him a vaine man : for you
make him to fpeake contrarieties. He
had faied before, that the word of God
was of fuch force, that it brought men
from vice to vertue. He lamenteth afterward, that, although he were ftirred vp by the might and power of the
word of God, yet he could not poffi-
bly bring the people from their wickednes. Wherefore he fpeaketh contrarieties, and difagreeth exceedingly
with him felfe. As you did therefore
in S.Paule, euen fo doe you now. You
improue not my faying, but you make
the man of God to fpeake contrarie to
him felfe. But I faie on the other fide :
that it may moft eafily be prooued by
                                    this

this reason onely , that you could not vnderstand the meaning of the Prophete, bicause you thinke, that he dissenteth from him selfe. For it is not possible , that there should be any disagreement in the worde of God, of the which Ieremie was a minister . And yet you, to impugne more openly the meaning of the Prophete, you earnestly alleage the example of S. Peter, yea and of Christe him selfe , by whose preaching , say you , not al suche , as heard them , were fraied from their synne, vice, and wickednes.

And at the length you goe so farre, that you affirme, that whereas one man yealdeth to the warning of God, an other doth not , it is not in the free wil of euerie man , but that it was so ordeined before the beginning of the worlde : and so you confirme againe that fatal violence or necessitie . And whereas you heare the complaint of our Lord him selfe, whiche is very la-

GG men-

mentable, wherein he bewaileth the infidelitie of the Iewes, which would not be receiued vnder his winges, being thereunto very mercifully moued: yet do you impute their damnation, not to the wickednes of the naughtie men, but vnto God as the author therof. The which impiety of yours is already sufficiently confuted, (so much as the place required.) But neither you neither your maisters doe vnderstand the Prophets: and therefore they imagine, that the Prophets should speake contrarieties.

Thinke you, that God by Ieremie gaue that token to discerne a true Prophete from a false: that al such, as were present at the sermons of a true Prophete, should foorthwith be withdrawen from wickednesse, the which thing the false Prophetes could not doe? If you imagine, that the Prophete spake so, you are much deceiued. For our Lord him selfe, by whose

spi-

spirite all the holy Prophets were enkendled and stirred foreward, spea-
king vnto those men, that were obstinately bent in synne, that shutte their
eyes, and stopped their eares will-
fully, that the light of heauen might
not shine vppon them, or the Worde
of God moue their heartes, made them
not to forsake their wickednesse.
And therefore he complayneth of the
Capharnaites, and suche other as
withstoode his Doctrine verie obstinately.

What is that then, that Hieremie
said? Dowbtles this. That such as be-
leeued the Prophetes, suche as hadde
them in good estimation, suche as
tooke their sayinges to be the verie
answeres of God, (if those Prophetes
were sent from God) there is no doubt,
but that they were easily brought
from vnbeleefe to faith, and from vice
to an honest ordre of life. The
whiche thing when it folowed not,

it was

it was a moste sure argument , that they were not sent from God . For example.

Phasur the Priest was in high reputation . He bent him selfe earnestly against Hieremie . Hananias desired to be called and esteemed as a Prophete. He was in lyke manner an enemie to Hieremie . Hieremie in those daies threatned the people, that ther háged a great plague ouer them:but the other signified vnto the people with manie circumstances of words,that al should be wel. Many men folowed them,but very fewe folowed Hieremie. Nowe sir,when there was such a great dissension betwene these twoo factions, by what token might a man discerne, whether of them was sent from God? By the vertues and vices of suche as folowed either part. Therfore if it had ben diligétly marked at that time,that such as folowed Phasur and Ananias, or other the lyke false and deceitfull

Pro-

Ier. 20.6.

Prophetes, prooued neuer the better, but rather walowed ftil moft filthily in the felfe fame vice, as they did before: might it not haue ben eafily perceiued, that thofe Prophetes, vnto whom they had addicted them felues, were not fent from God? And contrarie wife if it had ben noted, that thofe fewe which folowed Ieremie, which reforted vnto him, which gaue diligent eare vnto his doctrine, did forfake finne, embrace godlines, and feare the iudgementes of God: they might haue iudged very well, that he was fent from God, and that the thinge which he fpake came not from him felfe, but that he vttered fuche thinges onelye, as he hadde learned of God.

Wheras therfore ther were at that tyme many men, which tooke vppon them the name of Prophetes, and faid: thus faith our Lorde: when in deede they had neuer heard the voice of our

G G iij   Lorde:

Lord:and clawed the common people and brought them in hope of a merie worlde,and said peace,peace,whē no peace,that is to say,no great quietnes, and abundaunce of thinges,but an extreme calamitie hanged ouer the state of the Iewes,and the common people, whose eyes were wholly bent vppon them , who esteemed them as menne of God, were nothing the better for them , but continued still in as muche wickednes,as they did before': doubtlesse it was euident , that those menne were false Prophets and craftie crowders,and that they did poison suche,as they tooke vpō them to instruct,with pestilent errours.

The lyke might be said of the tyme of Christe and his Apostles . There were Priestes, and Pharisees, and Saducees , and Herodians , all contrarie to the Doctrine of Christe . Suche, as folowed Christe, and applied them selues with al diligence to learne his

do.

doctrine, withstood synne, and were
inflamed with the desire of godlinesse
and vertue : but suche as solowed the
Priestes of that time, and the Pharisees,
were disteined with many foule vices.
By this token therfore it might be perceiued, that Christ wrought by the holy ghost, and spake the worde of God:
and that the Priestes and Pharisees
tooke a pride vpon their owne conceite which proceded of an vnsetled
and vndiscrete mind.

We may say the like of the Apostles,
who had much a do with false Priestes
and Philosophers, whiche were fro-
wardly bent against the truth. For such
as herkened vnto the Apostles, were
beautifully fournished with the ornaments of true vertue : but such as went
vnto the contrary part, were clogged
with most heinouse vices. Any man
therefore, that was in his right wittes,
might well perceiue by the testimonie of Hieremie, that the Apostles

G G iiij were

were sent from God: and that their aduersaries were moued and stirred forward by the enemie the diuel.

That this is the meaning of the Prophete, al men, which are not obstinatly set in their owne mad and frantike opinion, may see very plainely. For otherwise the wisedom of God, which spake in the holy Prophete, should speake against it selfe: the which thing if a man should but once conceiue it in his heart, it were a moste wicked synne, and horrible offence. Wee may nowe applie it vnto these newe Prophetes.

There was a certayne woorshipfull Prophete, whom you thinke vndowbtedly to haue ben sent from heauen. Many men went after him, and commended him highly, and garded him both with their bodies and armes, and fournished him with their gooddes. I will therefore demaund not of al, but of such onely, as did not onely loue

Lu-

Luther as a bowntifull and helping
man, but also esteemed and reuerenced him as a Prophet sent from heaué,
and receiued his doctrine most willingly both with eares and heartes:
whether they were foorthwith chaū-
ged in hert, and whether they became
any thing the better for it . No , they
were rather made by the hearīg of him
much more presumpteous and proud,
much more incontinent and seditious,
much more dispiteful and outragious ,
yea so farre foorth , that Luther him
self, which had schooled them, was not
able to kepe them in order. That therfore might haue ben a full proofe, that
Luther stoode neuer in the counsell of
God. For if he had stoode in the counsell of our Lord, and had declared the
verie wordes of God vnto such as folowed him and were named after him,
dowbtles there should haue ben seene
some wonderfull alteration of life in
them.

The

The like maie be saied of Melanchthon, Zwinglius, Bucer, and Caluine,
and other the like Prophets. For these
men were none such, as might by good
example of their cōtinent and honest
conuersation asswage the heate of in-
cōtinency in those that folowed them:
but rather out of their schooles proceded verie often vicious and incōtinent
men: yea and not only incōtinent, but
also violēt churchrobbers, destroiers of
good lawes, wily practisers of treason
against princes, felowes mischieuously
bent to deface al places of holines and
deuotion by manslaughter, bloudshead
and fier. Wherfore the teachers of this
doctrine were not sent from God :
for if they had ben sent from God ,
doubtles they had tourned those men,
that honoured them as goddes , from
their wicked life .

Moreouer , for so much as there is
no disagreement in the spirite of God,
if they had ben sent from God , there
must

muſt needes haue ben a moſt perfecte
cóſent and agreement emógeſt them.
But the world knoweth, that there is a
moſt bitter diſſenſion emongeſt them:
wherfore it foloweth neceſſarily, that
they were not moued by the inſtincte
and inſpiration of the holie ghoſt, but
driuen with burning fyer brandes of
the findes of hell, and that they applied them ſelues, not to inſtruct men,
but to ouerthrow them.

You ſaie, that there is a meruelous
goodlie agreement emongeſt you. I
ſpeake not of you as nowe. For it
maie be, that you maie by feare of
pouniſhmente ſtaie for a lytle time
the furie of raging felowes, (the
whiche remedie, when the minde
is not well ſettled, can not endure
longe.) But of others, ſee you not,
howe great diſſenſion there is emongeſt them, that ſprange of Luther ?
See you not, howe they fall out a-
bout woordes ? How they alter and
chaunge

chaunge their opinions? Howe confusely, doubtfully, and intricately they speake? With what fond reasons they labour in vaine to prooue that thing, which they are bent to mainteine: in so muche that they can neither agree with other men, neither yet within them selues? They choppe and chaūge their Creedes, they affirme now one thing and now an other, they are established in no one opinion. They can neuer agree within them selues, to whome they maie referre the determination of dowbtes.

You referre the matter to your parlament (as you terme it): or els to your babling Bucerans, as the Bishoppe of Angra not vnfittely termeth them. Diuers men referre the decision of questions in religion to diuers Confessions of the faith, which are wont now and then to be altered and chaunged. Thinke you, M. Haddon, if, as I doe now reason with you in writing, so I

might

mighte be presente wyth you, and
presse you with wordes, and wind you
to and fro by the force of argumentes,
that you were able to stande to your
tackelinges? No without dowbt. But
you wculde deuise a hundred diuers
shiftes of descant to face out the matter, and seeke out all the starting holes
and blind corners in the world: in such
sort, that it might easily appeare, that
neither your tongue, neither yet your
wit were in perfecte good plight.
Howbeit one poore shifte you would
finde, (which is a singular good helpe
to you in all your distresses.) that is, to
brawle, chide, schold and reuile. You
saie afterward.

That you maie acknowledge the autho-
ritie of this Churche, if you dowbt of it, I
referre you to the Apologie. I know you
haue written an Apologie, wherwith
you labour to set out your Churche
merueloufly. If you haue written it
more wittyly and finely, then this
booke,

booke, which you set out against me, surely you haue done me great wrōg. For you made light of me, and therefore did not vouchesafe to put out the vttermost strength of your eloquence, when you encountered with me. If you vse the like stile and the like argumentes, that is to saie, if you contend with the like arrogancie and reprochful language: I haue not so much time to spare, that I wil desire to take it once in my handes. For you define nothing, you speake nothing sincerelie, you conclude nothing by good argument. You saie at the length.

Confute it if you can. But you can not. That was verie arrogantly spoken. Who hath made you so loftie and high sprited? Your eloquence? Or elles the loue of the truthe? If you truste to your eloquence, you are a very babe. If you beare your selfe vppon the truth, you imagine manie
thinges

thinges to be true, that are not.

You saie, that one hath barked a-
gainste your Apologie. I haue not
reade it, and yet I knowe, that your
Apologie, whiche, you saie, can not
possiblie be confuted, is alreadie excellentlie well confuted, by a manne
of muche grauitie, godlines, and lear-
ninge. which thing you denie.

But this lesson haue you learned of
your maisters: who beinge openlye
conuinced, fall a crying, being sette a
gogge, kepe a raging stirre: and when
they are able to saie nothing to the
grownde of the matter, they heape
together manie woordes without order and besides the pourpose, aud yet
they vaunte them selues emongest
their adherentes beyond all measure
and modestie. But I regard not your
brauerie and lustines, I esteeme not
your haughtie and prowde vauntes:
I weye the truthe, reason and argumentes. And suche is the noblenes of
this

this your Iliad, the glorie and renoume
of your kingdome so bright, that neither can anie vice lie hidden in it, neither yet anie vertue vnknowen.

Wherfore you labour but in vaine to
conceale that thing, whiche is euerie
where cõstantly reported. What you
say touching the immortality of soules,
I wote not. I neuer saied, that your
maisters denied the immortalitie of
sowles. Howbeit I am not ignorant,
by what degrees or steppes men are
wont to clymme vp vnto the highest
point of that most detestable opinion.

Whereas you saie, that there hath
ben manie men emongest you, which
haue confirmed the truth of the gospel
by banishment, nakednes, hungre, yea
by sheading their bloud and yealding
their liues : I graunt it. For so did the
Bishop of Rochester, so did Moore, so
did the holy Carthusians (to passe ouer
a numbre of others) these men died a
most honourable death for the glorie
of

of Chriſt. So doe your holy Biſhops, whō you haue defeated of their goods depriued of their dignities, and caſt into priſons. So do we ſee many others, Biſhops, Prieſts and Monks, very godlie and Religiouſe perſons, driuen out of England and Ireland, liuing like baniſhed men and outcaſtes: the which, if they had not ben able to eſcape out of your clammes, had peraduenture ben put to a moſt crewel death, by the miniſters of this your Goſpel.

If you meane any other of your men, heare what S. Cyprian ſaith: that, ſuch as being without the bowndes of the Church, doe ſuffer death for the glory of Chriſte, they doe not receiue the Croune of Martyrdome, but beare the puniſhment for their vnbeleeſe. If thei therefore, that breake vp the incloſure of the Church, and ſeperate them ſelues from it, although they yeld their bloude and liues for the Religion of Chriſt, which the Church holdeth, are

H H   not

not to be accounted as Martyrs, but as naughty packes and Church robbers : what is to be thought of such, as being without the Church, are not ashamed to spil their bloud and liues in the main tenance of rebellion and vngodlines?

I am nowe come to that place, whiche is by you, (who are a man naturally abhorring the sleightie occupation of flatterie and lying) verie clerkely handled. Your woordes are these.

You confesse that you haue gone further in the matter , then you had thought to doe. Truth it is , that you haue gon a great deale further , then it became you to doe : especiallie in the most learned and prudēt eares of the Quenes Maiestie, whose sharpe witte and iudgement you woulde haue ben afraid of, if you had wel weighed with your selfe , how much pitthinesse there is in her . O right excellent Syr Waulter, you appeare nowe in your owne likenes. Tel me, I pray you, doe
you

you not fee, that excefsiue prayfinge doth not aduaunce the dignity of Prin-ces, but rather vtterlie peruerte their minde and iudgement oftentimes? Do you not know, that the moft fine and fharp wit, loueth truth, and abhorreth excedingly all lying and flatterie? For what other thing is it to praife Princes excefsiuely, but to fet them out to the world as mocking ftocks? Truly if your Quene be fo witty, as I may wel think fhee is, not by your talke, but by the reporte of other men, fhe will tourne you out of her courte and companie as an open and detected flatterer, and wil not fuffer her felfe to be moft im-pudently mocked of you.

If you fet out her wit, if you com-mende her knowledge in the Latine and Greeke tongue, if you praife her courtlie grace and comlines of fpeach, it is well donne. But when you make her no meane Diuine, when you aduaunce her witte fo muche,

as though I ought to be terriblie afraid
of it, you affault her Maieftie by verie
wilie and craftie meanes. Is this your
loialtie ? Is this the part of a kind hert,
mindefull of the benefites beftowed
vppon you ? Is this well done, that a
moft noble Quene, a Princeffe endu-
ed with moft excellent wit and fingular qualities, fhould be gibed and fcor-
ned of you, M. Haddon, who haue,
as you faie your felfe, ben foftred and
brought vp by her Maiefty ? Did you
fo little efteeme her iudgemente, that
you thought her meete to make your
laughing ftocke ? To pull her downe
from the fetled ftaye of her minde by
your clawing and flatterie ? To deceiue her for your gaine and lukers
fake ?

If, when you fette for this bootie,
you had made your entrie more co-
uertlye, your fowle flatterie needed
not to haue benne repelled with fo
greate inforcemente. For a manne
might

mighte haue thoughte, that you had
mildowbted the sharpenesse of the
Queenes witte, and therfore hadde
deuised to vndermine secretelie, that
you might the better haue scaled the
forte, whiche you haue desired to
take.

But now, wheras you mock so opély,
ascribíg vnto her maiesty, such cómen
dable qualities, as can not possibly stád,
neither with her age, neither with her
nature, as being a woman, neither with
her tender and delicate bodie, neither
yet with her estate, (which is otherwise employed to weightie and carefull affaires) : is it not manifeste, that
you make lighte of her witte? Doe
you so recómpence the benefits which
you haue receiued of her bowntiful-
nesse? If shee be so wise as you make
her to be, if shee haue so many excellente vertues, as I desire her Maiestie to be alwayes decked and bewtified withall : the moderate praises,
            H H iij   which

whiche I geaue her, fhee wil accepte
with good hearte, but that immode-
rate flatterie of yours fhee will refufe
and reiecte : neyther will fhee fuffer
her felfe to be mocked of fuche pre-
fumptuoufe felowes to the greate a-
batemente of her eftimation and honour.

As towchinge the quietneffe of
thinges, whiche you talke of at large,
I faie this muche. It is the parte of a
madde man, yea of one, that is ignoraunte of the common frailtie of man,
to truft to much in profperitie, and not
to caft long time before by caufes paf-
fed, fuch aduerfities, as peraduenture
hange ouer his heade. Moreouer,
there canne be no quietneffe, where
the faithe of the holie Churche is fhut
out. For the minde is troubled, yea
and oftentimes fhaken quite out of
the hengies, by the remorfe of fynne,
the which the moft prefumptuous and
bolde felowes in the worlde are not
able

able to suppresse, (although many are
able to dissemble it).

As for the comparison of your
Church with the Primitiue Churche,
which you saie may be confirmed by
the Histories, I saie that, either you
haue not read the Histories, or els you
are past all shame . You shoulde haue
brought some example or testimonie
out of the Histories, with the whiche
you might ouercharge vs . But you
can neuer doe it , forsomuch as all the
antiquitie maketh against you .

Whereas you saie, that your nobilitie is verie well agreed, would God
it were so : but it is otherwise reported commonlye . I passe ouer manie
thinges of purpose, partly bicause they
are nothing to the purpose , and partly
because they are alreadie confuted before. But wheras you saie these words:
Ah be not disquieted gentle Syr : I acknowledge your pleasaunt manner of
speach. As for your heauenly kindred,

H H iiij   of

of the whiche you faie, you are verie
defirouſe : you doe well in it . But I
woulde you had ſome other menne of
this ſtocke and kinred, more ſkilful in-
terpretours of the law of God . Then
how wittilie was that ſpoken of you ?

*Wherefore ſaie you , that menne haue
benne caried awaie by vs from that moſt
aunciente and holie Religion , which
was grownded vppon the bloude of Ieſus
Chriſte , and hathe continewed alwayes
one euen vntill our daies , and that they
haue benne trained in an other Religion,
which is moſte curſed and deteſtable ?*
Then you adde , *Doe you beleeue theſe
thinges , as you haue ſpoken them? No
trnely doe you not.* Theſe thinges were
very merrily ſpoken of you, M . Haddon. Doubtleſſe your pleaſant gyrdes
procede of ameruelous wit: eſpecially
when yon thinke your ſelf to be cocke
ſure.For then,as though your diſcourſe
had eſcaped the rockes , you pleaſure
very much to ſport and dalie .

But

But whereas you saie, that I doe
not beleeue those thinges whiche I
haue saied, you are fowly deceiued.
For I doe bothe beleeue and confesse
them, neither shal the outrage and vn-
brideled wilfulnesse of a sort of rascall
varlets euer bring me from the cõstant
confession of my faith. What argumentes of yours thinke you, to be of
such force, that thei might cause a mã,
which is in his right wittes, not to beleue that, that is confirmed by the testimonie of holie Scriptures, by authoritie of the holie Fathers, by the recordes of al the antiquitie? You saie,
afterward.

For in the olde and beste time of the
Church, neither was their any Popedom,
neither leaden redemption for synne,
neither the marte of Purgatorie, neither
woorshippinge of Images, neither run-
ninge vppe and downe to visite Sainctes,
neither offering in the Masses for the
liue and for the dead, with other like.

These

*These shamefull pointes, whiche dooe
dishonest Relligion, at what times they
crope in, and by whome they were deuised, you are not ignoraunte. But you
dissemble it, to serue the eares of your
companie.*

Belke out M. Haddon, streine your
selfe, as muche as you can, ridde your
stomake of this surfeicte, of most barbarouse surie and rage: cast vppe your
poison, spewe out your venime: and
then shall you openly triumph emongest your compagnions with this peeuish and vaine talke. When you haue
said nothing, prooued nothing, alleaged no true testimonie of the antiqui-
quitie: when you haue broughte nothing elles but railinge for argument,
madnesse for reason, impudencie for
true exaumples: you keepe such a ra-
ginge stirre, as though you hadde alreadie wonne the fielde with greate
honour.

But we on the other side are wont

to

to declare, by authoritie of the holie
Scriptures, by teſtimonies of the holy
Fathers, by fetching the Monumentes
and Recordes of al the Antiquitie, finally by reaſon, by vſe, by experience, by a number of examples, that
thys kinde of gouernement hath all-
waies bene in the Churche: and that,
who ſo euer goeth about to appaire
it, is a breaker of peace, an ouerthrower of Religion, a woorker of
ſedition, a puller downe of the Churche, whiche is one, and a ſetter vp of
diuers and ſundrie churches, diuerſly
ſundered and diuided within them ſelues, a bringer in of infinite moſt filthie
vices, and trowbleſome errours.

As for the mart of Purgatorie, which
you ſpeake of, we anſwere you, that
there is no ſuch thing. If at any time in
ſo many hundred yeares ther hath ben
any bying and ſelling of holie thinges
vſed, the holie Churche alloweth it
not, but baniſheth it out of the bounds
of the

of the Chriſtian common weale, as a moſt peſtilent and pernicious abuſe.

Likewiſe of Images, we ſay, that al we, that liue in the holy catholik faith, are able to prooue both by reaſons, argumentes, and examples, that euen frō the primitiue church, (eſpecially after it might be done for tyrannes) there hath ben Images ſet vp in churches, to the euerlaſting remembraunce of vertue, to moue men to godlines and religion, to the glorie and honour of Chriſte, the whiche is ſeene in the wonderfull vertue of holie men. We ſaie moreouer that the errour of thoſe men, that threw downe Images, was condemned by manie authorities of the holy Fathers, by diuers decrees of generall councels: the whiche thing your maiſters, be they neuer ſo ſhamelès, can not denie, vnleſſe they wil firſt burne al the writinges of holie fathers, al hiſtories and records, all the decrees of general Councels.

What

What shoulde I here reason of the reuerence and honour, which was of old time geauen vnto sainctes? Could you neuer spare a litle time from the fine woorkes of Accursius, to bestow in the reading of Gregorie Nazianzene, Basile the Greate, Hierome and Ambrose? If you coulde doe it, you shoulde see it in their bookes, howe many times godlie personnes came together in the olde time, what resortes and assemblies there were made, what eloquent Orations were pronounced in the commendation of Sainctes, how greate multitude of the common people pressed thither to heare them. But nowe, if I woulde shewe you, with what feruente zeale and deuotion verie many men were wont to continue all night at the Tombes of Martyrs, it were a hard matter to expresse it.

None of al the holy Bishops in those daies, did once put backe the common people from hearing the cōmendation

of

of Martyrs : no man diſſwaded them
from that moſte earneſt deuotion towardes the Saintes: no, they did rather
exhort al ſuch as were preſent, to viſit
their Monumentes, to praiſe and honour them, to obſerue and keepe ſuch
woorſhippe, as was dew vnto them.
For they ſawe in thoſe aſſemblies,
when the name of Martyrs was ſette
out with heauenlie prayſes, that not
the nature of the bodie, but the grace
of God, and the almightie power of
Chriſte him ſelfe was dewlie honoured in them. For if the Chriſtian
menne in thoſe daies kept the ſignes
of the holie Croſſe, and the Images
of Sainctes, whiche were of deuotion ſette vppe in Churches, with ſuch
reuerence : if they were oftentimes
put in minde by thoſe ſignes to plucke
vppe their heartes, and to remember
the vertue whiche thoſe domme Images did repreſente : was it not muche
more conuenient, that the liuely Images

ges of Chrifte fhoulde be honoured with greater feruencie, and that all fuche as ferued God truely and heartilie, (to doe this honour the better) fhould vifite the Tombes of Martyrs, and Churches builded in the honoure of them? And is it not euidently fene, that the Sainctes are by the operation of the holy Ghoft fhapen to the likenes of God, and that they beare a very true and expreffe Image of Chrift?

As touching your paftime that you make with Purgatorie (for you muft needes haue a fnatche at euery thing) can there be broughte any grauer teftimonie againft you, then that, which the manne, that was fent (as you faie) from heauen, hath geuen openlie? Who is that faye you? It is that Luther, whome you honoure and reuerence, whome you make a God, whome you affirme to haue ben borne for youre faluation. Hee fayed more then once or twife, and abidde

by

Purgatory proued by Luther.

by it, that there was a Purgatorie, and that he did not weene, thinke, or beleue it, but certainely knowe it to be so. For proufe whereof, he constantlie alleaged that place of S. Mathew, where Christe said, that the synne of suche, as did wilfully resist the testimonie of the holie Ghoste, shoulde neuer be forgeauen, neither in this worlde, neither yet in the worlde to come: by the which wordes it is signified, that some hope of forgeuenes is mercifully shewed by God vnto many men euen in the worlde to come.

Matt.12.c

He alleged also that place out of the Machabees, where Iudas made oblations for the synnes of such as were departed. With these and other the like argumēts and allegatiōs he was earnest to proue that there was a Purgatorie.

2.Macab. 12.g.

How then? If Luther saied there was a Purgatorie, and you will warrant it, that Luther was sent from God: and, if he were sent from God, so long

as

as he was in that embassage, he coulde
not lie : it is manifestly prooued by his
authoritie, (the whiche you maie not
gainsaie) that there is a purgatorie. If
there be no purgatorie, Luther lied. If
Luther lied, he was not sent from
God, but from him, that is the father
of lying. Choose therefore whether
you like better. For either the authoritie of Luther shal cōfirme, that there
is a purgatorie, or els the feined tale of
purgatorie,(as you terme it)shall conuince Luther of vanitie and madnes.

But he afterward denied purgatorie. That is no wonder. For not only
he, but all his offspring saie nowe one
thing, and now an other: they correct
and alter manie thinges, neither can
they staie them selues in anie one degree, but rather when they haue once
begonne an errour, they heape and increase it with a numbre of other errours.

But I would faine learne of you M.

Haddon: whether of these two opinions, whiche are mainteined both by Luther, think you to be the truer? The later, saie you. Well then the former he receiued not of God. Then was he not as yet sent from God. But after he had disteined him selfe with incestuous wedlocke, after he had allured his contrei men to rebellion, after he had defied chastitie and all holines, after he had stirred vp such broile and sedition in the common weale, that he coulde not appeace it him selfe afterward, when he had railed against the state of the church with most reprochfull and shamefull language, when he had vttered most horrible and diuelish blasphemie, when he had wasted, spoiled, and burned all holie thinges, when he had committed all these outrages and villanies: then was he thought a meete man to be taken into gods prieuie counsell, and a persone woorthie, to whome God, besides all other se-

cretes

cretes, fhoulde mercifully reuele that myfterie alfo of the deuifing of purga-torie. Then did this great wife man vnderftand at the length, that S. Augu-ftine, which held that we fhould praie vnto God in our Sacrifices for the dead: that S. Cyprian, which laied this moft grieuous punifhment vpon fuch, as appointed Prieftes in their teftamét to be tutours or gouernours to their children, that there fhould no facrifice be offred vp for them in the churches: that S. Chryfoftome, whiche referred this ordinaunce to the tradition of the Apoftles: that S. Denife (to paffe ouer a numbre of others) which wrote ve-ry diligently of the care, that is to be had for the departed in the faith, and of praiers, that are to be made vnto God for their deliueraunce : Luther, I faie, vnderftood, from heauen that al thefe men had ben in great errour and folie.

Trulie the capitaine of this your faction had a great commoditie of his

II ij   naugh-

naughtines and folie, if, after the rei-
sing of such broiles and troubles in the
worlde, he was deliuered by the benefite of God from that errour, in the
which those holie Fathers, most Godlie and wise men, excellently wel learned in the Scriptures, linked vnto
Christe with a most streight band of
heauenlie loue were quite drowned.

If no man can thus perswade him
selfe, vnlesse he be peeuish, frantike and
starke mad, void not only of al godlie
religion, but also of common sense:
who doth not see that this opinion of
Luther is wicked ād detestable, taught
and set out by none other, then by the
enemie the diuell.

But this, saie you, is not witten in
the scripture. What then? The thing,
which the Apostles taught by word of
mowth, which their schollers deliuered to the posteritie, whiche hath ben
most constantly holden and beleeued
from the primitiue Churche till our
times,

times, whiche hath ben approued by
the beleefe and full agreement of the
whole Church for fo manie hnndred
yeares, fhall Luther a feditious mad
felowe, after fo manie ages garifhly
auowch it to be a feined matter? Shall
men, whiche take vpon them to be
both Godlie and religious, folow him
as a God of heauen, that attempteth
moft defperatly to affault heauen? For
he maketh warre againft heaué which
taketh vp armour againft the faith of
the Church.

No, no, faie you, *you would not thinke,
what manner of man he was. For he, I tel
you, woulde allowe nothing, vnleffe he
fownde it written in the holie fcriptures.* Well fir, I will not nowe handle
that matter, whiche is by the holy Fathers difcuffed long a goe: howe the
gofpell confifteth not only in thinges
written, but alfo in cuftomes and ordinaunces receiued without any writing, deliuered vnto the Churche by

II iij   word

worde of mowth and order of the A-
postles: how much the sure and grou̅-
i. Tim. 3. c. ded authoritie of the Church, which
is the piller and staie of truth , is to be
esteemed: of howe great value and
importaunce the agreement of all holy men in one minde without anie
varietie ought to be : all these thinges
I will nowe omit , and aske you one
question, how Luther , when he saied
there was a purgatorie , to prooue it,
alleaged the testimonies of the holie
scripture, if there were no testimonie
in the scripture, that proued that there
was a purgatorie?

Then againe when he saied, that
there was no Purgatorie , by what
testimonie of the Scripture thought
he, that Purgatorie might be vtterly
disprooued ? Brought he anie one
place, by the whiche he might conuince that there is no Purgatorie ?
Dowbtlesse not one . Such therefore
was his presumption , that , what so
euer

euer came into his head, that woulde
he conftantly affirme : and againe, the
felfe fame thing, if it mifliked him,
would he vtterly denie.

And yet his difciples for footh find
no fault at all, neither with his incon-
ftancie, neither yet with his lewd faf-
fhions : but what fo euer the drowfie
blowbol draueled out ouer his pottes,
that toke they vp fo griedily, as though
it had ben good gofpell.

But left you fhould faie, that it can Purgato-
not be fhewed by the teftimonie of rie.
the fcripture, that there is a purgatory,
although it be not neceffarie, yet, befides thofe places, whiche are wont
to be alleaged for the proofe thereof,
I thinke it good to bring a fewe : of
the whiche that is one of S . Marke :
where our Lorde, when he had faied,
that hel(into the which al fuch fhalbe
throwen downe, as efteeme more
their bodilie pleafure, then their dewtie towardes God) fhoulde haue this

II iiij   pro-

propertie, that the worme of them, that shall be tombled down headlong into it, should neuer die, and their fyer neuer be quenched : he brought in *Marc.9.g* foorthwith these wordes : for euerie man shalbe seasoned in fyer, and euery sacrifice shalbe seasoned in salt. In this place there are two thinges to be noted. One is, that there is a worme, that is to saie, a vexation or torment of cōscience gnawing and molesting the minde, the whiche shal haue an ende : and that there is a torment of fyer also, the whiche in like manner shall haue and end in some men. For otherwise our Lorde woulde neuer haue *Esaie.66.a* brought that place out of Esaie : their worme dieth not, and their fyer is not quenched. By the whiche place we are taught, that there is one torment euerlasting, and an other that lasteth but for a time. For so muche therefore as this worme and fyer is a torment or vexation of minde, and of tormentes

tormentes there is one, whiche is appointed by the iudgement of God to laſt but a time, and the other to continew for euermore : is it not euidently prooued, that there is a purgatorie? (for ſo is the place of puniſhment called, in the whiche by the ſentence of God the ſowles are purged within a certaine time of ſuche ſpottes of venial offences, as they had gathered in this life.)

An other thing worthy to be noted is this, that no ſynne ſhal eſcape vnpuniſhed. For euen as in the old lawe it was not lawful to offre vp any Sacrifice without ſalt, ſo is it not lawful for our ſoules to approch vnto the throne of Gods maieſtie, vnleſſe their vncleanes be before clenſed by ſalt and fyer, that is to ſay, by the rigour of Goddes iudgement, and by dewe puniſhment: that, when al the ſpottes of vncleane affection be put out and quite conſumed, the faithful ſowles may come to haue

haue such a puritie and cleerenes, that thei may be able to receiue the brightnes of God in them selues, and be likened and confourmed to the glory of God. For although by the mercy of God synne is taken quite away in such as stay them selues vppon a liuelie faith, yet are they for the most parte so bounde with some knot of the law, that they must needes satisfie the iustice of God. For almightie God is mercifull, but so, that he is not vnmindfull of his iustice: he is also iust, but in suche sorte, that in the ministring of his seuere iudgement he sheweth manie pointes of great mercie.

Moreouer this puritie or cleannes, which is gotten by the grace and benefite of Christ, hath certaine degrees, so, that he that is cleane, may be yet cleaner, and come vnto a cleerer knowledge of the nature of God. And the encrease of this cleannes consisteth

steth in salt and syer, that is to say, in
such pounishment, as is appointed to
pourge the remnantes of synne : that
the Sacrifice may be purer and holier
and more acceptable to God. Wherefore it is necessarie, that the Sacrifice,
whiche is to be offered vppe vnto
God with suche rites and orders, as
are appointed by Christe our high
Priest, be first cleansed, yea and perfectely well pourged, by laying on
some pounishment vppon synne, either in this lyfe, or elles in the lyfe to
come. For euen as God, when he
pardoned Dauid, quited him not of all
punishment, (for he lost afterward his
sonne, and was chased out of his kingdome by the heynouse treason of his
sonne Absolon, and his howse was
dishonoured in the face of the world)
in lyke sorte, although God forgea-
ueth synnes, yet, that notwithstan-
dinge, hee wyll require some penaunce, that there maye be made a
satis-

2. Reg. 12.
d.

satisfaction or amendes for the offence committed. The which satisfaction resteth not in the weight or estimation of it selfe, but in the infinite merite of Christ. For otherwise there should be no end of punishment, for so muche as the offence was endles : in so much as the maiestie of God was offended, (which is endles.)

Vnto this penaunce, which is to be abiden of al such, as haue not thorughly pourged the vncleannes of their sinnes in this life by dew labours, looked S. Peter, when he said, that the iust should hardly be saued, wherefore the wicked were farre from that, that they could assure them selues of saluation. That there is a most certaine hope of saluation offered vnto the iust, he denieth not : but that it is geuen, vnlesse they take great paines and trauaile before, that he denieth vtterly.

S. Peter againe in the selfe same epistle, to teach vs, that the entraunce

ŧ. Pet. 4. d

vnto

vnto saluation is not shut vppe to the
dead, saith, that Christe preached the
gospell to those sowles, that were in
custodie or ward. He saith not, that
Christ going downe to hel declared
that ioyfull and glad tydinges to the
holy Fathers onely, but also to menne
which were committed to ward, that
is to say, to men which were shut vp
in prison for offences committed. And
lest it might be thought, that those mē,
whome Christ at that time instructed
with a more cleere and exacte know·
ledge, had ben before vtterly voide of
faith, he added : Such as had ben some
time vnbeleeuing. And againe lest
some man might suspect, that that sentence had ben spoken by them, the
which, although they had sometyme
cōmitted some offences, yet had spent
the greatest part of their life in faith
and religion, he saith : that the gospel,
that is to say, the tidings of euerlasting
saluation was brought to them, which
in the

1.Pet.3. d

Ibidem.

in the daies of Noe made light of the
counsel and aduertisement of the holy man : the whiche notwithstanding,
(before thei were cōsumed in the flud)
were better aduised, and gat pardon of
their synnes and offences : but yet so,
that for their long offence, they suffred
in hell a long penaunce. Out of the
which place it is gathered by the autoritie of S. Peter, that such, as repent
them selues in lyke māner of their vncleane and synful liuing in the ende of
their life, and depart out of this bodie
with a burning faith, shal after the same
fasshion be kepte in prison, vntil they
haue suffred suche punishment as God
hath appointed, and vntil being more
cleerely instructed in the thinges apperteyning to God, (in the whiche instruction and receiuing of the light stādeth, as S. Denyse saith, the somme of
the purgation) they may be caried vp
into those ioyfull dwelling places of
heauen.

S.Paule

S.Paule alſo writing to the Corinthians, ſaith. What ſhal they do, which are baptized for the dead, if the dead riſe not at all? Wherefore are they baptized for them? To be baptized in in this place, is to offer vppe him ſelfe as a ſatisfactorie or pourging Sacrifice to waſſhe and clenſe the ſpottes of ſowles. Wherevpon our Lorde him ſelfe ſhewed, that he was very ſore pained with the earneſt deſire that he had of baptiſme, that is to ſay, of that moſt wholeſome waſſhing, wherein he ſhould offer vp him ſelfe a Sacrifice vpon the Aulter of the Croſſe for the ſynnes of mankind. And of the two brethren, whiche ſought to haue the higheſt roome with him in his kingdom, he demaūdeth, whether they be ready to beare him cōpanie in the ſame baptiſme. To be baptized therefore for the dead is nothing els, but to honour God with ſome pourging Sacrifice or offering for the ſaluation of the dead,

and

*1. Cor. 15.
d.*

Luc. 22. b

Mat. 20. c

and to offer vp with good heart euen
the Sacrifice of our body for their saluation.

   The which thing S . Paule did, as it
appeereth, not only for the dead, but
also for the liuing. For immediatly after he saith thus . Wherefore doe we
also put our selues in ieoperdie euerie
day? I doe die dayly for your glorie,
which I haue in our Lord Iesus Christ.
By the whiche place it may be gathered, that S. Paule, so often as he aduen-
tured his life for the state of the holy
Church, so often did he administer the
Sacrament and Sacrifice of this baptisme : the whiche thing he did then
most worthely, when he died a moste
honorable death for the glory of Christ
and saluation of al men. For he sayde,
that he was to be offered vp as a Sacrifice, at that tyme especially , when
death, by the which he should be deliuered out of the prison of his bodie,
approched neere . By the which place
it is

2. Cor. 15. d.

2. Tim. 4. 6.

it is euidently prooued, that many o-
ther also haue offred vp most holy Sacrifices for the dead, that is to say, for
the saluation of the deade. The which
thing if it were alwayes done in vaine,
then might it be concluded, that such,
as are deade, should neuer returne a-
gaine to liue.

But now, for so much as it was not
done in vaine, (for otherwise S. Paule
would neuer haue borne withal) it foloweth necessarily, that prayers made
for the saluation of the dead are not
superfluous, and that the sowles of
such, as are departed this lyfe, are holpen by the prayers, vowes, and Sacrifices of the lyuing. The whiche
sowles so departed, for so much as thei
are neither buried in euerlasting dark-
nesse (for then could they not get out
by any mans prayers) neither yet placed in heauen (for there should they
not neede any mans prayers) it followeth, that they be in some other
K K   place,

place, which we are wont to call purgatorie.

Many other thinges might be spoken to this purpose. Many things haue ben verie well alleaged of diuers godly and holy men to confirme this matter: but if there had ben no such thing, yet the faith of the holie Churche, which hath alwaies continewed vndefiled euen from the Apostles tyme till our daies, might haue suffised vs abundantly. But you, when you see most euident testimonies, when you are not able to shift our argumentes, when you are conuinced by the autoritie of the holy Fathers, when you may see the agreement of the whole Churche, yet wil you of an vncredible stubbornesse continewe in the wicked opinion, which you haue once taken.

What shal I here say of prayers and vowes made in Sacrifice for the liue

and

and the dead ? Is there any tyme, in the which it is not lawful for Christiã men to vse charitie, the perfection of whose Religion resteth in charitie? Can there be deuised any greater deede of charitie then that, wherein we praie vnto God most feruently for the saluation of our brethern ? Is there any tyme more meete and conueniét to doe this holy woorke, then that is, when we goe about to appeace the maiestie of God, not with the Sacrifice of brute beastes, but with the bodie and bloude of Christe? Is there any thing more agreable to the ordre of our Religion, which doe beleeue, that suche as departe out of this mortall bodie with true faith, doe not die, but lyue, then to ioyne them with suche, as remayne in this lyfe: and to praye vnto Christe, whiche was offered vppe for vs, both for the lyuing, as also for them, that are departed out of this life?

Cal you this godlie point of Religion, this holy worke of moſt feruent charitie, this wholeſome Sacrifice offered vppe not onely for vs, but alſo for our brethern, vnto whome wee are knit with an euerlaſting bande of loue, call you this, I ſay, the diſhoneſtie of Religion? Is this no outrage? Is this no madneſſe? Is this no impudencie?

To refuſe lawefull authoritie, to breake the ancién ordre of the Churche, to deflowre holy virgins, to robbe good matrones of their chaſtitie, to cancell the verie remembraunce of of vertue, Religió, and iuſtice, to quéch the loue of honeſtie and gentlenes, to prophane and robbe Churches, to take holy men, and ſome to murder, ſome to ſpoile and put to all the villanie in the worlde, ſome others to banniſhe out of their countrey, to awrecke the malice your beare towardes godlines vpon the relikes of Sainctes, to

vaunt

vaunt your selues like helhoundes in
the waste and sacke of holy thinges,
shal this be accompted as honest and
gloriouse, shall this be esteemed as a
matter worthie of immortal commendation and praise? And to be bound to
obeie authoritie grounded vppon the
commaundement and ordinaunce of
Christ, to conserue the band of peace
and concord, to honour and reuerence
the iustice and mercie of God ioyned
together in one, to cal to remembrāce
the goodly monumentes of holines, to
offer vp that most holy and noble *Sa-*
crifice(the vertue whereof we cā neither expresse with woordes, neither
yet conceyue in heart) for the liuing
and the dead, and for the good estate
of the whole Christian cōmon weale:
shal this be such a dishonestie as may
not be borne? And yet you are not
afraied to cal al these thinges the dishonour of Religion, and to say, that
I am not ignorant, by whome these

thinges are cropen in, but that I diſſemble it to ſerue the eares of my
compagnions.

Of lyke, Sir, all theſe thinges,
whiche you miſlike, and call the diſhoneſtie of Religion, were deuiſed
and brought in, by brothels and baw-
des, or elles by ſuche felowes, as ſerue
the bellie, luſte, or vnſtedfaſtneſſe of
the people for their commodities ſake,
and not by the ſpirite of Chriſte, and
by moſt continent and holy menne, in
whome was the ſpirite of Chriſte.
But you are neuer able to prooue that
you ſay. For both reaſon and the teſtimonie of all antiquitie, as alſo the
authoritie of holy Fathers doe vrge
and preſſe you, yea and conuince
you of impudencie: but wee haue
putte backe the violent puſſhe of
this your vngodlyneſſe and malice,
with argumentes moſt ſure, with teſtimonies moſt graue, with examples
moſt true.

Where-

Whereas you say, that I speake o-
therwyse then I thinke, to serue the
eares of my compagnions, I see well,
you are wel acqueinted with my behauiour. I am lyke to be suche a man,
as would spend my tyme with all diligence to learne to flatter, and to
write, not what I thinke, but what I
imagine may be best liked of my compagnions. I besech Christe the iudge
of the liuing and of the dead, if I
write not, in matters concerning Religion, those thinges which I thinke,
whiche I iudge to be true, whiche I
beleeue assuredly, that he suffer me
not to enter into that most glorious
and euerlasting Citie of heauen, and
that he let me not to haue the ioyfull
fruition of his owne light and brightnes for euermore.

For what is the Popedome els, but
a ministration of an authoritie, which
is lawefull and ordeyned by God?
What is our beleefe of Purgatorie,

KK iiij   but

but a declaration of Gods iustice and mercie together? What is the honour geuen vnto Sainctes, but a reuerent consideration of the worke of God in the which appeereth the almighty power and bountifulnes of God muche more, then in the making of heauen, yea or in al the works of nature. What are the praiers made in our Sacrifice for the liuing and the dead, but a work of moste perfecte holinesse, of moste excellent Religion, of moste feruent charitie?

These be dishonest points, which you haue take away. There is good cause, why you should glorie in it, and haue your name recorded with honor to al the posterity. for you haue brought in, for obeying of holy and lawful autho-ritie, rebellion: for the feare of purga-torie, a rash affiaunce of licentiousnesse vnpounished: for dewe woorshipping of Sainctes, the contempte of holi-nesse and iustice: for the religious ob-

ser-

seruation of the most holie sacrifice, and charitable behauiour of men, a despising of religion and forgetting of charitie : yea moreouer and this, you haue brought in a scornfull laughter exceding al modestie together with a sawcie talke passing all ciuilitie. Are these thinges comelie, M. Haddon ? Are these thinges honourable ? Are these thinges to be commended ? Are these thinges to mabe a shewe of?

But you saie, that the Bishoppes of Rome keepe warres, that in Rome is kept a market of purgatorie, that holie thinges are there set out to sale, that manie men are to muche incombred with superstition in the woorshipping of Sainctes, that Priestes liue not very continently, and that they abuse their sacrifices now and then to their luker and gaine.

First of all as towching warres you must thinke, that we can not of reason and equitie condemne all warres. For they

they are some times begonne for the
defence of Religion, and maintenance
of a iust cause.

As for the buying and selling of holie thinges, if in so manie hundred
yeares some suche matter haue ben
vsed, it is no wonder. For(as you saie
your selfe) it can not be chosen, but
that sometimes in the good corne
there will growe some weedes. And if
anie such abuse haue ben, it is now taken quite awaie.

If superstition trouble mens mindes
now and then, it is verie easily taken
awaie by the labour and diligence of
Bishops. The vicious and vncleane life
of Priestes is verie seuerely punished.
And there are at this time emongest
vs a great manie moe of them, that liue
verie continently, then of such, as will
disteine them selues with vicious and
vncleane liuing.

Last of all, to passe ouer all other,
the vertuous, godlie, and religiouse
example

example of this moſt holie Pope Pius
the fifth, (whome neither ambition,
neither coueteouſnes, neither the fauour of the people, neither yet the
raſhnes of men, but the holie Ghoſte
hath placed in this roome of highe
honour and dignitie)bringeth to paſſe,
that all thinges waxe better and better euerie daie, and that verie manie
are ſtirred to the loue of true godlines.

But admitte there were no ſuche
matter at this time, as I talke of : admit
that al went to naught, and that there
were no man to reſourme the church
where it is decaied : ſhould it be well
done by and by to euerthrow all ſuch
thinges , as haue ben wiſely ordeined,
ſo ſoone as men doe abuſe them to
naughtines? No truly : but rather to
prouide, as neere as we maie, that holy
thinges maie no more be abuſed. For
otherwiſe all would decaie, and there
wold folow a meruelous diſorder and
confu-

confusion of thinges in the Churche.

If you, as you haue for the misbe-
hauiour of a fewe monkes (as you saie)
taken quite awaie the whole order,
and for the lewdnes of certain Pristes
ouerthrowen the dignitie of Priest-
hood, and authoritie of Bishopps: so
you woulde procede, (for it standeth
with as good reason as the other doth)
and for the default of a Magistrate, or
Prince, or King, which hath not done
his dewtie, take awaie the orderly gouernment of the common weale, together with the Kinglie honour and
authoritie: the worlde shoulde come
againe to that confusion, which (as the
Poetes report) was, before that nature
was disposed and set in comelie order.
For what thing is so holie, the whiche
men maie not abuse sometimes to doe
much harme and mischiefe? For, that
we maie goe no further, wedlocke it
selfe, (which you preferre before perpetuall virginitie) is it alwaies kept in
                                    such

such chaste, godly, and religious order,
as it ought to be ? Doe the housbādes
neuer looke besides their wiues? Doe
the wiues neuer beguyle their hous-
bandes? Are there no aduowtries cōmitted nowe and then emong ? Yeas
questionles are there: and manie fowle
and shameful actes are done of maried
men oftentimes, with great rashnes
and impudencie. Shall we therfore, for
the lewd demeanour of some maried
persones, breake the band of man and
wife, and take awaie the holie state of
lawfull wedlocke ? No truly. For then
woulde men and women runne vnto
it without order, and there woulde be
no differéce betwene them and brute
beastes. Wherfore although all our
doinges were voide of al good order,
honestie, and religion: yet are not such
thinges, as haue ben for a most godlie
pourpose deuised and ordeined, forthwith to be disannulled, but rather order woulde be taken, that thinges,
                                    which

which are amisse, might be amended.
Neither are suche thinges, as maie be
cured, to be cut of: neither yet, if the
festered and corrupt partes of the body must needes be pared of, is it necessarie for that to destroie the whole
bodie, whiche maie be recouered: neither is the state of a common weale
to be altered, so soone as anie disorder happeneth in it, but rather reason
woulde, that al such matters, as are decaied, should be brought again to that
comelie order, in the whiche they
were at the begynning.

　Aristotel telleth, that there was a
certaine man called Hippodamus of
Milesium, which wrote of a common
weale. Emongest other matters he re-
citeth a lawe of his, by the which he
decreed, that a great rewarde shoulde
be geauen out of the common trea-
sure to him, that coulde deuise anie
lawe profitable for the commō weale.
This decree Aristotel misliketh. For he
thinketh,

thinketh, that there woulde be an end in making of lawes, bicause the often chaunging of them is wont by litle and litle to bring them into contempt: and the lawes being once despised, the good estate of a common weale can not long continewe. Wherefore that excellent learned man counselleth al such, as make lawes, to foresee, that there be not more euyll in the often altering of the lawes, then there is in that disorder, which they goe about to resourme by the new lawe. For he thinketh it more safetie to keepe indifferét good lawes, then to make others not muche better. Wherein he hath good reason. For whie, that constant and perpetuall reuerence towardes the lawes causeth a certaine seare and bashfulnes, and linketh men together within them selues with a sure and inuiolable band of equitie. But this fond appetite that men haue to alter and chaúge the law (without som weighty cause)

Often chaunging of lavves daungerous.

cawſe) engendreth a preſumpteouſe
boldnes, and maketh a waie by ſubtile
and wilie meanes to take the lawe
quite awaie, and to bring in tyrannie.
And although there came none other
inconuenience of it, yet at the leaſt it
diſordereth the common weale.

Nowe this, whiche is to be feared
about the innouation of lawes, is to be
determined about religion ſo muche
the more conſtantly, the greater the
perill is to offend in religion, then in
anie other thing. This thing cõſidered
the ſownders of common weales of
olde time, puniſhed ſuch, as brought
in anie new tricke of religion out of
other places, with death or baniſhmẽt,
and decreed, that the rites or faſhions
of the countrey ſhoulde be moſt conſtantly reteined. Wherin, although
they had ſhaped them ſelues a religion
after a very bad ſort, and liued in great
errours, yet was this their ordinaunce
not altogether voide of good reaſon
and

and confideration. For if it were poffi-
ble, that fome one religion might be
more commendable then fome other,
he, that fhould take awaie an old religion, whiche were not vngodly, to fet
vp an other religion, that were but a
litle better, fhould do a fhrewd tourne
to the common weale.

Whie fo, faie you? Bicaufe he fhould
bring in a cuftome to alter Religion,
and, by confequent, to bring Religion
into contempt. And fo it might come
to paffe, that diuers and fundrie religions coming in one after an other,
being either deuifed by craftie wittes,
or els taken out of other countreis,
might moue great debate about the
eftablifhing of religiō: and while euery
religiō fhould difprooue one an other,
the matter might by litle and litle fo
fall out at the length, that all religion
fhould come to naught.

The which thing being true, (that
we maie retourne to our difputation
LL   againe)

againe) how is this to be taken, that a
religion, which, is moſt true, holy, and
auncient, approoued and confirmed
by the teſtimony of God, by the bloud
of Chriſte, by the faith of holie men,
ſhoulde be diſcredited by reaſon of a
new goſpel deuiſed bi the wit of a ſort
of filthy varlets? Is it not a conſequent
(as we now ſee it fal out euery where)
that there ariſe a nomber of religions
of diuerſſe ſortes, all vngodlye and
naught, yea and iarring within them
ſelues? That they ariſe one againſt an
other? That euerie one of them diſ-
prooue the folie of others? That neuer
a one of them being able to mainteine
it ſelfe by grownded reaſon, and ſtrõg
argument, they come all at the length
to be deſpiſed and ſet at naught?

By theſe ſteppes or degrees are mẽ
come to that point at the length, that
manie a one raiſeth vp the damned
ſprites of Arius, Sabellius, and other
moſt deteſtable heretikes from hell,

and

and reneweth their errours, whiche were before buried: fome others thinke, that there is no Religion true at all, and perſwade them felues, that the worlde is not gouerned by God. This fruicte haue the brochers of your newly deuiſed and freſh tapped goſpel brought into common weales, that euerie man maie profeſſe him felfe to be a fetter vp of a newe Religion, and take vp the fweard againſt all other, that are deuiſers of the like peſtilent fectes: whereby it is like at the length, that al order of Religiõ maie be taken quite awaie. O what bountifull and profitable felowes are theſe, whiche haue fo woorthely prepared a waie to al miſchiefe and vngodlines?

And yet you aſked me, what came into my head, to affirme, that theſe fectes are daungerous and hurtful vnto Princes. Tel me fir, I praie you, fuch as haue preſumed to doe fo great villa-nie, as to ouerthrowe the wonderful example of chaſt and cleane life, to deface al monumentes of religiō and holines to burne the holie Canōs or rules of the Church openly at a ſermon, to raſe the ſtate of the church with their weapons (where they might be ſuffred to doe it) to bring the people to hate the lawe, and ſo to plaie outragious and mad partes, to deſpiſe all lawfull authoritie, to ſet God and al godlie order at naught, to fil the Churches and chapples of religious men with bloud, to egge and allure the ſimple people through the hope of to much libertie to take vp armour: think you not, that theſe felowes (when ſo euer they ſhal finde occaſion) will tourne the ſelfe ſame furie and rage vpon the Princes them ſelues? Is it not wel knowen (as it is ſaied before) what they haue wrought and practiſed againſt the emperour in Germanie, againſt the eſtate and life of King Henrie in Fraunce, againſt Edward, whome they made

awaie

awaie with poiſon, and afterwarde
againſt Quene Marie in England? Is
it not knowen, how traiterouſly and
furiouſly they bent them ſelues againſt
the maieſtie of theſe Princes? What
ſhal I here ſaie of the King of Scotlãd,
whome the worlde knoweth to haue
ben moſt crewelly murdered? What?
Haue they not wrought the like treaſon againſt many other Princes alſo?

I leaue out a number of examples
of this barbarous villanie, whiche I
could here recite. And, although there
were none ſuche, yet woulde I not
dowbt to ſaie ſo much, as I haue ſaied.
For it is not the part of a wiſe man,
when he ſeeth the cawſe, to dowbt of
the euent, whiche ſoloweth neceſſarily of the cawſe. For when I ſee the
common people void of feare, vnrulie
and fearce through a pretenſed name
of libertie, outragiouſely following
their owne vnbridled wil and pleſure,
haughtely flingyng vp and down, bea-

ring them felues vppon a falfe opinion
of Religion : maie I dowbte, but that
they are moft fpitefully bent againft al
authorititie, wherby they thinke, that
their libertie, (which they fo griedely
long after) maie be hindered?

These are the thinges, M. Haddon,
thefe are the thinges , that doe difho-
neft Religion , and not thofe matters,
which you fpeake of. For what is more
comely and honeft, then to obey fuch
authoritie, as is ordeined by God? To
dread and feare the iudgemēt of God?
Reuerently to confider the mercie of
God, in them, whome he firft trieth by
dewe punifhment , and fo admitteth
them into life euerlafting? To call to
mind the monumentes of iuftice, godlines and holines? To yeld vp humble
praiers vnto God in the moft holie fa-
crifices , for the good eftate of the liuing, and for the faluation of the dead?
But in the meane time, while you
dowbte not to faie , that thefe moft
godlie

godlie orders are the thinges, that doe
dishoneft religió, you marke not how
great the difhoneftie of your religió is.

For, that I maie faie nothing els, can
there be anie greater difhoneftie of religion, then that all Sacramentes and
ceremonies, al decrees and ordinaunces of the Churche, al priefthood and
holie orders fhoulde be vnder the rule
and gouernement of a woman? I
meane not hereby to difgrace your
Queene, whome I defire to fee fo
beawtified and fournifhed with moft
excellent vertues, that her name maie
remaine as a thing of holie remembraunce vnto all the pofteritie. Neither doe I fo muche blame her, as
you, whiche haue by your flatterie
brought her to this inconuenience,
that fhe taketh her felfe to be gouer-
neffe of the Churche. Tel me fir, if it
like you, where haue you readde, that
euer anie Prince tooke vpon him the
office or charge of the high Bifhoppe?

LL iiij   No

No rather, all suche Princes as loued godlines and iustice, whose name is for their noble actes set out to the posteritie for euer, did reuerence the iudgemét of Priestes, refused not to be obedient vnto Bishoppes, and thought like verie wise men, that it would tourne to their euerlasting commendation, if they were gouerned by them. So did your great Cóstantine, the most woorthie ornamét and beawty of your Iláad: so did our Theodosius, so did Lewis King of Fraunce, so did a number of others, which with most noble victories enlarged their Empiere verie farre: when they had subdowed al countreis with armour, they did so obey the decrees and ordinaunces of Bishops, that they seemed to glorie not so much in their Empire, as in that obediéce. But you haue brought al holie thinges not only vnder a king, which (as I shewed before) were to be esteemed as a most heinous offéce, but also vnder a quene, againſt

againſt all right and reaſon, againſt the
inuiolable reuerence of moſt pure religion, againſt the ordinaunces of almightie God : you haue taken awaye
the moſt holy dignity of the high biſ-
ſhoprike from the lawful biſhops, and
haue tranſpoſed it to be adminiſtred
by a woman. The which, I ſay, was a
moſt wicked deede, a moſt barbarouſe
acte, a moſt deteſtable and curſed offence. Whereby it may be gathered,
that mans heart can imagine no miſchiefe ſo horrible and diuelliſh, that
theſe flatterers wil not take vpõ them
to practiſe it, with deſperate boldneſſe
and impudencie.

Here do I paſſe ouer many thinges,
and vnto the railing words, which you
heape together againſt me, I anſwere
you nothing, for in deede I regard
them not. Neither is it my meaning
to confute your railing wordes, but to
take vppon me the defence of moſte
holy Religion, for the which it were
a good-

a goodly matter for me to die. Al other thinges therefore I let paſſe, that I may come to that place, in the which you drawe bloud of your owne body, yea and geaue your ſelſe a deadly wound with your owne handes. Your wordes are theſe.

What then? This holy doctrine of the goſpel, in the which we haue continued more then thirtye yeares together (the moſt troubleſome ſpace of ſix yeares excepted) in the which the Queenes maieſtie hath paſſed oner all her life, in the which ſhe hath founde God ſo mercifull vnto her, in the whiche the ſtates of the realm are fully agreed, in the which many noble ſtatutes and lawes haue enſewed: this true and ſincere worſhipping of almighty God, which is ſo diligently enuironed and fortified on euery ſide by the Quenes maieſty, ſhal the voice of a ſeely felow of Portugal breake it downe? What a deale of matter you heape vp together, M. Haddô, how vnaduiſedly you*
                                    ſpeake

ſpeake(that I may not ſay, how raſhly and madly). for firſt of al, this, whiche you cal the holy doctrine of the goſpel, is the doctrine of Luther, Zwinglius, Bucer, Caluin, and other the like brainſicke felowes, which haue, not only by their moſt peſtilent decrees and ordinaunces, but alſo by the example of their filthy and vicious liuing, quite ouerthrowen al chaſtitie, holines, modeſtie, meekeneſſe, and obedience: which haue broken and caſt away true faith, and in ſteede of it haue ſet vppe a raſhe and preſumpteouſe boldneſſe: whiche haue taken awaie libertie (although in their talke they pretende otherwyſe) and for that haue rewarded their adherentes with a licence to lyue in naughtineſſe vncontrolled: whiche haue taken awaie the gyft of iuſtice (which is the greateſt and largeſt grace that man maie receyue of God) and for true iuſtice haue brought in a feyned and counterfeyte iuſtice: which,

which, of a mad and vngodly minde, haue not ben afhamed to impute the cause of al synne and wickednesse to God that most perfecte goodnes, from whome no euil can proceede: which, (whereas they tooke vppon them to scoure or purge the gospel throughly, and to repaire the Churche againe, which tendeth to ruine) haue not only not persourmed so muche, as they prowdly and rashly promised to doe, but haue moreouer beraied the Chürche (the vncleanes whereof religious menne could not beare before) with much filthinesse of vice and naughtines, and haue brought it to be rent and riuen in peaces,

What should we thinke to be the cause, wherefore, when any man infected with the contagion of this doctrine is taken emongest vs (whiche is counted here a very straunge matter) although he set neuer so sad or graue countenaunce vpon it to make a co-
lour

lour and fhewe of holineffe, yet will the concealed trickes of a difordered and carnal mind fhewe them felues, and manie fowle vices, whiche were before hidden vnder the couert of hypocrifie, wil foorthwith appeere. For the more a man geueth him felfe to this doctrine, the more is he contrarie to bafhfulnes and continencie.

I omit to fpeake of your earneft talke, wherein you fay, that this newe broched Church, which is difteined with innumerable vices, may be compared with the Churche of the Apoftles, which was moft flourifhing with heauenly gyftes, with religion and holineffe.

As for that comparifon of myne, wherein I fhewed, what great difference there was betwene the twoo Churches, I would not haue you vainly and without any fruicte to find fault withal. For as yet you haue not confuted it, neither fhal you euer be able

to

to doe it . And who so euer shall attempt to do it, shall doe nothing elles, but only set out to the world his owne madnes and impudencie together, and cause al men to laugh at his folie, and abhorre his malice.

That I may therfore omit that foolish and shamelesse talke of yours, I would you would compare this your Church, but onely with the Churche of your auncetours: the which thing if you doe, you shall finde , that there is brought in for the religious conuersation of your forefathers , a presumptuouse boldnes : for their grauitie and constancie , a light and vnsetled harishnesse : for their continencie , sensualitie: for their manhood nicenesse. And will you call this the holy Doctrine of the gospel, which hath ouerthrowen and defaced so many holie thinges , and in steede of them hath brought in such a deale of naughtines and disordre ?

Call

Call to remembraunce I pray you
the firſt founding of this your Churche. For you maie not wel diſſemble
ſuche thinges, as are commonly talked of all menne, and in writing commended to the euerlaſting remembraunce of all the poſteritie. Wan-
tonneſſe and loue were the firſt ſetters vppe of it : the breache of lawe
and ordre, and a hatred towardes the
Pope for geauing ſentence agaynſt
the offender enlarged it : the flatterie of lewde ſelowes with the healp
of lying walled it : inordinate deſire
and coueteouſneſſe fenſed it : the pu-
niſhinge of holie and innocent perſonnes halowed it : the putting of al
menne in feare confirmed it : final-
lye the Doctrine of ſuche menne, as
were ſent into thoſe coaſtes not from
Godde, but from Satan, infected it
with moſte peſtilent and ſeditious errours. Dare you call this a religious,
godly, and holy doctrine, whoſe beginning

ning , proceding , increase , and ende
you see (vnlesse you be in extreme and
miserable blindnesse) to haue ben set
vppon , folowed , and finished with
naughtinesse , incontinencie , hatred,
coueteousnes , creweltie, outrage and
madnes ?

Then , what a sopperie is that , to
say, that you haue continewed in this
doctrine, more then thirtie yeares together? O reueret horeheaded gospel.
O auncient heauenly doctrine . O old
vnspotted religion . But you thinke,
that you being a wittie and wilie in-
terpretour of the law forsooth, neede
not recke much for the antiquitie of
your doctrine . For you seeme to
plead prescription, and therefore you
content your selfe with the space of
thirtie yeares, within the which tyme
you thinke, that the ordre of your religiō may be lawfully possessed. Howbeit if you take awaye from thyrtie
yeares the space of sixyeares, whiche
you

you call a troublesome time) it is euident, that this your holy Gospel is not yet fully thirtie yeares olde.

But admitte that the thirtie yeares were fully expired, if this title of prescription be good, then may the Arabians much better mainteine their sect, then you can yours. For you defende your heresy by the prescriptiō of thirty yeres: but they wil vphold the wicked superstitiō of Mahumet by the possession of more then nine hundred yeares.

You saie moreouer, that the Quenes Maiestie (for such a pleasure haue you to flatter, that you neuer call her the Queene, as though in the name of a Quene, there were litle dignitie, or els her Maiestie should decaie by and by, if you should cal her Quene). You saie therfore, that the Quenes Maiesty hath passed ouer al her life in this doctrine. That this is true, I haue none other warrant but your word. But if it be so, the fault is not so much in her, as in her

M M   tea-

teachers, who had the bringing vp of her, when shee was of age tender and weake, and therefore the more meete to be abused by such subtile and craftie felowes.

Last of all, it is not as yet euidently seene, so long as shee is not free from your tyrannie, which vnder her name, as men saie, doe possesse the kingdom, what waie she woulde take in al these matters. Of thys I am righte well assured, that her singular wit is not by nature so obstinately bente to mainteine an opinion once conceiued, or so muche geauen to naughtie and false doctrine, that it is not very flexible to yealde vnto good reason, and verie willing to forsake false doctrine, and to folowe that which is true and incorrupted. Wherefore I doubte not, if she be so wittie, as you say shee is, but that shee will (so soone as euer shee may doe it for your importunitie) turne from this your wicked doctrine,

to

to the honeſt, godly, and profitable doctrine of the Church.

And wheras you adde theſe words:
*In the which ſhee hath found God ſo mer
ciful vnto her*: Me thinketh, you vnderſtand not in what thing the teſtimonie
or proufe of Gods mercy ſtandeth. For
it ſtandeth not ſo much in the glory of
the people, or in the proſperouſe ſucceſſe of worldli matters, as in the peace
ād quietnes of cóſciéce, in a mind beu-
tifully decked with the giftes and graces of God, in faith and vpright cóuer-
ſatió, in true and vncorrupted doctrine,
in that ſtate of life, which is abundantly
furniſhed with heauenly vertues. Furthermore, if ſhee haue had God very
merciful vnto her, and haue not tryed
or fealt as yet his iudgement, ſhe ought
to be ſo muche the more carefull, that
ſhe do not offend him, and that ſhe doe
not abuſe his mercy and clemencie to
the contempt of his moſt pure and holy
Religion. And to make ſo much of fiue

M M ij   yeares

yeares prosperitie, it argueth a merueilouse great rashnes in you. When
Solon warned Cresus, that he shoulde
not trust to much to prosperouse fortune : he taught him, that the prosperitie not of fiue yeares, but of manie
yeares, is to be feared : and he shewed
withal, that no man is to be accounted
happie, so long as he liueth. This Cresus being afterward ouercome by Cyrus and set vppon a pile of wood to be
burned, called with a lowd voice vpõ
Solon, by whome he had ben warned
before of the cõdition of mans frailtie,
and of the sodaine alteration of worldlie felicitie. Cyrus hearing the name of
Solon, demaũded of Cresus what that
Solon had ben. To whome Cresus answered that he had ben the wisest man
in al Greece, of whom he had learned
this lesson, that it is the greatest madnes in the worlde, to be lifted vppe to
much with prosperitie. Cyrus foorthwith, caused Cresus to be taken doune
                                    from

from the pile , and vſed him very honourably , and himſelfe in all his proſperitie held a goodly meane.

These and the like examples are ſo
wel knowen, and daily experience geueth vs ſuch occaſiō to know the vn-
certaintie of this our condition , that
there can not be any greater token of
madnes or folie, then to waxe proude,
when the worlde ſerueth vs at will .
For who ſo euer is puffed vp with the
proſperouſe ſucceſſe of things, neither
doth he vnderſtand, how ſodainlie all
the wealth of the worlde vaniſheth a-
waie , and from howe high a grieſe or
ſtep many of the greateſt Princes haue
fallen, to the great wonder of al men :
neither doth he conſider, what a violent kinde of ſeueritie that ſupreame
Iudge vſeth, whē he mindeth to ſhake
as it were with a whirle winde , and
throw down the eſtate of ſuch as truſt
to much to them ſelues. Who is able
to ſaie, that al things ſhal proſper with
M M iij   him,

him,euen vntil his dying daie? Who is able to aſſure him ſelfe of one daie, yea of one hower voide of all calamitie or miſhappe? For as darkenes enſeweth vppon lighte, as the tempeſt is wonte to come vppon the watermen and mariners vnwares : euen ſo doth heauy chaunces oftetimes marre the flouriſhing ſtate of fortunate men, and ouerwhelme them in the waues of al aduerſity,and driue them againſt the rockes of euerlaſting thraldome and miſerie. And the more careleſſe men are, the more grieuouſly are they pained,when any ſuche calamitie falleth vpon them.

Wherefore it is the parte af a wiſe man,to conſider long time before all ſuche miſchaunces , as maie happen euery daie and hower , yea euerie minute of an hower: but it is a token of a fooliſh and madde felowe , in proſperitie to forget the weakeneſſe of manne : eſpeciallie whereas we ſee often-

oftentimes, that almightie God nowe
and then suffereth suche, as he is moſt
offended withall, to haue the longer
enioying of their apparente felicitie,
that he maie of a ſodaine ſtrike them,
that will not repente, and geue them
the deeper wounde. And therefore
our Lorde warneth vs, that we be *Gen.7.c.*
not like vnto them, which in the daies
of Noe liued a recheleſſe life, and ſo cō
tinued euē vnto the time, in the which
they were oppreſſed ſodainly with the
floud, which they could not poſsiblie
auoid. He teacheth vs alſo by the ſo- *Gen.19.e.*
daine fiering of thoſe Cities, that his
iudgement catcheth improuidēt men,
as it were with ſecrete grynnes or
ſnares, in ſuch ſort, that they can not
eſcape from euerlaſting pouniſhment
and tormentes.

If theſe thinges be true, what a
madnes was that in you, for fiue yeres
proſperitie, to vaunt your ſelfe ſo arrogantly and vainely? To triumph

MM iiij ſo

so insolently? to build so great an argument of Gods fauour towardes you vpon so slender a ground? See you not howe manie nations there are in the worlde vtterly voide of the faith of Christe, whose estate is a great deale more flourishing then yours is? If this argument were any thing woorth, see how easily the Turkes shall be able to auouche their pestilent secte, wherein they are drowned. You mainteine your cause with fiue yeares felicitie.: but they wil proue their Religion to be true by their great victories, and by the very prosperouse successe, which they haue had in all their affaires for the space of many yeares.

Last of al, are you wel ascerteined, what alteration one day, or rather one hower, may bring vnto your state? Wherefore are you then so bragge? Wherefore do you vaunt your selfe so farre beyonde all modestie, as though you were free and past al daunger, yea

as

as though you were altogether exempted from the bondes of the condition of man in fuche forte, that you coulde not pofsibly be ouertaken with any fodaine mifhap?

As for the agreement of your councel in bringing the auncient Religion to be fet at naught and forgotten, (if it be fo as you faie) and in makinge the Quenes Maieftie Superintendent in al fpiritual matters, I haue already declared, that neither of them both coulde be donne without incurringe the grieuoufe difpleafure of God. If you think, that you fhall efcape vnpunifhed, bicaufe it is delaied, take hede, if you repēt not, while you haue time, left you doe increafe through this your prefumption, the plague, that hangeth ouer you.

As for the hope, which I conceiued (as you faie) of your Quene, and therfore wrote thofe my letters vnto her, it repenteth me not, as yet of my doinges

inges. If I haue donne any good,
it will appeare at the lengthe. If I
haue donne none, yet the signification of my good heart towardes her,
can not be but wel taken of her, if shee
wil continue in her accustomed courtesie and gentlenes.

You saie, I shall not bring her to
be of myne opinion, no, althoughe I
should write sixe hundred millions of
Philippicall Orations. I would faine
knowe, how you are able to auouche
that. Thinke you, that she is of nature
so barbarous and sauage, that although
I doe detecte the craftie dealinge and
priuie practises of naughtie felowes,
and prooue them vnto her by Argumentes inuincible, by reasons more
cleere then the sonneshine at noone-
tide, if I set before her eyes the filthines
and lewdnes of this counterfeict religion, which they haue most wickedlie
and heinoufly deuifed, if I declare vnto
her in plaine words, how childish your
reasons

reasons are, wherwith you goe aboute
to mainteine their cause, and how il fa-
uoredly thei hang together: think you,
I sai, that she wil, notwithstãding althis
rather imbrace your most detestable
opinion to her certaine and vtter vndoing, then cal to mind againe the true
Religion, which hath ben forgotté for
a time through the default and naughtines of such as should haue put her in
remembrance of it, to her most assured
saluation and glory euerlasting? If reason shal ouercome her, if the authoritie
of holie Fathers shall cause her to
yealde, if the Lawe of God shall put
it into her heart, that shee wil desire to
forsake and detest this your secte: yet
haue you so good affiaunce in your
owne force, and so little estimation
of the sharpenesse of her witte and
iudgemente, that you dare warrant,
that vnlesse you geaue her leaue, shee
shall neuer retourne (doe what shee
can) vnto that godly order of Religion,
which

whiche her moſte noble Progenitours
obſerued and kepte very honourably,
to their great profit and immortal glorie? Shall you Syr, haue her at your
commaundement and becke: ſhal you
take order with her:ſhal you preſcribe
her what ſhee ſhal beleue, in ſuch ſort,
that for ſeare of ſalling into your diſpleaſure, ſhe ſhal not regard her owne
life and dignitie : but ſhal rather ſuffer
her ſelfe to be carried awaie into euerlaſting tormentes and damnation,then
to gainſaie your opinion,be it neuer ſo
vngodlie , heinouſe , and wicked, yea
and mainteined with neuer ſo fond and
peeuiſh kinde of talke?

But bē it. Admitte ſhe be ſo much
an vnderling vnto you , that ſhee dare
not for her life once diſſente from you
in any thing. What if ſhee ſhalbe moued by the inſtinct of the holy Ghoſt?
What if Chriſt him ſelfe ſhal ſtirre her
heart to conſider and enioye his gra-
ciouſe giftes? What if God wil ſet vp
ſuch

such a light before her heart, that shee may see how certaine wicked persons woorke priuie treason againſt her lyfe and perſone? And, that I may ſay nothing els, what if ſhe ſhall receiue but onely ſuch a ſmal quantitie of the light of God, that ſhee may ſee, that Luther with his diſciples and folowers, were neuer moued by the holy Ghoſte, but pricked foreward by the fendes of hel, and that they came not to inſtructe men with wholſome doctrine, but to infecte them with moſte peſtilente errours? What? Wil you this notwithſtandinge, holde her backe, will you ſhackle her in ſuch ſorte, that ſhe ſhall not poſsibly geue eare to the holy warninges and counſels of God? To continue in a wicked opinion being once conuinced as erroneouſe, is the parte of a dul and blunt wit: to be afraid of the vniuſt diſpleaſure of her own ſubiects, is a token of a baſe and cowardlie heart: but to refuſe the gift of Gods
mercie,

mercy,to reiect his gratious aid,when
it is offred, is an argumté of an vngodli
ād naughty mid.So ſhal it com to paſſe,
that you , while you deſire to put the
worlde to vnderſtand what a perilous
felowe you are,ſhal falſely charge that
Princeſſe , whome you reporte to be
moſte excellentlie fourniſhed with all
vertues,paſsingly well adourned with
many ſingular qualities, with dulnes of
wit, with feintnes of heart, and with
the crime of impietie.

Truely M.Haddon ſhe is very much
beholdinge vnto you for your goodly
ſeruice, if you haue by your diligence,
ſo beſette her on euery ſide, that, although ſhe ſee her ſelf tombled doune
headlong into euerlaſting death and
damnatiō, yet ſhe may not be ſo hardy
in her hert(if you ſaie nay to it)as once
to whinch or ſtep aſide, to auoide the
daunger, that hangeth ouer her, leſt in
ſo doing, ſhee might trouble your patience (more grieuouſlie perhappes
                                   then

then a man would thinke).And yet am
I moued to refreine to write vnto her,
any more of the fame matter for verie
iuft and good caufes.For I think I haue
very wel difcharged my duety,both in
my letters which I fent vnto her,as alfo in this anfwer,which I write againft
your booke,if it happe to come to her
hands. Either therfore the things that
I haue already written fhall haue fuffi-
ciente force and ftrength to make her
heart to yelde, or els I fhal not be able
to doe it,although I write againe.And
in deede , I haue not fo much vacante
time, that I may fpend it without any
fruict or profite .

Let vs now come to your good coūfel,
wherin you aduertife me,that I fhould
not once hādle the holi fcriptures.you
cōmend my wit,and my eloquēce you
do not miflike. But you fav , that I am
to be reckoned emongeft the Ora-
tours and Philofophers,and not emongeft the Diuines.My bokes of nobility

(for

(for it is like you neuer read any other bookes of myne) you saie you like very wel. I am right glad, that my writinges are commended by a manne so finely learned, and so trymly nourtered: and your friendly counsell I take it in good worth. And therfore it liketh me to speake vnto you (Syr newe Diuine) with the selfe same verses, as Horatius feineth him selfe to haue vsed to Damasippus a new Stoike.

Damasippus had no thing of a Philosopher but onely a beard. The barber therfore shauing his beard, toke avvai his Philosophie.

Syr Waulter for your counsel true,
   a barber maie you haue :
Sent from the Gods and Goddesse eke,
   your worthie beard to shaue.

But howe came you to be so well acquainted with me ? Who tolde you, that I haue not bestowed a great deale more studie in Diuinitie, then in Cicero, Demosthenes, Aristotle and Plato. You comend my wit. what then? think you that the study of Diuinitie is mete for dul heads onely and drawlatches ? You like my eloquece: wene you therfore

fore that the holy Scriptures would be handled of rudeſbies only and homly felowes? Wheras you geue authoritie to women, to tinkers and tapſters, to the rifferaffe of al occupations, to iangle and prate at rouers in Scripture matters : wil you forbid me, being not only a biſhoppe and Prieſte, and long tyme exerciſed in the holy Scriptures with ſome profitte, but alſo a man (as you report your ſelfe) both wittie and eloquent, to followe this moſt godlie trade of learning ? Then by what equitie, by what power, by what autoritie doe you this ? ſhal it be lawful for you being a man of lawe, to geaue ouer the ſtatutes made for walles, lights, and eues gutters: to deſpiſe and caſt a ſide your obligations, bargaines, and couenantes : to lay away the drawing of writes and ſuites in lawe : and to take vppon you in Diuinitie as bold as blind baiard: and to me, to whom it apperteyneth by office to inſtructe the

N N Churche

Church committed vnto me in the holy Scriptures, wil you not geue leaue, to beſtome much tyme and diligence in the ſtudie of them ? You are iniurious two waies. For you doe both violently intrude your ſelfe into other mens poſſeſsions, and wrõgfully thruſt me out of myne owne by your vniuſt iniunctions.

Now thoſe threates of yours, howe weighty and graue are they ? What a great terrour doe they put into me? You ſay thus. If ſo be that you mind to vaunt your ſelfe to certaine men , and ſo to aſſault vs any more, I warne you now before, that you come with farre better furniture , then you haue done at this tyme.

You tel me moreouer, that , in caſe you be dead before, yet there ſhal not lacke ſuch, as ſhal breake the dint of my ſtroke. Whereby I ſee, that you could neuer ſo much as geſſe, what my meaning is. I knowe, that there are in that

Iland

Iland many excellēt men both, for wit,
learning, and godlines, which wil neuer moleſt me, for ſo much as they a-
gree with me in religion meruelouſly
wel: (although you thinke it a matter
not to be borne.)Then if any man doe
write againſt me, in caſe he wil cōtend
with reaſon, argumētes and examples,
I wil not reſuſe to diſpute with him.
But if he fal to railing and reprochfull
wordes, I can not poſsibly be perſua-
ded to make him anſwere. For neither
am I moued with any reproch, neither
can I looke, that that victorie ſhould
tourne me to honeſtie, where the ma
ner of fight is ſo vnhoneſt. If I ſhal ſee,
that there is any hope to win you and
ſuche as you are to God, I will not
doubt to trie both by letters and prayers, what good I am able to do. Otherwiſe I wil not ſuffer my tyme, wherof
I haue litle to ſpare, to be ſo il beſtowed. For ſo doth S. Paule teach vs, *Tit.3.6.*
that after one or two warnings wee
NN ij   ſhould

fhould fhonne the companie of fuche menne as are obftinatly bent in erroneoufe and wicked opinions, for fo much as they are condemned by their owne iudgement. Wherefore I geaue you leaue, to bende your felfe mofte fiercely againft me with tautes and reproches. Rore as much as you lift, crie out as lowd as you can . For neither is it conuenient for my perfon , neither yet comely for the office I beare, to be moued with railing wordes , or elles to make anfwere to euerie flaunder. I neuer reuiled you, whome I knewe not.

As for my epiftle , which you rend and teare with fpitefull languague, it hath not one reprochful word in it, vnleffe perhaps you wil cal the moft iuft bewailing and moft true declaration of errours and wicked vices a reproche. And yet like a wilde bore thruft thorough with a venemous dart, you rane vpo me, as though you had ben wood.

But

But I was not only nothing difquieted
with your reprochfull words, but alfo
moued to laugh at your fond talke. I
take my God to witneffe, that, if the
loue, which I beare to true Religion
and godlines, had not earneftly moued
me, I had neuer put pen to the paper
to write againft your booke. But if you
knew, how much I pity your cafe, and
what a hartie defire I haue of your faluation, (for I would with all my hart,
as the dewty of a Chriftian man requireth, yeald my felfe to die for the faluation of you and your countrei men)
you would furely be at one with me.
For I was not moued by anie euyl wil
I beare you, but it was verie charitie,
that prouoked me inftantly to write. I
praie Chrift our moft bowntifull and
almightie Lord, I humbly befech him,
by his precious bloud fhead for the faluation of al men, by his woundes and
moft bitter paffion, by his death, by the
which he ouercame death, by his vi-

&orie whiche he atchieued ouer the
kingdome of Satan, to deliuer that
kingdom, in the which hath ben sometime a dwelling place of vertue, religion, grauitie and iustice, and is now
disordered thorough the lewdnes of
desperate felowes, from errours and
heresie : to make the brightnes of his
light to shine ouer them:to bring them
againe to the faith and vnitie of most
true Religiō:to carie them backe vnto
the fold of the catholike Churche: to
gouerne and mainteine them by the
assistance of his holy spirite:that al we,
which are now sundered in opinions,
maie at length agree in the vnitie of
faith, and loue of true Religion, and so
come to that euerlasting glorie,
to the great reioysing of al
the holie companie
in heauen.

Liber iste lectus est & approbatus à viris sacræ Theologiæ et Anglicani idiomatis peritissimis , quibus tutò credendum esse existimo:maximè cùm tantùm translatus sit ex Latino legitimè approbato.

Cunerus Petri, Pastor Sancti Petri Louanij. 3.septemb. Anno. 1568.

RESPICITE VOLATILIA COELI, ET PVLLOS CORVORVM

I F